# THE TWICE-BORN

## LIFE AND DEATH ON THE GANGES

AATISH TASEER

FOURTH ESTATE • *New Delhi*

First published in hardback in India in 2018 by 4th Estate
An imprint of HarperCollins *Publishers*

HarperCollins Publishers India, Cyber City, Building 10-A, Gurugram,
Haryana-122002, India
www.harpercollins.co.in

2 4 6 8 10 9 7 5 3 1

This edition published in paperback in India in 2019 by 4th Estate
An imprint of HarperCollins *Publishers*



P-ISBN: 978-93-5357-337-9
E-ISBN: 978-93-5302-389-8



Typeset in 11.6/15.2 Arno Pro at
Manipal Digital Systems, Manipal

Printed and bound at
MicroPrints India, New Delhi

FSC MIX Paper FSC® C218906

This product is made of FSC®-certified and other controlled material.

HarperCollins Publishers, Macken House, 39/40 Mayor Street
Upper, Dublin 1, D01 C9W8, Ireland

# THE TWICE-BORN

The most rewarding [book] written by a contemporary writer on the perpetually romanced—and sacred—geography of India

—*Open Magazine*

Taseer writes like he always does, relentlessly, intensely, sometimes unkindly, in a complex way, raising questions with a deep intelligence that disturbs more than it quietens

—*The Telegraph*

Makes the reader think about religion, caste, culture and the idea of modernity, and most rewardingly, about where she stands in relation to all of these

—*Hindustan Times*

Doesn't sit squarely in the camp of memoir, travelogue, or long-form reportage. It hovers among the three—but with such lilting grace as to make that limbo feel like a lovely hybrid

—*Vogue*

Moving ... For Taseer, Benares incarnates a curious quality of modernity: the city makes anthropologists of the devout and believers of the skeptical. The book's charm resides in the way the author orbits this tension between faith and rationality

—*The New Yorker*

A gorgeous, sinister portrait of Benares ... Taseer's wonderfully atmospheric rendition of landscapes and gnarled social psychologies make for an engrossing dissection of India's discontents

—*Publishers Weekly*

## ALSO BY AATISH TASEER

FICTION

*The Way Things Were*

*The Temple-Goers*

*Noon*

NON-FICTION

*Stranger to History:*
*A Son's Journey Through Islamic Lands*

TRANSLATION

*Manto: Selected Stories*

*For Ryan,*

*and in memory of Martand "Mapu" Singh*

*1947–2017*

India affords the most tragic spectacle of the world, since we see there a living and magnificent organisation, akin to, but infinitely more complete than that of medieval Europe, still in the process of destruction. Inheriting incalculable treasure, she is still incalculably poor, and most of all in the naiveté with which she boasts of the poverty that she regards as progress. One questions sometimes whether it would not be wiser to accelerate the process of destruction than to attempt to preserve the broken fragments of the great tradition.

—ANANDA K. COOMARASWAMY, *The Dance of Shiva*

One cannot launch a new history—the idea is altogether unthinkable —there would not be the continuity and tradition. Tradition cannot be contrived or learned. In its absence one has, at the best, not history but "progress"—the mechanical movement of a clock hand, not the sacred succession of interlinked events.

—OSIP MANDELSTAM, "Peter Chaadaev"

# CONTENTS

# 1

# FOREIGNERS IN THEIR OWN LAND

**FOR A LONG TIME,** I had a recurring daydream of the ancient Indian city of Benares, superimposed onto the geography of New York. From my open window on West 86th Street, my mind's eye followed the westering sun over a roofscape cluttered with heat pumps and slim steel chimneys. In the distance, the curved blades of a turbine vent glinted in the late-afternoon light. A sign on the exposed flank of a building read SOFIA STORAGE CENTER.

Beyond, out of view, was the Hudson.

I imagined it, like the Ganges in Benares, taking a deep bend north and flowing toward its source in the high Himalayas. The traffic on the

Henry Hudson Parkway was stopped, and on the steep escarpment of Riverside Park were acres upon slanting acres of humanity. Bathers and pilgrims, Columbia University students, and old ladies with coiffured blond and copper hair watched the glittering river with vacant intensity. Ghats went down in two-hundred-yard flights of steps, like stone bleachers, to the edge of the river, where long wooden boats rocked gently in the bilge water. Corpses, wrapped in their gold brocade, lay on bamboo biers, awaiting cremation.

The sky darkened, and silhouettes appeared in the yellow rectangles of the tall apartment buildings on Riverside Drive. The air was high with clouds of incense, the crashing of bells, and frantic chanting in Sanskrit. The people of two cities, and myriad systems of belief, poured out onto the riverside.

The liminal hour stretched out. A daytime darkness silvered the city. Thousands watched through special glasses; thousands more stood waist-deep in water, their heads lowered, muttering prayers. Old men with knotty hands leaned on their wooden staffs; women carried babies on their hips. There were farmers and laborers, bank clerks and UPS delivery-men. A party of schoolchildren observed the changing shape of the sun through a steel colander. As its disk went dark, some cried, "Beautiful!" Others stood in solemn terror as Rahu, the eclipser—a demon riding a chariot drawn by eight black horses—swallowed the sun.

**BENARES—VARANASI, AS IT IS** known officially; Kashi, as it has been known for millennia by the Hindus, who regard it as their holy city—is only eight hundred kilometers from Delhi, where I grew up.

In my midtwenties, after college in America and a couple of years spent working as a reporter for *Time* magazine in New York and London, I found myself living in Delhi again. I was working on my first book, *Stranger to History*, a memoir about my father, who lived in Pakistan, and from whom I had been estranged for most of my life.

My time in the West had given me an outside view of my world in Delhi, robbing my life there of its easy, unthinking quality. I thought I should do something, by way of traveling or learning, that would help me establish a connection with India at large, the country that lay beyond the seemingly impermeable confines of life in Delhi. I wondered if I should learn Sanskrit, the ancient language of India. In the early centuries of the Common Era, it had served as a lingua franca for the learned in a region that stretched from modern Afghanistan to Indonesia. Sanskrit was no longer spoken, but, like Latin or ancient Greek, it retained its liturgical function among India's Hindu majority. I would have had some notion of a vast body of literature in Sanskrit, but, as more an absence than a presence, it was further proof of an intellectual inheritance that had not come down to me. Absences can be suggestive, and I wondered if a voice from the past might serve as a beginning point in my quest to reconnect with India's history and language. That was why I went to see Mapu, an old friend of my mother's. He was among the few people I knew who had sought to regain what a colonial education had denied him: he had attempted a version of Frantz Fanon's "return to self."

We sat in Mapu's office in a lush enclave of New Delhi. The room was bright and bare, save for a painting of a blue dancing Shiva. Mapu was dressed in a white kurta, ribbed and starched. He had a classical face, prominent eyes and cheekbones. He was in his sixties but could still erupt into fits of childish laughter.

When I told him of my interest in Sanskrit, he began to speak of Kamlesh Dutt Tripathi, the former head of Sanskrit at Banaras Hindu University. Mapu described Tripathi as steeped in Indian myth. "He is someone who can pass a flowering tree, pick one, and say, 'Mapu, you know, this is the flower Kalidasa uses as an earring in such and such a play.'"

"What?" Mapu would say. "How do you know that?" Then Tripathi would show it to Mapu in a text.

This was the kind of knowledge Mapu had seen disappear in India from one generation to the next. The lines of transmission had gone dead, not centuries ago, but in his own lifetime. He felt the loss more acutely than most because he had worked in conservation.

"And I did it all wrong!" he cried.

He recalled one project in which he laid stone over all the ghats. When it was done, he went up and down the Ganges in a boat, proudly inspecting his achievement. On the shore, an old man approached with a troubled expression. He said, "But where will I read my Ramayana?"

"What do you mean?" Mapu said. "Here. There. Anywhere you like."

"Have you ever walked on the stone in the heat? It becomes very hot. I won't be able to sit on it."

Mapu was so upset that he went back to Delhi and resigned his post. He hadn't realized that that particular ghat had always been left unpaved. Trees grew there; it was a place of shade and cool, where people could come to read their scriptures and epics.

"Isn't there anyone to tell me these things?" he cried, seeing in this one crisis many others. "No writers, no historians, no architects?"

Mapu belonged to an aristocratic family, the second son of the second son of the maharaja of Kapurthala, a princely state in Punjab. His family were renowned Francophiles, but his parents were of a generation of Indians who were still culturally and linguistically bilingual. I had childhood memories of Mapu's mother, Aunty Sita, a tiny woman with a cap of woolly white hair. I had a passion for the Hindu gods as a child, and Aunty Sita would recite the Sanskrit hymn associated with the destructive dance of Shiva. Its dark dithyrambic beat gave me goose bumps. Aunty Sita, dressed forever in a widow's white and so at home in Indian ritual and custom, had seemed to me the picture of a traditional Hindu woman. As an adult, I was surprised to learn that the same woman had been a celebrated beauty of Europe in the 1930s. She was the muse of Man Ray, was dressed by the American designer Mainbocher; Barbara Hutton, Mapu's godmother, was a close personal friend. Mapu had inherited something of his mother's luminosity and grace, but by the time he grew up, the age of Indian bilingualism was over. Mapu's generation of upper-class Indians could barely complete a sentence in an Indian language, let alone move between cultures.

As a young man, Mapu paddled in the shallows of café society. He wore leather trousers and listened to the Eagles. He went abroad to meet the grand friends of his parents' and was spotted arriving at JFK in a peacock-feather cape. It was a pared-down version of the life his parents had led. Colonization overlaid by socialism had beggared the Indian aristocracy. They had lost their money, but they had also lost the style and confidence that comes to people who know their own culture before they know another.

That generation, educated in convents and English-style public schools, accepted cultural loss as inevitable. Mapu did not. He broke with his world, with its emptiness and ennui, and set himself on a course of restitution. He taught himself about Indian textiles and redesigned a jewel of a museum in Ahmedabad called the Calico Museum of Textiles. He was a founding member of INTACH, one of the country's first and most important conservation organizations. He went to Benares over and over, educating himself in Hindu tradition and ritual. He could explain what each element in a ceremony stood for, from the flowers that were used to the colors that were worn, and the Sanskrit verses that were associated with the different deities.

India ceased to be background for Mapu, ceased to be an interlude between foreign trips. The country his mother had so easily been part of, participating in all its ritual and customs, became his again. Mapu's quest earned him the scorn of his friends, who accused him of having gone native. "He used to be so glamorous," a friend of his once told me, "but Ahmedabad was the ruin of him."

It was nonsense; Mapu's time in Ahmedabad was his making. He could never fully regain what had been known when tradition was intact. Once that break occurs, it is final; it cannot be undone. But loss, like absence, need not be inert; it can allow one to look with curiosity and feeling upon that which others, more culturally intact, have taken for granted.

When I mentioned Sanskrit, Mapu said, "You're a very intense young man. And this is a language whose every nuance will come to intrigue you. It is important to know where to stop, important not to be sucked in by Sanskrit."

In the same breath, he brought up Kamlesh Dutt Tripathi. Mapu said he hoped Tripathi would agree to be my teacher and spoke romantically about the relationship between master and student, guru and *shishya*.

"Just as the guru chooses his shishya," Mapu said, "so too must the shishya choose his guru."

Mapu's own search for a guru had brought him to Ram Shankar Tripathi (no relation to Kamlesh Dutt), the head priest of the Kashi Vishwanath Temple. The meeting Mapu described, between himself and his guru, was every bit the mystical union that Arthur Koestler likens to "a soul in search of his assigned body," a search that ends in master and pupil instantly recognizing each other. When Ram Shankar Tripathi set eyes on Mapu, he simply said, "*Aa gaye ho, Raja Saab?*" (Ah, you've come, Raja Saab?) And that was that.

Mapu had first gone to Benares at the age of nineteen. "I fell in love with the city as a young man," he said, "and it has always been my first love." He stayed in a palace, and what he remembered above all else was the sound of bells. He would always think of it, he said, as the city of bells.

I was getting up to leave when Mapu's expression darkened. His mouth grew small, his lips arched.

"But you have to be able to hate it as well. You have to be able to look at that river and say, 'I hate you.' And when it gets too much, you must flee."

**THAT WAS DECEMBER 2007. IN** February of the next year, I was aboard the Kashi Vishwanath Express from Delhi bound for Benares. The carriages of the overnight train were striped in two shades of blue. I was traveling with an American friend, and we found our names on a passenger list glued to the outside. The platform was crowded with travelers, some asleep on their luggage, some sharing food from pink and white plastic bags. We traveled deep into the Indo-Gangetic Plain, which like the Nile or Indus Valley had been one of the basins of early civilization. The darkened landscape was dotted with redbrick buildings bathed in white fluorescent light. The train stopped along the way at medieval Muslim towns set on the banks of sluggish rivers. We passed brass-producing Moradabad, then Lucknow, the capital of the state of Uttar Pradesh. The stations, with their high-pointed arches and little canteens, were teeming despite the late hour, and anxious crowds awaited the arrival of the train.

In the morning, a sun of dull gold rose through tinted windows. The flat green fields smoked. The air in the sleeper grew close. The relative anonymity of the night before, with passengers boarding and disembarking into the early hours, gave way to the intimacy of waking up among strangers. Some stirred and stretched, others belched frankly. I felt the manners and indifference of the big city fall away, and the laws and customs of rural and small-town India come into effect. A few passengers took plastic vessels with them into the toilet; others brushed their teeth with sticks of neem out of the open door of the moving train. All this was a preparation of sorts. Delhi and Benares are only eight hundred kilometers apart, but the real distance, the sense of traveling across centuries, was not physical. Distances in India rarely are.

"Kashi," writes the historian Diana Eck in *Banaras: City of Light*, using the oldest name for the city, "is a place that gathers together the whole of India. Kashi is a cosmopolis—a city that is a world."

In Benares, it was possible to see in miniature every major event that had etched itself onto India's consciousness. The entire history of the subcontinent lay in bits and pieces on its river shore. When, twenty-five centuries ago, the Buddha burst out of Bihar, with a sermon ready on his lips, he delivered it at a deer park in what is today Sarnath thirteen kilometers from Benares. When Buddhism in India declined, and a resurgent Hindu faith arose, it was in Benares that a city of temples sprang up. When, in the twelfth century, the Muslim slave king Qutb ud-Din Aibak rode east from Delhi in a destructive fury, he laid waste to this ancient city of the Hindus, as would a succession of Muslim rulers who rose in Delhi over the next five centuries. In Benares, great mosques stood on the bones of old temples, and when Islam grew languid and over-refined, this city exerted such symbolic power over the Hindu imagination that a Hindu king took advantage of the decadence of the Muslim governor and founded a dynasty. It was in Benares, too, that the descendant of that dynasty was outmaneuvered, in the eighteenth century, by the new European power on the horizon. Warren Hastings, the British governor-general, came himself to face down Chet Singh, the Hindu king of Benares, in 1781, and fifteen years later the city came under British rule. Benares is the place that best embodies the India described by Jawaharlal Nehru, its first prime minister, as "an ancient palimpsest on which layer upon layer of thought and reverie had been inscribed, and yet no succeeding layer had completely hidden or erased what had been written previously."

I had been to Benares once before, as an eighteen-year-old, on my way to college in America. It was not my idea to go; I had wanted to spend the summer before college backpacking around Europe. But to this request of mine, my mother responded with surprising urgency: "You can do that anytime. Please go to Benares. Benares is the key to secret India."

I have a picture of myself from that first trip. My hair is cut short, and I am sitting on the stone steps of the riverfront, dressed in a black long-sleeved shirt, patterned with white oms: ॐ. I'm wearing baggy pants and sandals, and what the picture makes clear to me is that I have understood my mother's wish for me to visit Benares as encouragement to don a kind of fancy dress. I am a Western traveler, a modern-day hippie in search of "secret India." Denied permission to go backpacking in Europe, I have gone backpacking in India instead, like a child camping out in his own backyard. It was easy then to brush off any discomfort I might have known in Benares. I was on my way to college in America. The glamour of a future in the West propelled me forward without any thought to the past.

Things were different now, in 2008. I had returned to India for good, I thought. My time in the West had not led to a life there, but it had grafted a layer of anxiety onto my way of looking at India. I saw everything as an Anglicized Indian watching an imaginary European or American visitor watch India, and I had my heart in my mouth as I tried to guess what he would make of it. It was an embarrassment twice removed. Anything that made India seem like a freak show filled me with a double horror: my own, and the vicarious horror I felt on behalf of the white man I carried on my shoulder at all times. I hated the presence of these intervening selves. I wished I had a more direct relationship with my country. But any attempt to do so only made the self-observing selves multiply.

We were staying—my American friend and I—at the Ganges View, a lovely riverside hotel run by an effete Benares grandee.

The weather was beautiful, but the trip had gone badly. The city was in a black mood. That blackness, to which Mapu had obliquely referred, had a name—*tamas,* etymologically related to "tenebrous," was the term Benares gave to an underlying menace that was an accepted part of its character. "Those who are unfamiliar with Benares," writes Richard Lannoy, the author of *The Speaking Tree,* "can feel almost overwhelmed by the tamasic darkness they see there ... People shudder not only because of the physical decay and the craftiness and trickery of those who prey on the pilgrim trade but, more insidiously, because that physical and moral decay contributes to a creeping fear of familiar structures breaking down, all safeguards and moral boundaries dissolved by an aberrant and subversive power."

Tamas is inseparable from the chthonic energy of Shiva, the city's presiding deity, and the god of creative dissolution. Lannoy describes tamas as a downward pull as strong as gravity, "the dark ground" of Shiva's being. The city deals in equal measures of light and shade. There is dirt and squalor, death and disease; but there is also the transcendent spectacle of the river, and the utter beauty of people lost in meditation, waist-deep in water, as the sun comes up over the uninhabited opposite bank. So long as the balance holds, tamas is kept at bay. But when that darker element overwhelms the light, tamas can turn predatory. Then it is time, as Mapu said, to flee. It is to keep from becoming the victim of tamas that one is advised to seek the blessings of a fierce form of Shiva called Kala Bhairava before entering the city. Needless to say, we had not.

I wanted my American friend to see those eternal river scenes and the riveting life of the street, with its medieval artisans and workshops, the close air that had the cloying sweet smell of incense and linen in need of airing. But, despite my every effort, the city did not disclose its secrets. There was more shade than light. Benares was all surfaces. The river was flat and oily; beggars circled, more wretched than I remembered, their diseases more florid. Tumors ravaged one man's face, and flies covered the festering wound on a boy's lip. A darkling energy was abroad in the city. It was in search of a victim, and one morning it found him.

My friend and I stood on the riverfront, watching a group of Norwegians on a tour. A blond man in his forties, handsome, with a lined but youthful face, was dressed all in white. No sooner did our eyes settle on him than it was plain to see that something was terribly wrong. He looked stricken. He was trying to communicate something urgent to his guide. But his manners, his Scandinavian politeness, were too gentle for India. The guide smiled past the man's distress. Come on, I remember thinking, grab him, tell him that you need to go back to the hotel immediately. Instead, the guide prevailed and got the Norwegian to sit down on the steps of the river.

The sun was strong. The fear in the Norwegian's face was one I had known all my life in India: it was the fear of losing an individuated sense of self, which the West fosters, and India systematically undoes.

The group of tourists stood in front of a high rampart of rich honeyed stone. Its recessed arch was blind and frilled, the base festooned with red paan spittle. The Norwegian rose suddenly and lurched. He made one last flailing attempt to tell his guide that he was in bad shape. Then, before another word could be said, he crumpled into the arch. His face was deathly pale, his eyes rheumy. They fastened with blank intensity on the diamond-strewn surface of the river.

There was no way to shield him from the gaze of those on the riverfront. A crowd of twenty or so gathered around. For many moments, the man just sat there, in the arch, his internal discomfort gone, even as his external shame was amplified. Some moments later he was led away to the bus, the seat of his white trousers hideously stained.

**I HAD COME BACK TO** Benares in a cautious, noncommittal way. My wish to learn Sanskrit was an attempt to deal intellectually with a country whose reality perturbed me. I had not come to Benares prepared to do whatever it took to embrace that reality. I came hedging my bets. This second trip to Benares seemed destined to end like my first: in flight and oblivion. But then, on my last day, as if to deny me so easy an out, the city gave me a glimpse of its inner life. That was the day I met the twice-born.

My American friend was resting in the hotel. I had tried to meet Kamlesh Dutt Tripathi, but he was a hard man to track down. One of Mapu's contacts suggested I try the Abhinavagupta Research Library, where he was meant to be addressing a gathering of scholars. It was late afternoon when I arrived at the library, a pretty building with a façade of jalousie windows and sleeping columns, all in different shades of yellow, cream, and brown.

Inside, the Brahmins filed into the room, some bare-chested, some with foreheads emblazoned with caste marks. I had known Brahmins all my life, but I had not known Brahmins like these. The Brahmin, who sits at the top of the Hindu caste system, is "twice-born," or *dvija* in Sanskrit, for he is born once at the time of his actual birth, and then again when he is initiated by rite into his ancient vocation of the mind. The Brahmins I knew had not undergone this second birth; they were Brahmins in name only, and the life of tradition in a place such as Benares was as closed to them as it was to me.

Kamlesh Dutt Tripathi was among the twice-born. One of the younger Brahmins, seated on the floor next to me, pointed him out: a tall, thin-lipped man in his seventies, with a margin of fine white hair running along the shiny dome of his head. He was dressed that afternoon in a wrinkly off-white kurta, with a discreet dot of dark vermilion on his forehead. He addressed the others in Hindi, then switched to Sanskrit. For the next ninety minutes, I sat there in stupefaction listening to the Brahmins of Benares have a heated argument in Sanskrit. Someone explained that they were discussing *sphota*, an esoteric branch of Indian linguistics that dealt with the relationship between sound and meaning. Sphota, or "word-seeds," as the French mystic and poet René Daumal translates it, "evokes the blossoming of a flower, the development of a bud—thus a constant germinative power hidden beneath the appearances which manifest it."

I had never heard of the concept. I knew no Sanskrit. I did not know that ancient India had made a study of these things. I was ignorant of the Indian passion for grammar, linguistics, and hermeneutics, the obsession with literary theory and figures of speech. But I had studied Wittgenstein at Amherst; I knew of Hellenistic philosophy and the different Platonic schools. I had lived in two or three societies other than my own; I had traveled extensively in half a dozen more and written books about them; I had learned foreign languages; yet here I was, a few hundred miles from where I grew up, overtaken by an experience of the uncanny as powerful as any I had ever known.

Brahmins are sometimes described as members of a priesthood, but this is not quite right. Historically Brahmins were grammarians, logicians, writers, poets, astrologers, and scientists. They were men of the mind, as these men still were. I had seen Brahmins performing religious ceremonies and reading their scriptures. That interested me less. But I found the sight of these men engaged in an ancient form of scholarship utterly compelling. How strange that it had been right here all this while. Strange, too, that no connection should exist between their world and mine—that India's intellectual past should play no role in engendering its present and future. A link had been severed, but I knew too little about what had been lost to feel the pain of it. What struck me hard that afternoon was how automatic my incuriosity about old India had been.

I had felt a discomfort since my return, a melancholy, an odd feeling of being abstracted. Nehru had written of the "spiritual loneliness" he put down to having become "a queer mixture of the East and the West, out of place everywhere, at home nowhere." He wrote, "I am a stranger and alien in the West. I cannot be of it. But in my own country also, sometimes, I have an exile's feeling." Nehru no doubt felt a version of what the French intellectual Didier Eribon experienced in relation to class—"the discomfort that results from belonging to two different worlds, worlds so far separated from each other that they seem irreconcilable, and yet which coexist in everything that you are." That afternoon among the Brahmins of Benares, I knew an odd feeling of being impoverished by my exposure to other places. The legacy of British rule in India meant that I belonged to a zone of overlap that lay between East and West. It was what made it easy for me to go to college in America. The linguistic and cultural familiarity with multiple societies should have brought forth a rich cosmopolitanism; but instead it had been sterile, and it had left me feeling somehow poorer for my experiences.

Like so much of the old non-West, India was an ancient civilization reborn as a modern nation, twice-born in another sense. But it was amazing to consider how long it had been trying to cure itself of the trauma of its second birth. A hundred years ago, in this very town, the Banaras Hindu University had been founded with the stated intention of closing the gap between East and West. At its inauguration, in 1916, a little-known leader, freshly arrived from his activities in South Africa, had caused "a beautiful scandal."

"It is a matter of deep humiliation and shame for us," began Mohandas Karamchand Gandhi—addressing an audience comprising the viceroy, a pride of Indian princes, and Annie Besant, the leading theosophist and champion of self-rule for India—"that I am compelled this evening, under the shadow of this great college in this sacred city, to address my countrymen in a language that is foreign to me ... But suppose that we had been receiving, during the past fifty years, education through our vernaculars, what should we have today? We should have today a free India, we should have our educated men, not as if they were foreigners in their own land but speaking to the heart of the nation ..."

Gandhi was responding to a process that had been set in motion a century before. The British administrator Lord Macaulay was roughly my age—in his midthirties—when, in 1834, he was appointed to the Committee of Public Instruction. Macaulay had felt duty bound to create a "class who may be interpreters between us and the millions whom we govern; a class of persons, Indian in blood and colour, but English in taste, in opinions, in morals and in intellect." He envisaged an Indian elite that would gradually extend modern knowledge to the great mass of the population. But this is not what happened. Instead the class of interpreters grew more isolated with every generation, and by the time Gandhi gave his speech, the distance between the two Indias had become the cause of pain and anxiety, both for those who felt talked down to and for those who had been colonized and now lived at a great remove from their country.

In Mapu's generation, the sense of loss must have been painful enough to warrant a desire for return. In my generation, the memory of loss had been erased. It had been sublimated into a quiet, passionless aversion to one's own culture. A dullness of mind, an almost willful ignorance. Until that day in Benares "colonization" had felt like an abstraction, one of those overused words, such as "poverty" or "global warming," that seem to obscure meaning. But that afternoon in the Abhinavagupta Library, my colonization felt as real to me as a law of nature. It was as if my upbringing in India, innocent and unthinking on the surface, had been acted upon by a quietly coercive force that had the power to bend space and time. It could make New York feel culturally nearer to my Delhi than to Benares, and it could put centuries between those living next to one another, making foreigners of people in places they had never left.

The image of the Brahmins of Benares seared itself into my mind. But I now also found it impossible to approach Tripathi with my original intention of learning Sanskrit. Mapu had spoken romantically of the relationship between guru and shishya. Perhaps he was nearer the life of tradition and could imagine himself immersed in it again. I, for my part, could not. Incredible as it was to glimpse the antiquity of a sacralized form of learning, to witness was not to participate. The induction into the ancient language was a ritual part of a traditional Brahmin boy's passage into manhood.

The world of ritual was closed to me. To insinuate myself into it now would have felt like an unspeakable act of fraudulence. A break had occurred, and I was on the other side of it.

# SUMMER

# 2

# THE COLOR-FILLED ELEVENTH

**IT WAS MARCH WHEN I** went to see Mapu about going back to Benares again. Six years had passed since that February day in 2008 when I had seen the Brahmins at the Abhinavagupta Library and left soon after for Delhi, half in terror, half in wonder. I wrote to Mapu when I got home, thanking him for the introduction to Tripathi:

> Just back from Benares. I'm sad to say that it defeated me this time round. I got in touch with KD Tripathi, but when we went to see him he wasn't there. Later I caught up with him at a Sanskrit seminar he was organising. I've never seen anything

> more dazzling in my life: five or six grand Brahmins in a room full of people, sounds of cycle bells and horse carriages, coming up from the street, arguing passionately with each other in fluent Sanskrit. It was also at this moment that I was overwhelmed ... I felt I wasn't ready for him at all, felt that this was not the time to approach him with my beginner's interest in learning Sanskrit. Also, Benares, in the way only certain cities can, cities like Venice, started to go wrong. And in this new ugliness, I felt that there was a message for me ... I think I need some grounding in Sanskrit before going back there.

Mapu replied with understanding: "Thank you for your mature statement. There are many ways to begin learning Sanskrit..." But I sensed he was disappointed. He knew what it was for the distance at which westernized Indians held India to collapse, knew how unnerving that collapse could be, and was perhaps sad that I had not had the courage to see it through—that I had resorted to the simple option of flight. But from that day on, I had spent several hours of every day learning Sanskrit.

I came to Sanskrit out of a need to hear a voice from the past. That day in Benares it had struck me hard that there had been twenty centuries of continuous literary production in India, yet when I started out as a writer in Delhi, I had felt myself to be working out of a vacuum. "The historical sense," T. S. Eliot says, "compels a man to write not merely with his own generation in his bones, but with a feeling that the whole of the literature of Europe from Homer and within it the whole of the literature of his own country has a simultaneous existence." It "involves" a perception "not only of the pastness of the past, but of its presence."

I had no past as complete as that. Two thousand years of literary production in India and my perception of the past comprised little more than a handful of Victorian novels, a few snatches of Urdu poetry, and some Indian writing in English—R. K. Narayan, V. S. Naipaul,

Salman Rushdie. Sanskrit gave me more literature than I could have read in twenty lifetimes. There were treatises and court poems, epics and plays. I read for the first time the marvelous opening to the Ramayana in which the sage Valmiki summons verse (*shloka*) "from an access of grief" (*shoka*); I lost myself in the mournful quatrains of Bhartrihari, with their relentless pessimism: "Gone indeed is youth, fruitless, like a lamp burning itself out in an empty house!" I especially loved the Sanskrit commentators, who, each with a distinctive style of literary analysis, made up a parallel history of reading to go along with the trove of texts. One commentator in particular, Mallinatha, active in fifteenth-century South India, virtually taught me the poetry of Kalidasa, who had lived ten centuries before. It was amazing to read a paragraph of Mallinatha's thoughts beneath the impenetrable fifth-century couplet, now breaking up difficult compounds, now making wry observations. The link with the commentators—even more than with the poets and the dramatists—was electrifying. It was continuity; it opened the way to feeling whole again.

Sanskrit is the oldest, fullest expression we have of a shared Indo-European linguistic past. An underground stream of language had run parallel to the rise and fall of empires, connecting places as far apart as the western reaches of China and Ireland. To possess Sanskrit was to look afresh at the history of language. My relationship to English—the language I thought, wrote, and dreamed in—changed. I stopped seeing it as merely the legacy of colonization, but part of a history older and grander than that of nations. Sanskrit made it possible for me to take ownership of the Indian past, but I was only too aware that these thrills occurred in a kind of intellectual vacuum. And it was from my wish to close the gap between text and context that I sought Mapu out again. I was ready to return to Benares on firmer footing.

Mapu asked me to lunch at his house in Noida, a suburb of Delhi. It was an afternoon swept with windy shadows. The doors and windows of the Spartan bungalow where Mapu lived had been thrown open—

the heat was almost there—and the white muslin curtains blew inward very gently. Mapu served a vegetarian meal and then we sat outside. When he heard what I had come to see him about, he said:

"But I'm going to Benares next week! Why don't you come with me?"

Mapu's access in Benares was legendary. "He keeps the keys to secret India in his pocket," my mother had said. Mapu explained that at the Kashi Vishwanath Temple, where the former priest was his guru, there was to be a great spring festival. The Rangbhari Ekadashi, literally the Color-Filled Eleventh, which occurred on the eleventh day of the lunar month of Phalguna, marked the beginning of the festival of Holi in the city.

"It is the night Shiva and Parvati consummate their marriage," Mapu said. "And it's wonderful. I'm too old to hack it. But you should definitely go."

I asked after Kamlesh Dutt Tripathi.

"K. D. Tripathi lost his son some years ago. And he's not been the same since."

I asked Mapu why—since he was not attending the festival—he was going to Benares at all.

"I want to see my guru before I pass on."

Mapu was in his sixties; his guru was in his nineties. Surely, Mapu meant, before *he*, the guru, passed on.

"My chart says I have two more years at best," Mapu said casually.

"How do you know?" I gasped.

"Birth and death, we know," he said, and his eyes gleamed.

**BIRTH AND DEATH HAD ALSO** played their part in bringing me back to Benares. In January 2011, three years before my return to that city, I was woken by a phone call from my mother in Delhi: "Your father is dead. He was killed a few hours ago in Islamabad."

I was in New York, in a borrowed flat in Alphabet City. The sky in the two westward facing windows was dark.

My father was the governor of Punjab in Pakistan. He and my mother had met in Delhi in 1980. He was there promoting his biography of Zulfikar Ali Bhutto, the Pakistani prime minister, who had recently been deposed in a military coup and executed; my mother, a cub reporter on a national daily, had been sent to interview him. They had a brief, passionate affair, conducted between London and Dubai, which eventually fell apart. My mother returned to Delhi with me. My father went on to a career in politics in Pakistan. We had a relationship for some years, starting when I was twenty-one. Difficulties arose between us after the publication of my first book, *Stranger to History*. I had not seen or spoken to my father in three years, since the night Benazir Bhutto, the former prime minister of Pakistan, was killed. He had in the meantime become the governor of Punjab. And now he was dead too.

An architecture student whom I had been dating for the past six months lay asleep next to me. I woke him. "My father's been killed."

We made coffee and checked our phones. A friend of my mother's in Lahore had emailed, "Your father has been shot. He was killed by his gunman. We are here."

A few minutes later she called. My father, she told me, had been killed by a member of his elite guard in Islamabad. He had finished lunch with a friend and was about to get into his car when Malik Mumtaz Qadri shot him twenty-seven times. He died before he reached the hospital. Qadri said he killed him because of his position on Pakistan's blasphemy laws.

In the weeks leading up to his death, my father had taken up the cause of a poor Christian woman accused of blasphemy. The blasphemy laws, which had been given sharper teeth in the 1980s by a military dictator, were draconian; they had become an instrument in the hands of the Muslim majority to persecute the country's few religious minorities. My father spoke out against the severity of the laws; he called them "man-made," "black laws." He thought he was protected by his class and stature—he joked in drawing rooms about how the clerics had declared him *wajib-ul-qatl,* an Islamic designation given to a man "fit to be killed." The judgment of clerics and television hosts fell hard on my father. He came to be a blasphemer himself in the eyes of many. They burned him in effigy; they issued fatwas against him and made threats on his life. He responded with a bravery that was in part real, in part a feeling of class security tantamount to blindness. He quoted poetry; he tweeted prophetically, "I was under huge pressure sure 2 cow down b4 rightest pressure on blasphemy. Refused. Even if I'm the last man standing."

One by one the calls began to come in from Pakistan.

A family friend rang in tears. "Just the other day, I was telling him to be careful. I can't believe it, I just can't believe he's dead."

She had used exactly the same words for Benazir Bhutto three years before. But it was not so unbelievable that my father had been killed. The story was nothing if not a lesson in the fragility of the power of the colonial classes. In the hours, days, weeks, and months to come, my father's killer would become a hero in Pakistan. Lawyers showered him with rose petals on the night he killed my father; ordinary people sent him food and money in jail, named a mosque after him, and had their children blessed by him. It was practically impossible to bring him to justice. During the trial, the killer's lawyers gestured to my father's "lifestyle," "his character and associated matters." My father was also a kind of foreigner in Pakistan. His mother was English; he was liberal, westernized; he had no religious faith in a country where the decade after 9/11 had given Islam a new vitality. My father's foreignness, not unlike my own in India, had made his position in Pakistan far more precarious than he had realized.

The day he was killed wore on. More calls, more emails. I looked at the news on my phone. When at last I got my sister on the line, she said again and again, fighting tears, "Such a bad day to die." The news showed scenes similar to those I had seen in Pakistan when Benazir was killed three years before. The same flags, the same slogans, the same billboards—"How many Bhuttos will you kill? From every house a Bhutto will emerge!"—but now, in place of Benazir's face, there was my father's. The more I watched, the more the story of my father's killing slipped away from me, becoming something remote in the world beyond. The only image that remained in my mind was of a pool of blood on a dusty stretch of road. Security men in dark blue uniforms stood around. It was hard to believe it was blood, *his* blood.

There was press interest, and I thought I should say something:

> We had our differences, but he was the bravest man I knew, a man without the capacity for fear. And if there was one thing I never doubted about him, it was his love of Pakistan. It never allowed him to believe what had become of the country his forefathers had fought for. Today he joins that sad procession of martyrs—every day a thinner line—standing between Pakistan and its inexorable descent into fear and nihilism.

My agent suggested I remove "inexorable."

The next morning, I trudged past the small hillocks of begrimed ice that had formed on the curbs and bought *The New York Times* at a deli. My father's killer's picture was on the front page. It would be five years before it was possible to carry out the death sentence he had been given—such was his popularity—and then a crowd the size of a small city would pour out into the streets to bid him farewell. It would be one of the largest funerals in the country's history. My father's, in comparison, was a small affair, from which many senior leaders, including the president, stayed away for fear of reprisals. My father's death was part of my reason for wanting to go back to Benares.

It showed me that the isolation of people such as myself on the Indian subcontinent was not merely undesirable; it was dangerous.

**I WAS IN BENARES A** week after Mapu and I had lunch.

The riverfront curled around the Ganges in a four-mile crescent, less than a mile wide. This was the labyrinth of sunless streets, the city of palaces and temples, the warren of infinite variety. Beyond was a drab and nondescript Indian town that graded into open fields. With half of India at its back, and the Ganges before it, the city felt like an island. The name Varanasi came from the two smaller rivers—the Varuna to the north, and the now-extinct Assi to the south—that enclosed between them all that was considered sacred: a slim sickle of consecrated land watched over by Shiva.

"Benares is older than history, older than tradition, older even than legend," wrote Mark Twain, "and looks twice as old as all of them put together." In fact, little of brick and mortar was older than five hundred years. But the city was older as an idea than a reality. What the Belgian Sinologist Simon Leys says of China—"the Chinese everlastingness does not inhabit monuments, but people"—was true of India too: it was "a past of the mind," and the material reality was almost actively disdained. "All of us alike can see her obvious form," said the renowned monk Swami Karpatri, but Kashi has a "subtle form" too. It is this, added Anant Maharaj, another of the city's great teachers, that "is like the sun behind the clouds. I know it is still there although I cannot see it."

The ghats of Benares are encrusted with history and legend. From these four miles of riverside it was possible to know every major historical event, every religion, every region, caste, and community that had for three thousand years seeped into the memory of India.

The Tulsi Ghat, in the far south, was where, in the sixteenth century, a rebellious Brahmin named Tulsidas composed his retelling of the story of Ram in simple vernacular, thereby freeing it from the hold of the Brahmins, and releasing it among ordinary people. Farther along was the first of the cremation ghats, where funeral pyres burned all day and night. It was named after Harishchandra, a king who gave away his kingdom, sold his family into slavery, and worked as a *dom*, one of the low castes designated to handle the remains of the dead. He was about to cremate the body of his own son when the gods appeared, to release him from his suffering. Ahead was the Piazza San Marco of ghats—the Dashashwamedh—where every evening a great spectacle of river worship was performed before an armada of pilgrims and tourists in long wooden boats. Just beyond that was the second of the burning ghats, the Manikarnika, where the earth was black and exposed, the logs piled high, and mourners in white peaked caps were visible through a screen of smoky orange fire. This was the great cremation ground where Arthur Koestler, watching corpses wrapped in cotton sheets that appeared bloodstained because they were printed in pink and white patches, had been reminded of the crematoriums at Auschwitz. Then there was the Ahilyabai Ghat, in front of which that picture of me as an eighteen-year-old in Benares was taken. It was named for Ahilyabai Holkar, a warrior queen from central India who had rebuilt the Kashi Vishwanath Temple in 1669 after Aurangzeb, the last of the great Mughals, razed it during the final Islamic assault on the city. The riverscape was threaded through with such stories, and at the far end, in the very north, the arc of history stopped abruptly at the Raj Ghat, the verdant setting for the Krishnamurti Foundation. Running parallel to the life on the river was the life of the streets, with their uneven patchwork of paving stones, their blue-washed buildings, their wrought-iron balconies and projecting oriel windows, their deep overhanging eaves and carved brackets, the saw-toothed dentil ornaments creeping in fits and starts along the walls, all winding their way, slowly but surely, in the direction of the Kashi Vishwanath Temple.

The temple sat in the shadow of a great white mosque. I was met by one of the sons of Mapu's guru, the old priest, and was led swiftly through the network of tight surrounding streets. Bright shops sold everything from cosmetics and copper vessels to religious offerings. We went deeper into the market, nearer the temple, and the police presence grew heavy. They were guarding the mosque, which was occasionally visible through the bars of a towering metal fence. I stopped to look, and a policeman in olive green ushered me on. I could tell from the name on his badge that he was Hindu; they *all* were; and there was something strange about this Islamic building, which must still have caused offense, guarded by Hindus from, I suppose, themselves. From what they might do if their passions got the better of them.

Tonight, especially, was a night when passions would run high, and the ecstasies of faith would merge with the very real intoxication of bhang. Tonight was one of four nights in the year when the temple was open all night, and we were about to witness a raj puja.

Mapu's guru's house was on a downward-sloping street covered in crude strips of bright green artificial grass. A narrow strip of sky, suffused pink, was visible past the crowded houses and the vines of snaking thick black wire creeping overhead, naked bulbs hanging off them like fruit. We were led through a small shop, with powdery-pink walls and glass cabinets filled with silk saris, and upstairs to where the old Brahmin sat, chewing his lips.

He was wizened and sparrow-chested, with gray leggings covering his thin, exquisitely wrinkled legs. He sat in a tiny room, no bigger than an attic, which was cluttered with offerings for the ceremony that was soon to begin in the temple downstairs. The temple had been confiscated from the old priest decades ago and put in a trust managed by the state; he had spent his life in courts, and was old and embittered. He was practically deaf, but the odd phrase did make its way through. He looked hard at me with his small intent eyes, and then, chewing his lips and flaring his eyes, he said, "I see that these swines in Congress have put up that young whippersnapper Rahul!"

Rahul was Rahul Gandhi, and his grandmother, Indira Gandhi, had been the old priest's great enemy. It was her government that had taken his temple away.

Mapu's guru now became philosophical. "*Sarvam khalv idam brahma*," he muttered: all is indeed Brahma. "Time beats on, forward, forward. Man must find himself within the confines of time."

The thought comforted him for a moment, then rancor returned. "Everything has been destroyed."

The walls of the room were hung with paintings of the old priest's father, grandfather, and great-grandfather, and pictures of the guru with various members of the Nepalese royal family. Princes had once patronized the priests; now it was all businessmen. A picture of the sanctum sanctorum of the temple showed the *linga*, an aniconic representation of Shiva, in a silver basin embedded in the floor.

A monkey appeared at the window and looked longingly at the offerings. An expression of pure delight crossed the old priest's face.

"Look!" he said, his eyes brimming with light. "He's picked up the fragrance of the food."

It was time to go in. The ceremony was about to begin. I asked Mapu's guru if he would join us, but he looked away in sadness. "You go on," he said, "I am too old now."

Downstairs we met his grandson Golu. He was the last member of this Brahmin family who was directly connected to the temple. He was in his early thirties and wore a black Nehru-collared coat and pink-stemmed rimless glasses. There was little to suggest he was a priest at all, save for the top-lock of caste on the crown of his head: the *shikha*, which means "crest" or "summit," is the mark of the twice-born. Many older societies, from the Native American to the Persian and Jewish to Edo Japan, have a version of this uncut measure of hair.

Golu's was a particularly impressive example, thick, oiled, and plaited. He disappeared behind a curtain to change and reappeared a moment later in full ceremonial gear: two measures of unstitched white cloth, with necklaces of coral and rudraksh hanging from his neck. Golu enjoyed the effect his transformation had on me. He flashed me a roguish smile, and I saw that his gums were encrusted with the reddish grit from paan.

Golu led me deep into the walled precincts of the temple, which was a small building with a red base and spires of dull beaten gold. The energy inside was electric. A breathless swarm of devotees rushed from shrine to smaller shrine. Corpulent priests snatched money from the devotees' hands and pressed offerings into them in exchange. Young Brahmins, their thin bodies smeared with sandalwood paste, carried sloshing brass pails of milk to and from the sanctum. Golu was in constant demand. Everybody needed him to do something—now a group of women who wanted access to the inner sanctum, now the agent of a rich businessman who wanted offerings to be made on his behalf. Important people had paid serious money to witness the ceremony up close. Golu tended to them all, gentle and coaxing to the rich and powerful, abrasive and rough with the poor.

In the sanctum, devotees clawed and groped their way to the linga, which was never more beautiful than when it was unadorned, smooth and black. The sanctum, a small tube-lit room, was heavily ornamented with marble carvings. It contained almost nothing save for the silver basin with the linga, and the simple austerity of the black oblong stone that represented Shiva was especially striking amid all this marble and silver.

The devotees were greedy for *darshana*. The word derives from the Sanskrit verb for "to see" and suggests an audience, or a beholding. The idea is of a spiritual enrichment that comes entirely from setting eyes on, or even being in the presence of, a revered object or person, and having the deity set eyes on the devotee. Nothing need be said or done. Seeing is all, and the benediction passes soundlessly from the eyes to the soul.

Shiva and Parvati, the bridal couple, were waiting in a temple across the street. Their arrival here was to be the focal point of the ceremony. The linga, in the meantime, was washed and honored.

Golu smuggled me right to the door of the sanctum, past the policemen, who seemed rattled. Charged with protecting the mosque next door from the zeal that was about to be unleashed in the temple, they had to balance their duty to the modern state with the primal demands of religion. It didn't seem like much of a contest, and as I watched these representatives of the "secular" state, in their uniforms already red from the colored powder with which the worshippers were smearing each other, I felt that the ceremony would reclaim them.

I had been seated at the door of the sanctum while a moving mass of bodies swayed over me, occupying every inch of available space. A steady flow of consecrated items was passed by the priests inside the sanctum to the faithful outside: rose water, attar, sandalwood, flowers. The crush around me was unbearable. The air was warm and over-breathed. My right leg fell asleep. Inside the sanctum, Golu was swinging languidly from a red cloth tied to the doorway. He was completely at ease, laughing and joking with the officiating priests, who sat on the floor, even as the hypnotic cry of the Samaveda—the Veda of song, a wild and choral hymn beloved of Shiva—reverberated through the sanctum. The priests, like a troupe of performers, were engaged in an activity that was commonplace to them but of great importance to their audience. The faithful were treated roughly by the younger priests. Old and young alike were pulled and pushed out of the way, some wrenched by their limbs, their faces intent and desperate for more darshana.

Other blessed items began to pour out of the sanctum. The crush intensified. Arms reached out from the wall of humanity for a little turmeric, sandalwood paste, or scented oil. All these things had touched the linga and were sacred by association. I could not bear the fervor any longer. I broke out of the crowd into the clearing of the open courtyard. I was able to breathe again. The throng closed behind me. The sky was dark. I got a glimpse of the night sky overhead and the silhouettes of armed men standing on rooftops. The song of the priests was reaching its crescendo within the sanctum. Bells were crashing inside; I glimpsed an eruption of white light—and fire! Smoke wafted out of the narrow doorway and I had an odd feeling of synesthesia: I could taste and smell the colors. The mouth of the inner sanctum was blocked with human bodies. But a rumor had begun to spread through the walled confines of the temple, whose doors were now locked: Shiva and Parvati were in the building. Drummers appeared in the passages of the temple, beating the two-headed drum of Shiva. The idols, glimpsed for a second, vanished into the crowd.

The tempo quickened. Sudden eruptions of red appeared throughout the temple. We were all covered in powder and silver mica. It was part carnival, part riot. Then I saw something that captured the breakdown of boundaries that I had sensed was imminent earlier: a policeman who, moments before, had been patrolling the precincts of the temple, yelling orders into a handheld microphone, was swept up in the ecstasy. His olive-green uniform was covered in red; his eyes were rheumy from bhang; and using that same government-issue microphone into which he had been barking orders a moment before, he now bellowed a primal invocation to Shiva: "*Hara hara bom bom, hara hara Mahadev.*"

In the background, past a lattice of barbed wire, was the white mosque, the heavily defended symbol of a fragile historical peace.

**THE LEGACY OF BRITISH RULE** in India was one fault line, the legacy of Islamic rule another. The night after the ceremony at the temple, Mapu told me a story that gave a partial view of how India had dealt—or perhaps not dealt—with the physical remains of a history of invasion.

I had hardly seen Mapu until then. I had arrived and gone straight to the temple for the ceremony, and then Mapu was busy tending to his many friendships in the city. We talked at last at some length over dinner at the Ganges View Hotel. I told Mapu how strange it had been to see the mosque, adjacent to one temple and standing on the ruins of another, protected by Hindus. It was then that Mapu told me the story of Marshal Tito, the Yugoslavian dictator, in Benares:

"He was greeted by the Kashi Naresh"—the king of Benares. "The two men took a river tour of the city. Drifting up the Ganges, the Kashi Naresh pointed to the site of a major Hindu temple. Tito was surprised to see that there was no temple there at all, but a large red mosque. And he questioned the Kashi Naresh about this."

Mapu paused, his eyes glittering. Here were two men who came from places with very similar histories—several centuries of Muslim rule over a non-Muslim population. The Balkan approach to the unwanted reminders of that past had been different from India's. When I traveled through the region in 2005, I remember people telling me that Sofia once had sixty-nine mosques, of which only one still stood. This historical attitude was summed up in Rebecca West's *Black Lamb and Grey Falcon* in which a Macedonian wishes to remake Macedonia as it had been five hundred years before. Whenever he saw a ruined church or a castle that belonged to the Serbs and was destroyed by the Turks, "he would take Turks and Moslem Albanians away from where they lived until he had enough labour to rebuild them, and then he made them work under armed guards. And when people said, 'But you must not do that,' he answered, 'But why not? They knocked them down, didn't they?'"

"So, what did the Kashi Naresh say to Tito?" I pressed Mapu.

"He said"—Mapu suppressed a smile—"that every day the shadow of the mosque's minaret comes and falls at the feet of Lord Ram!"

Now it was Tito's turn to smile. "You're a very tolerant people."

"But was he so tolerant, this old king of Benares?" I asked Mapu.

"No!" Mapu cried. "He was an old bigot!"

Yet the story stood as an example of how singular India's approach to its past of invasion and conquest had been. This was the sophistication of Nehru's palimpsest country. Save for the demolition of a sixteenth-century Mughal mosque in 1992, which had marked the beginning of the rise of Hindu nationalism, India's approach to its varied and difficult history had been synthesis and assimilation. It had rarely sought erasure.

Mapu told the story on the eve of the rise of another kind of leader in India. While we were in Benares, news had broken, spreading through the clogged streets of the temple town, that Narendra Modi, the prime ministerial candidate of the Hindu nationalist Bharatiya Janata Party (BJP), had chosen Benares as one of his two constituencies for the general election two months away. Modi was not from Benares, or even Uttar Pradesh, and the significance of his choosing the eternal city of the Hindus as his parliamentary seat was not lost on anyone. He was repurposing its symbolic power to fit his politics of revival.

**I HAD FIRST HEARD MODI** speak one September morning in Delhi, six months before. It was a dazzling day of crystal heat—the kind that follows the rains in India. An editor friend and I had come far too early to a dengue-infested wasteland in west Delhi called Japanese Park. The press enclosure held mainly cub reporters and Hindi-language journalists. There were no senior commentators, no one from the foreign press.

The mood at first was lackluster, the crowd small. The prodigious heat, the greasy packaged breakfasts, the tiresome looping slogans made my friend and me restless. We were half considering leaving when the strangest thing occurred: the sky darkened; a cool wind began to blow; the temperature dropped by many perceptible degrees. A poster of Modi, tied to the steel frame of the tent, came free and began to flap in the wind. The effect was magical. It was as if Modi, arm raised, were waving at us. The crowd began to cheer. Photographers in the press enclosure captured this small miracle, not merely because it was wondrous to see the apparition of the leader waving at us, but because the change in weather corresponded exactly to Modi's arrival on the dais.

I stood up on my chair and looked behind me. The crowd had grown into a throng. They had been arriving all the time, quietly filing into the open tent from all sides. Now, as far as the eye could see, down the length of the vast tent and pouring out of it in every direction, I saw great multitudes of restless young men. These people were a world away from the old base of the Congress Party. Those had been the faces of a rural class, infinitely patient, weather-beaten and lined, eyes yellow from undernourishment. These were men of jeans and sneakers and fashionable haircuts—"spice cuts," as I was later to learn they were called. They were slightly built, the bones small and prominent, their thin wrists bandaged in red religious threads. The wiriness of their bodies seemed to intensify the seething male energy they projected.

They were spread across a wide income bracket. Some wore blue rubber slippers; others, fashionable sneakers. Some came on bicycles and scooters, others in small cars. Some wore polyester shirts, with baggy trousers in dull colors; others, cotton and denim. These were the temple-goers: Hindi speaking, deliriously nationalistic, young and full of idealism. That they were middle-class had less to do with their income, and more to do with their aspirations and self-image. When Modi began to speak—after the interminable bugling of a conch and cries of "Victory to Mother India!"—he was able to convert their belief in themselves into the political pain of dreams deferred and the wasted promise of youth.

He began with humor, which was rare. Indian politicians are not by and large funny. "The prime minister," he said, referring to the frail Sikh gentleman, regarded by many as a puppet who reported directly to Rahul Gandhi and his mother, Sonia Gandhi, "is in America at the moment. He is groveling before Obama, telling him we are a poor country. America must help us."

Silence fell over the crowd. In imitation of the prime minister's thin, plaintive voice, Modi said, "We are a nation of some one and a quarter billion, but we are poor. Help us!" There was some laughter. "I have only one question," Modi now said, in a low growl. "Is this real poverty? Is this the poverty of our towns and villages? Or is this also that 'state of mind' poverty of which the Prince speaks?"

The Prince was Rahul Gandhi. Modi used him as a metonym for the Indian elite. Gandhi was reluctant, effete, and—oddly enough for a Gandhi—charmless. No communicator, he had just referred to Indian poverty as "a state of mind." It came off sounding like a modern version of "let them eat cake," and translated into Hindi, it sounded even worse, like a medical condition.

The crowd roared with laughter; but Modi himself was no longer laughing.

He implored his followers to tell him how the prime minister of Pakistan, who had at the United Nations recently described the Indian premier as a "village crone," could dare insult India's prime minister abroad. Modi's anger grew, and it was a frightening thing to behold, a crescendo of outrage and humiliation. "In honor-and-shame cultures like those of India and Pakistan," writes Salman Rushdie, "male honor resides in the sexual probity of women, and the 'shaming' of women dishonors all men." Here, India was the shamed woman, and Modi the man who would restore her honor, and thereby the honor of his vast male audience. He would give her back her dignity and return her to the glories of eons past. She would once again stand, head high, among the comity of nations.

If India's shame dishonored the tens of thousands who had come out to hear Modi speak, they, in turn, knew a shame of their own through joblessness and lack of opportunity. Their male pride had been hurt. Modi would empower them. His belief in these people was absolute. He saw in them a potential even their own mothers had failed to see. He felt their ambition as they felt it; he was kept awake at night by their restlessness; and he promised to ennoble that youthful energy with an outlet. He would give them jobs. The rest would follow. The dream was vague and short on details, but that was so much part of its charm.

That morning after Japanese Park, I came home and wrote in my diary:

> His victory will decimate the opposition. Not just in terms of numbers, but philosophically too. It will be a long time before they find their way again. The pundits in Delhi will say, *How will he find the numbers?* The numbers will come. This is going to be one of those elections when all the old calculations cease to apply.

**THE RISE OF MODI WAS** part of a historical awakening. In 1992, Hindu mobs destroyed a sixteenth-century mosque in Ayodhya, which they said stood on the birthplace of the epic hero Ram. Riots ensued, and the BJP profited politically from the atmosphere that was created. A few years later, they formed their first government in Delhi. Modi had been one of the organizers of the movement that led to the demolition of the mosque. Modi knew that the historical wound left by the Islamic invasions of India had a violent potential; the demolition of the mosque showed him how history could be made to serve politics. He positioned himself squarely at the center of a triangular historical antagonism. He made out that India had endured a thousand years of slavery, first under Muslims, then under the British. The inheritors of that history were the anglicized classes, a small elite as represented by the Nehru-Gandhi dynasty, and India's 170 million Muslims, a largely converted population that comprised some of its poorest citizens. Modi's genius was to open a culture war on two fronts, in which he used the passion generated by anti-Muslim feeling, especially virulent in his home state of Gujarat, to attack the ruling Congress Party, accusing it of coddling minorities to the detriment of the Hindu majority.

In 2001, Modi became chief minister of Gujarat, where he presided over some of the worst religious violence in recent years. In 2002, some two thousand people, the majority of them Muslim, were killed in riots, and the state looked the other way. It didn't hurt Modi politically. He won, and won again. The senior leadership of his party were unable to prevent his rise. He now stood at the precipice of becoming prime minister, and as with other leaders adept in the politics of revenge and revival, he played down the element of revenge as he grew more powerful, speaking only of development and progress. He became many things to many people, while never entirely disabusing the party faithful of their implicit belief that when he came to power, he would find a way to settle the scores of the past. Modi would usher in an age when Nehru's palimpsest would be scraped down to its bottommost layer, where Hindu purity, free of British and Islamic accretion, could be found.

In 1998, my mother interviewed the writer V. S. Naipaul for television. "Well, I am probably not as horrified by Ayodhya as most people are," Naipaul said. "I see that Babur was no friend of India, had little regard for India. And, in Babur's building of a mosque there, there would have been an expression of contempt. So, if you behave in this way, you challenge hubris. If you are a builder and a conqueror, and nemesis catches up with you a few centuries later, really, one shouldn't complain."

Naipaul's view was received with dismay on the left and exaltation on the right. It was an election year, the BJP was poised to form the government in Delhi, and Naipaul was seen to be giving intellectual support to the worst elements in Indian politics. Naipaul had also made an important clarification that was missed in the hysteria of that time:

> Let me talk about the other matter, the matter of the invasions and why a political idea of taking revenge doesn't make sense. I think that after a cultural death, a true revival comes about when we accept that the past is truly dead. As I said earlier, the Dark Ages in Europe came about when there was a strong belief among the people that the old world was continuing, that the classical world was just going on, and on, and on. People feel continuity is what they are expressing, but the renaissance doesn't come about by people trying to pretend that the past is still going on. The renaissance comes when people accept that the past is over. I think this is where I would probably part company with the political postures of the BJP!

**THE MEMORY OF THE BRAHMINS,** holding forth in Sanskrit, from that afternoon six years ago made me want to come back to Benares for an extended time. A conjunction of events—a meandering line that ran between my private awareness of my isolation in India, the circumstances surrounding my father's death in Pakistan, and now the rise of Hindu nationalism in India—made Benares, on the eve of a revolution at the ballot box, feel like the right place to be. I wondered if this city's Brahmins, living as men had in classical times on the banks of a river in a temple town, might serve me as a prism of sorts—that it would be possible to observe in them what old societies, such as India's, went through in their quest to be reborn as modern nations.

Soon after Mapu told me the story of the Kashi Naresh and Tito, I found the place where I would live in Benares in the weeks and months to come. A friend of Mapu's, also a textile man, suggested I try the Alice Boner House, which was next door to the Ganges View Hotel, where we were having dinner. He said it was basic but well situated. We could go there afterward.

The nights were still cool. The moon, coming into fullness for the festival of Holi three days later, was high on the river. It was not late, but the city was fast asleep. We passed an ascetic with matted hair spooning with his pet monkey. Mapu's friend led me into a side street, no wider than a corridor. A beam of white tube light was overhead. The flagstones ran with water. We knocked on a low wooden door with an iron hoop. A fearful tiny man, with beetle brows and a mouthful of crowded teeth, opened it. He was reluctant at first to show us in. The house was full, he said; and besides, permission to stay could only be obtained through the director in Zurich.

We persuaded him that we were, to use his phrase, "big people" too, and he let us into the house. We came into a lotus-crested courtyard. The city beyond retreated. The house, with its dim electrical light and long slanted shadows, was a sanctuary, and, unlike so many modern buildings in India, not at war with the climate. It had thick walls and cool stone floors, excellent proportions, complete with an aperture at the top. The house spoke, with quiet self-assurance, of tried solutions to old problems. It was perfect.

I wrote to Johannes Beltz, curator of South and Southeast Asian art at the Museum Rietberg in Zurich. He responded almost immediately: "May I know what you think to write about Brahmins? As an old student of Sanskrit, I would like to know. I'm just curious."

I knew too little then to answer him. I knew of course that Brahmins sat at the apex of the Hindu caste system—above the Kshatriya (warrior), Vaishya (merchant), Shudra (worker or laborer), and the Dalit (the Untouchable, who is outside the system, outcaste). But, in the India I grew up in, we possessed little knowledge of caste. I could not tell a Brahmin name, such as Mishra or Mukherjee, apart from any other; and even if I could, I would not have held it in any special esteem. India has infinite systems of inequality: exquisite composites of class, caste, language, education, and wealth. Our markers were all to do with class, which originated in our familiarity with the West, in general, and our comfort with English, in particular. The inner workings of caste, no less than to any foreigner, were a mystery to me.

"It is much easier to say what caste is not," writes the journalist Taya Zinkin in *Caste Today*, "than what caste is." Caste is not class, not religion or race, or even occupation. It is above all a religious or metaphysical idea, concerned specifically with the purity of the soul through the ages. Our deeds on earth—our karma—determine the progress of the soul, which in turn determines what caste we are born into. Our caste tells us who we may or may not marry, what work we may or may not do, and with whom we may or may not break bread. Nobody knows if the original categories of priest, warrior, merchant, and laborer—the *varnas*, as they are known in Sanskrit—were once fluid and hardened into the reality of caste today. But what we do know is that there is no escape from caste, save death or renunciation. Caste in India, as the Mexican writer Octavio Paz had observed in the 1990s, is still "the first and last reality."

"No sense yet," I wrote, replying to Beltz's question. He was understanding. He said stay at the house was free, as were meals; but that guests were expected to "manifest their gratitude through a little donation."

Ten days later he CC-ed me on the brief email he wrote to the manager of the Alice Boner House:

> Please receive Mr. Aatish Taseer at the airport in Varanasi. Arrival: 1 April, 2014, 14:10

# 3

# THE HOUR OF JUNCTURE

**THE STARS ARRAY AND HARMONY** constitutes itself gradually," wrote Alice Boner in her diary in February 1936, "This house is a strangely soothing and exciting matter. In it I feel withdrawn into myself, my house, my home ... It encloses me with love and opens the world for me. It spreads the blossoming earth out in front of me, the colourful life, and surrounds me with the simple peace of a monastery. I feel fulfilled, happy, settled, and supported, like on a gentle stream."

I had been given Alice's room. A narrow river-facing room, sparsely furnished, with rust-red walls and a wainscoting of Indian matting. The ceilings were high and coffered, with black metal hoops hanging from the stone beams. Small grille windows, shabbily curtained, gave onto the river. Beyond was the sandy waste delineated by a pale line of trees. The light inside the house, though harsh and white outside, was pale and diffuse. A daytime darkness welled up out of the central courtyard. A steep internal staircase led downstairs, where a plaque read ALICE BONER, SWISS ARTIST AND SCHOLAR, LIVED IN THIS HOUSE FROM 1935 TO 1978.

I came to know Alice through reading her diary, a published copy of which was kept upstairs in her library, as the days grew hotter and the election raged below.

She came from a wealthy Swiss family—her uncle was one of the founders of the engineering firm Brown, Boveri. She had expressed an interest in being an artist, but was immediately disenchanted with "the pert, lewd atmosphere" of Paris in the 1920s. In 1926, she saw Uday Shankar dance in Zurich: "Evening in the Kursaal: a lot of kitsch, and a revelation, the Indian dancer," she wrote in her diary. In Shankar, Alice saw "a living source of Indian sculpture." She was not alone. Shankar was causing a sensation in Europe at the time, a cultural event equal to the stir caused by his brother, the sitarist Ravi Shankar, in the 1960s. "In recent years," wrote René Daumal in *Rasa*, his collection of essays on Indian art and music, "something extraordinary occurred in various European cities ... Uday Shankar, perfect and all powerful master, governs some four hundred and fifty muscles of his body; each one does exactly what he wishes it to do, obeying the head and ignoring the neighboring tissues." Daumal believed that he was witnessing "Hindu thought, alive, authentic, in flesh and bone, in sound, gesture," presented in their midst.

Uday and Alice became lovers, and she accompanied him to India for the first time in 1930. Five years later, after their affair was over, she returned to India alone to live in this house on the Ganges. Like her hero, the Sri Lankan art historian A. K. Coomaraswamy, Alice devoted herself to the study of Indian art and lived in Benares until a few years before her death in 1981.

In those first days in Alice's house, as I was waiting for Tripathi to call, but also waiting more generally for a sign of some kind—a bit of luck, a synchronicity—to tell me that what I was doing was worthwhile, Alice's anxieties about belonging assuaged mine. Her decision to come to India was something of an intellectual experiment. And India was hard. Not in terms of discomfort—which Alice never mentions—but hard on her nerves. "Every day I have to invent a reason to justify my being here," she writes. India is the country "where the soul feels best," but Alice is also intensely lonely. She misses Europe. She comforts herself: "One thing I know now: my centre is here and not there"; but the more she stresses feeling centered, the more one suspects she isn't. "My entangled nerves are now loosened and vibrate in accordance with the constant, eternal rhythm of this country." But surrender is not easy. She digs "into the chambers of the soul," in search of a way to support the varied selves she contains.

"On an evening like this," she writes, months after moving to Benares, "in the loneliness of this house, in front of the river glittering in the moonlight, in the ringing stillness where only sounds from unknown people, unknown dogs, unknown temples reach me, where nothing overshadows the inner existence, one comes to oneself, so it is said. The multidimensional identity of being rises up. The thousand different individuals and lives that are in me, all hopes, all opportunities, all experiences are aroused and press against each other, forming a clew, a firm block."

Alice finds she cannot take a step further without the consent of her whole being, but no wholeness is at hand; she has "outgrown the inherited world of Europe," and though India is part of that outgrowing, traditional India is a closed world: all community, all instinct, the group above the individual. Alice can no more enter it than she can banish the "inborn individualism" of being raised in the West, the feeling of "being-thrownback-to-myself." She finds herself plagued by the scrutiny of "the self-observing self." And so, she writes, she oscillated between worlds.

Alice came to be a friend across time. She had an acute understanding of the trouble India would be in if it failed to close the cultural gap that was emerging between the modern state, the legacy of British rule, and the ancient culture upon which it had been grafted.

On June 25, 1946, the year before Indian independence, Alice met the freedom fighter Sarojini Naidu, the quintessential anglicized Indian in the mold of men such as Nehru, and credited with a famous witticism about Gandhi: "Ah," she said, on seeing Gandhi living in an Untouchable quarter equipped with modern amenities, "if the Mahatma only knew what it costs us for him to live the simple life."

Many in the India I grew up in shared the sentiment behind this clever remark, but they also failed to see what was plain to Gandhi: if one was to change India, one would have to change it from within. It would never work for a colonial class to speak down to India. I was deeply struck by this entry in Alice's diary:

> I asked [Naidu] whether, when India would have her own government, they would not consider calling Coomaraswamy back from America to give directives for the new education in art and other fields. I thought that he was the man who could really put India on the right path and help her to keep her own tradition intact, while recognizing her whole social and economic life ... "Oh no!" she said. "We have other things to do now! We have to rebuild India politically. Those things will come much later! And, besides, he is old now, and out of touch with India." I felt disappointed and wondered who was more out of touch with India, whether a man living in America and devoting all his studies and deep penetration to

the exact meaning of Indian tradition, or people living in India and looking all the while towards Europe for inspiration and direction of all their activities?

**ON MY FIRST DAY IN** Alice's house, I went for a walk along the Ganges. The auspicious hour of juncture—*sandhya:* when day meets night—was near. I hadn't gone far before I noticed a young man who could only be a Brahmin. He sat on a wooden platform gazing out at the water. He was handsome, though the marks of poverty were manifest in him no less than those of high caste: his small teeth were crested yellow and lodged high in his gums; he wore a light beard, through which his skin, rough and beaded from exposure to the sun, was visible; and the whites of his eyes were faintly yellow. He was dressed in two measures of white cloth, one wrapped around the waist, the other draped lightly over the shoulders. A sacred thread hung loosely from his torso, and from the crown of his tonsured head, the trademark lock of rough unshorn hair was neatly knotted.

The young Brahmin sat speaking to an older man with kohled eyes and a Charlie Chaplin mustache. It was hot, and the young man used the edge of the lower garment to wipe the sweat from his chest and armpits. The conversation of the two men concerned arrivals and departures; since I had only just arrived in Benares myself, I tried to join in by asking the young Brahmin if he was from out of town.

The question—or perhaps my language, or the way I was dressed, or how I stood at a distance, not introducing myself—made him start. He looked up at me as if I had committed an impropriety. Then he beckoned me over and asked me to repeat my question.

When he heard it, he seemed dismayed by its banality. He had been in Benares since November and was staying at an ashram nearby. He had come to the city to read Tulsidas's famous poem and to gaze upon the Ganges. He wanted to have its darshana. That was all.

It seemed like an extraordinary indulgence. Did he do no work? What had brought him to Benares? How long would he stay?

"Someone I love told me to go to Kashi, so I came to Kashi." He didn't know how long he would stay. "Here"—he gestured to the great temple upriver—"nothing happens of one's own doing; it happens only by His will."

Pavan Kumar Mishra came from a family of peasant Brahmins from a small village near Hardoi, a town four hundred kilometers away. He had a wayfarer's air of drift about him, and as he spoke, I began to see how much religion in India was still threaded into life. It did not exist in a separate sphere as a set of precepts, or a private matter; it was a ritualized part of action, and it expressed itself in the instinctive, unquestioning way in which this young Brahmin, like a pilgrim in medieval Europe, had come to Benares. If there was work to be done in the monastery, he explained, he would "lend a hand" in exchange for food and board. But work was not the point, nor could he say what was. My trouble communicating with Mishra gave me a foretaste of what was to be one of the ironies of this journey: those in whom tradition was most intact were often the least able to speak of it. They could not see themselves from the outside. When tradition was intact, life itself was an expression of belief. And this particular life had been so cloistered, so walled in by tradition, that it made conversation hard. We lacked a shared vocabulary.

Mishra now turned my questions on me.

Where was I from?

From India, I said.

He stared at me in disbelief. No, but—really—where was I from?

From Delhi, I clarified.

He seemed unhappy. He was sure I was a foreigner of some sort, but he couldn't tell what sort. He tried to invoke a deeper level of identity: What was my dharma?

It is one of the great untranslatable Indian words. *Dharma* could mean "duty," "religion," "vocation"; but it is also the dharma of fire to be hot, and of water to cool. It is so basic a word, so central to the Indian scheme, that it would not do to say I had no dharma. Everything, even an inanimate object, has a dharma. As the Hindi writer Kubernath Sukul tells us, "The immensity of dharma is such that we sometimes say that all that is not adharma [i.e., not unjust, undutiful, or wrong] is dharma."

I said I was a Sikh. It was half a lie. My mother was a nonpracticing Sikh, but religion and caste in India were patrilineal. I was, however, afraid that if I said I was Muslim, practicing or not, our conversation might end on the spot.

The mention of Sikhism brought a look of puzzlement to Mishra's face. He didn't know anything about Sikhs, except that their places of worship were called gurdwaras. He wanted to know whose picture or idol they contained.

The older man sitting next to him—Shukla, a Brahmin too—explained that the Sikhs followed a book.

The young Brahmin's puzzlement grew. He was trying to decide, with his limited exposure to the world, whether Sikhism was part of the Hindu fold or not. He now asked with some impatience—perhaps because dharma was inextricably linked to caste, and caste to work—what I did for a living.

I said I was a writer. His exasperation grew. "But what do you want to do?" he stressed. "What do you want from life?"

It was an odd question coming from him. Mishra, who had drifted to Benares on a whim and had no plan other than to gaze upon the Ganges and read a sixteenth-century poem, was asking me what I wanted from life?

I said, "I want to write books."

His interest waned; he must have thought I was being deliberately obtuse. "Good. Write them, then."

Our conversation ought to have ended there, but the hour of ritual bathing was at hand and the two Brahmins asked me if I would partake.

I said I would not, adding that I was not religious—but I accidentally said I had no dharma.

The Brahmins' faces blazed with incredulity. It was like saying one had no soul, no nature, no parent, no personality, no country. It was absurd.

"What are you saying?" Mishra asked. "These books you've mentioned, they would not have entered your life if you had no dharma."

"But that is a literary interest," I said.

"It's the same thing!" the two Brahmins said in one voice.

"I have no religious faith," I said, now using a different word.

Mishra's face softened. That was not the same as not having a dharma. The religion was lived; that was the part that was important: belief was a separate matter.

"But you must try and have faith," Mishra said.

I said something about being modern in my thinking. The word in Hindi meant "new" or "recent," as it did in English, but it did not carry the same historical weight. The Hindi word contained no suggestion of the Renaissance or the Enlightenment; it simply meant "new." In the West, one could be modern and religious; in India, to say one was modern was to say one was English speaking and westernized, part of the class of interpreters. It implied familiarity with the mores and customs of a particular culture rather than the acceptance of a universal set of beliefs and ideas.

Mishra stared at me, uncertain of my mental processes. He did not see his world through the lens of the West; he was not even familiar with westernized India; and he did not recognize his India when it was recast in the image of European history. After a moment of silence, he gave me the only response he saw fit. Without a trace of malice, he said, "I have never met anyone like you."

We were stalled. Mishra tried again to find some common ground between us. He asked me about marriage.

I said I was open to the idea of marriage, though not perhaps ready yet.

"But you do want to marry?" he said with the relief of a man who, having feared his interlocutor to be an alien, discovers he is not merely earthly, but a mammal too.

"Yes," I said, steering my mind away from all the more modern iterations of marriage. But it was not the gender of my future spouse that interested Mishra.

"There must be a conversation going on, at least?"

"A conversation?" I asked in confusion.

"Between the families."

"Oh, no," I said, now surprised myself. "It's a decision I will definitely make by myself."

"Without the consent of your parents?"

"Possibly."

An expression of total amazement, bordering on consternation, appeared on the young Brahmin's face. Marriage to him was between families, not individuals; it was a social contract.

The sun, though still strong, had begun to decline. Mosquitoes swarmed. Mishra wanted to have his bath. His older friend began to sing a verse from Tulsidas's poem. He sang of a boatman who ferries Ram across the Ganges. Ram tries to give him a ring as payment, but the boatman refuses, saying that men of the same profession cannot accept payment from each other.

"How can you and I be of the same profession?" Ram asks.

"I ferry people across the Ganges. You ferry them across the ocean of life."

Shukla's singing was beautiful, especially so because we were on the Ganges surrounded by boatmen who, with their ravaged sinewy bodies and long wooden boats, could not have been so different from the boatman in the epic. They sang songs too, and one sensed from the metaphorical descriptions of their vocation that they traced a line to the eternal boatmen of myth—Charon and Urshanabi—who ferry souls across a river.

Shukla would sing one verse, then prompt Mishra to finish it. But this seemed to annoy Mishra, and I suspected it was because he had not memorized the poem—the poem he had come to Benares to learn to the exclusion of everything else. When Shukla began a new canto, Mishra left us abruptly and went down to the Ganges to bathe.

On the river, though it was not yet dark, tourists were setting lamps afloat on the water. Mishra stood among them, his back wet and catching the late-afternoon light. He went through a series of swift, fluid movements, taking dips, cupping the water, standing with hands folded, eyes closed, oblivious to the traffic of lamps and offerings eddying around him. Then he returned full of the effect of his bath. His actions were brisk and dexterous as muscle memory. He stood next to the wooden platform where we sat and changed quickly, removing his wet clothes and slipping into dry ones. They were not now the clothes of the Brahmin—those had been collected and wrung out—but a simple red-checked shirt of cheap cotton and a pair of beige trousers. The transition robbed him of his earlier grandeur. He was now like any number of vagrant young men on the riverside.

He let go of our previous misunderstandings as if they were part of a discarded self, too trifling to survive the renewal of a ritual bath in the river. He said that I should come and see him at the ashram.

Then, as if reflecting briefly on all that had been discussed earlier, and thinking perhaps now of his time in Benares, and to what it had amounted, he said:

"I don't know what reward it will bring. But it doesn't matter. It is all decided."

**I WANTED TO SPEAK TO** Kamlesh Dutt Tripathi in part because the memory of that afternoon at the Abhinavagupta Library had become a lodestar—the beginning of a decade of Sanskrit education for me—and in part because Tripathi seemed to me the very image of what a Brahmin was. I thought, here is someone who must know what it is to balance his commitment to his tradition with an onslaught of foreign influence. What had surprised me that afternoon six years ago was how, despite having lived in India all my life, I had so naturally gravitated toward the glamour of the West, rejecting all that belonged to old India. The force that influenced me thus did not feel coercive in any demonstrable way, but how could something so powerful not be?

"European rule in Asian countries," wrote Arthur Koestler in *The Lotus and the Robot*, "was based on force, but its cultural influence was not." He continued, "The Indian *élite* became Anglicized because Hindu philosophy, science and literature had come to a standstill a long time ago, and had nothing to offer them. We ruled by rape, but influenced by seduction."

I wanted to know what role the interplay of rape and seduction had played in Tripathi's life. I wanted a sense from him of that moment when Western power was withdrawing, even as its influence was increasing. But Tripathi was a hard man to track down. I waited ten days in the febrile brightness of that election summer for him to call. I left messages at his place of work, I called his mobile; a young woman answered and promised to have him call me back, but he never did.

In the meantime, I made a friend who showed me the other side of this temple town: the world of malls and gyms, of cinemas and college canteens. I met Vishal one evening as he was nosing his motorbike down the sloping street that led to the river. In the evenings, the riverside became a promenade of sorts. The crowd was young: knots of girls, laughing and gossiping as the boys circled. Vishal was a fixture on the river. He was a basketball player at BHU, tall and handsome, lightly bearded, with large solemn eyes. He took one look at me and asked if I wanted to go for a ride on his bike. In another country, I would have thought he was picking me up. But this was India; in small towns, such as Benares, it was still breathtakingly innocent. Vishal's main motive for befriending me was a simple curiosity for the world beyond.

"I've always liked being friends with foreigners," he said, even though we spoke in Hindi and I told him I lived in Delhi. But soon I saw that he was right: in certain cultural respects, I was as good as foreign to him, the most obvious indication being that I lived in a world where men and women mixed easily. Vishal, though outwardly polite and well-mannered, was a furnace of stifled passion. He would stop me midsentence and ask in frank wonder how it was possible to talk to women.

"What do you mean?"

"I mean, *how* can you talk to them?"

Once, as I was telling a story that had no sexual under-or overtones, a story in which men and women were simply present, Vishal interrupted, "And then did everyone just go home and have sex?"

But, for all his inexperience, Vishal was a millennial. No less than any young person in London or New York—maybe more—he lived through his smartphone, which was a constant source of overstimulation. The combination of a restrictive society and a private world of images, graphic without precedent, had turned Vishal's curiosity about the opposite sex prurient before it had even the most basic outlet. One afternoon I was alarmed to see this young man, manifestly a virgin, hooting with laughter over a video of a blond woman pulling a fish from her vagina.

I saw this unevenness—of a society overwhelmed by outside influence—everywhere in India. An unevenness of personality, of appetite, it even manifested itself physically in the ugliness of the cities, in the outsize overpasses and the stunted towns, in the little blue-glass façades, which gave an illusion of modernity and were freely pasted onto shoddily constructed buildings, like a metaphor for how thin the relationship with the modern West could feel in India. "A century of 'progress,'" wrote Coomaraswamy a century ago, "has brought India to a stage where almost everything of beauty and romance belongs to her past." Since then, another century of "progress" had wrought many more horrors. In a country such as India, in a city such as Benares, one felt the aesthetic failure to digest the West as the symptom of a deeper failure.

I was in a multiplex cinema with Vishal, in a mall, watching a Bollywood romantic comedy called *Main Tera Hero*, when Tripathi called at last. He asked if I would come and see him at once.

We left the cinema midmovie. Vishal gave me a lift on his bike. It was just before 4:00 p.m. The city was desolate. Dust marionettes staggered over the scorching streets. We stopped at a paan shop where a teenage boy stood in front of an urn draped in a moist red cloth. He was singing a song from the film we had only just been watching: "I'm all shook up ever since I saw you; my heart has jumped out of my breast ... Turn around! Your hero is here. Turn around!"

# 4

# THE RAPE AND THE SEDUCTION

**MAPU HAD MENTIONED THE DEATH** of Tripathi's son, but another death in Tripathi's life had occurred decades ago, and in an important sense, it had been the more traumatic.

Kamlesh Dutt Tripathi was six years old when his brother was killed. The year was 1942. Gandhi's noncooperation movement was in full swing. Tripathi's brother, an eighth-grade student, the first of this family of Brahmins to receive a modern education, was taking part in a demonstration when he was shot dead by British Baluch troops. The bullet hit him in the forehead and he was killed instantly. The colonial government did not allow the body to return home.

"From the hospital, itself," Tripathi said, "my father took him to the cremation ground." Tripathi said "hospital" and "cremation ground" in English, the alien language seeming to set him at a distance from the reality. "My mother," he began again in English, "was not allowed to see the face of the son." Tripathi's eyes shone. "So, this," he said after a long pause, "is the background."

The office of the Indira Gandhi National Centre for the Arts (IGNCA), Eastern Division, was located in a little bungalow, painted in dull shades of red and cream and set some distance from a busy road. Once the head of Sanskrit at BHU, Tripathi, in his late seventies, was now spending his retirement as an adviser at the center.

I entered a room that contained little save for a few pieces of government-issue furniture and a glass-faced metal cabinet that held a small but grand collection of Sanskrit books. Tripathi, dressed all in white, a tiny dot of vermilion on his forehead, glanced at me as I came in, then at a white plastic clock on the wall.

"We're on a war footing," he said with a smile. His mouth was crowded with long, gapped teeth. He had a beautiful domed forehead, thin lips, and paper-thin skin. He sat opposite a younger man, an assistant of some sort, a fellow Brahmin. Between them lay a photocopy of a palm-leaf manuscript, a seminal text of Indian poetics highlighted in neon green. The two men worked together for many minutes in silence, with the grace and economy of movement that comes to those who do what men before them have always done. At 4:30, a secretary appeared with a plastic thermos, from which he poured tea into small clay cups called *kulhars*. Tripathi rose and ushered me into an interior room. He had a tiny knot of silver hair at the back of his head—the mere hint of a shikha.

Gandhi's speech at the inauguration of BHU had fired an early shot across the bow. He had only just returned from South Africa the year before, and his demands of the British were still modest. Three years later, in 1919, the British massacre of unarmed civilians in an enclosed garden in Amritsar made Gandhi think again. He came to feel that nothing short of full independence for India would suffice. In 1920, at a session of Congress attended by many thousand delegates, Gandhi's resolution—noncooperation with the viceroy and a boycott of British titles and goods—was adopted in full. "The whole look of the Congress changed," Nehru writes of that special session in his autobiography. "European clothes vanished, and soon only khadi was to be seen; a new class of delegate, chiefly drawn from the lower middle classes, became the type of Congressman; the language used became increasingly Hindustani ... a new life and enthusiasm and earnestness became evident in Congress gatherings."

Through a program of celibacy, dietetics, and work, such as hand-spinning yarn, Gandhi raised an army of nonviolent soldiers impelled by the force of truth. The freedom movement went in fits and starts. The 1922 burning of a police station in a small town called Chauri Chaura, in which some twenty-two policemen were killed, led Gandhi to suspend noncooperation. In 1930, Gandhi restarted the movement through an inspired act of political theater. In opposition to the British salt tax, he and a band of committed followers marched two hundred and forty miles to make salt from God's ocean under the open sky. The march to freedom gathered pace through the 1930s, but by the end of the decade, Europe was at war again. Gandhi and Nehru at first sympathized with the British war effort; when the Bengali freedom fighter Subhash Chandra Bose made overtures to the Japanese, Gandhi demurred: "Better the enemy I know than one I do not." Still, by 1942, after the fall of Singapore, and with Calcutta well within range of Japanese bombers, Gandhi had called for the British to "quit India." It was into this last act of the freedom movement that Tripathi's brother was swept up.

"I remember so vividly what happened," Tripathi said, "the way people were running everywhere, the way the Baluch army went deeper and deeper into the city. There was such terror. I remember all that very well."

For Tripathi—and, I would learn, for his father—the killing was inseparable from the might of the colonial enterprise at large. Brute force and cultural power merged in their mind. When I asked Tripathi if he had felt his culture under siege as a young man, he said that the death of his brother was what first alerted him to the coercive nature of colonial power: "I understood it the day my brother was killed. What was his crime? Why was he killed?"

Brahmins were in every part of India. Nehru was a Brahmin, from Kashmir in the north; the great mathematician Srinivasa Ramanujan was a Brahmin from the southernmost state of Tamil Nadu. There were Brahmins in Bengal—the writer Rabindranath Tagore was one—and Brahmins in Punjab. Brahmins in Uttar Pradesh, and Brahmins in Maharashtra. Brahmins made up only a very small percentage of India's population, but they were part of an intellectual superstructure that existed everywhere. They were culturally specific to each region, but they also represented the underlying unity of Indian thought and spiritual life. Like Sanskrit itself, which served as a lingua franca in a nation as linguistically varied as Europe, the Brahmins were part of the solution to a problem India had always had to deal with: the problem of the one and the many.

The Tripathis were Brahmins from Allahabad, a town 120 kilometers from Benares. It stands at the confluence of three sacred rivers—the Ganges, the Yamuna, and the mythical Saraswati—and hosts a great festival called the Kumbh Mela every twelve years. Allahabad was another of those places where the full palimpsest of Indian history is visible: the British Civil Lines behind a cordon sanitaire; a medieval Muslim town standing upon an ancient Hindu site of worship. The site of the confluence was, as Alice writes in her diary, one of those "sensitive points on earth" that are cherished by religions, such as Hinduism, in which the sacred landscape of India, its natural contours marked with myth, has a special place. "It is one of those seven or eight cities that are very old, older than history," Tripathi said. "Not a single one of them has a past less than twenty-five hundred years."

This branch of Tripathis were physicians. The word Tripathi used was *chikitsak*, which implied they practiced traditional medicine. "We were physicians for twenty-five generations."

How was he able to go back so far? Most Indians could not go much further than the birth of a great-grandfather.

"Those who are *uprooted*," Tripathi said pointedly, using the English word—his use of English, I was beginning to see, was strategic—"they no longer have any of this. But for those who belong to tradition, this is their daily ritual."

"How so?"

"We have a fifteen-day period when we offer libations of water to our ancestors. We can all go back at least seven generations. Beyond this, we also know where we originated, how we came to be where we are, and the age that we are presently in. This is something we do every day as part of our prayers. I am such and such, I belong to such and such clan, at such point of a time, in such an age, in such a place, that place which is part of a great continent..."

Tripathi wanted me to know that he had moorings deeper than those modernity had given us, more organic notions of space and time than Google Maps could provide. They were threaded into ritual, and according to the older system, *to know where you are was also to know who you are*. But Tripathi must also have known that the older moorings were not as secure as they had once been; otherwise, we would not be having this conversation. The Tripathis, physicians for those twenty-five generations, lived in a town that had been invaded many times. In the sixteenth century, the old Hindu town of Prayag was renamed and made over to Allah, but none of this considerable upheaval had stopped the Tripathis from doing what they had always done. The line had held, until now.

"Everyone came through India," Tripathi said, "Huns, Shakas, Jews, Parsis, Muslims—and everyone was absorbed. India remained India. The Muslims had military power, but their ideas were no match for India's. They brought change, of course, but India's continuities remained intact. It was only with the coming of the British—and the West—that we were confronted with a challenge from a power that was not merely economic or political. Its *thought content* was *powerful* too," he said, emphasizing the English words.

The power of that thought content and the corresponding need to confront it with thought of one's own was the reason BHU was founded. The great university at Benares, an ancient Hindu seat of learning, had been set up twenty years before Tripathi was born in 1936. The university, where Tripathi would one day head the Sanskrit department, had been established with the express purpose of assimilating the new knowledge that had come out of the West. This was part of the background to Tripathi's life. What I did not realize immediately was the extent to which that life, especially in its early years, had manifested all the trauma, fear, excitement, and possibility of that time. When Tripathi came of age, it was not possible to separate British soft power from hard: he was able to put a face to the power that dominated him intellectually and culturally, as well as politically and militarily.

The founder of BHU, Pandit Madan Mohan Malaviya, was also an Allahabad man, a family friend who belonged to the same subcaste as the Tripathis. He had attended the same two-hundred-year-old Sanskrit school where Tripathi, aged ten, would go to learn the rudiments of Sanskrit grammar through the sutras of the ancient grammarian Panini.

Tripathi remembered his father going to treat Malaviya at his house. Sometimes Tripathi, aged nine or ten, would be taken along.

Tripathi recalled that once, when Malaviya was unwell, Tripathi was made to recite a Sanskrit verse that the great educator was especially fond of: "It is a verse about Krishna in the form of a cowherd, and a very difficult verse to recite, but I recited it very well. It made Malaviya-ji very happy, and he gave me his blessings."

"Do you recall the verse?"

A look of childish wonder appeared on Tripathi's face and he recited the verse in a soft, gurgling voice. It came back effortlessly and seemed grand—and out of place—in the drab government office where we sat on that hot April day.

"I grew up with the language in my ears," Tripathi said with pride. "And so, when people say it's dead, I have no idea what they mean. It was certainly alive for us. I think I must have been fourteen when I began to compose verses in Sanskrit."

Writing came to ancient India out of the West a little before the beginning of the Common Era; as with all new things, it was met with a pushback. There was "a nostalgia for the oral," writes the scholar Sheldon Pollock, "and a desire to continue to share in its authenticity and authority, with the same lingering effects of remembered oral poetry [that] mark other first moments of literary invention across Eurasia." In old India nothing was considered learned until it came directly from the mouth of the preceptor into the ear of the student.

As Tripathi spoke, I was given a glimpse of his enclosed and secure childhood world. Here is the little boy reciting a Sanskrit verse for an esteemed visitor whose life's work is the founding of a university where East and West are to be brought under one roof. The year is 1945, perhaps 1946. Malaviya is at the end of his life; the Tripathis are still grieving for the boy who was violently killed a few years before. He had been the first among them to attend a modern school. Now, as a direct response to his death, Tripathi Sr. does something radical: he pulls his other sons out of the modern system and puts them right back into traditional education.

It was amazing to contemplate the depth and scope of the hurt. In the father's mind, the blame for the killing grew, acquiring larger and larger proportions. It did not stop at a local official, or the colonial government, or even the colonial enterprise; it grew to encompass the entire alien civilization. The terrifying "thought content" that must have offered wondrous miracles to the medical man had now turned up the dead body of his child. Rape and seduction came to be one in Tripathi Sr.'s mind. His response was retreat, a clean withdrawal into the old certainties.

This family of Brahmins had tested the waters of a brave new world and found they were out of their depth: the new knowledge was part of a killing enterprise. They thought the security of their traditional world still awaited them; they were soon to find out a door had closed behind them. Their embrace of the modern system had seemed voluntary, but it was in fact part of the inexorable triumph of that other system over their own. The truth of their position was revealed to them when it came time to send another elder brother of Tripathi's into higher education. Tripathi Sr. thought it would be a good idea for his son to study ayurveda, and where better to do it than at the newly founded university at Benares?

Tripathi Sr. was in for a rude surprise. Malaviya had died, but his son Govind Malaviya was vice-chancellor. Tripathi Sr. went to see him, taking his son along, believing admission would be a breeze.

"I'm happy to have him," Govind Malaviya said, "but he has to have studied science." He meant Western science.

Tripathi Sr. was aghast. "Govind," he said, feeling the insult keenly, "we have been ayurvedic doctors for twenty-five generations. If my son is not to be admitted, who is?"

Reminded of his kinship to the family, Govind Malaviya said, "Okay, call the boy."

Tripathi's brother appeared.

Govind Malaviya said, "Son, what have you read?"

"I've read Panini's grammar." The boy named a few other Sanskrit texts.

"You've read Panini's grammar, fine. But have you read physics, chemistry, mathematics? How will you learn all this? And that, too, in English?"

"What is there in the world that a man who has mastered Panini's grammar cannot master?"

"This was my brother's response," Tripathi said, recounting the story and beaming with pride. "It was said absolutely innocently. 'When I've read that, then what is this science? This chemistry, this physics? I'll read it all.'"

Tripathi now used an English word of the utmost importance: *confidence*.

"Govind Malaviya found my brother's *confidence* so affecting that he changed the *rule* in the university. He gave the *order* that the other *traditional* students be admitted too. And so, with my brother's admittance, thirty other students who had come from *tradition* were admitted as well."

"What do you think was the source of your brother's confidence?" I asked Tripathi.

"It came," he replied carefully, "from knowing his own tradition, his own treatises. If I know my tradition, why can't I learn that of another? This was there within him. But afterward, he said to my father, 'You've trifled with me, you know. I won't now allow you to trifle with my little brother.'"

Tripathi Sr.'s grief-laden decision to withdraw his boys from modern education had hurt one of them. Tripathi's brother attended BHU, but he had to work twice as hard as the other boys. He was the only one of that group of thirty that came "from tradition" who was able to finish the course. He got his degree in six years. The university asked him to stay on and become a member of the faculty, but he declined. He said his father's clinic in Allahabad had closed. He was duty bound to go back and reopen it.

"So, he went back to Allahabad and started his practice," Tripathi said. "He lived out his years in Allahabad and died a very successful physician, both of traditional and modern medicine."

The experiences of his two brothers, each violent in their own way, were precursors to Tripathi's own.

His father returned from the ordeal at BHU and immediately hired a tutor to teach Tripathi English, as well as the other subjects that a traditional education would have denied him: world history, civics, political science, English literature. He read with wonder for the first time of Greece, Rome, and Egypt, of Phoenicia and Sumer.

"When my brother's admission stalled," Tripathi said, "my father thought, 'Now nothing will happen without English. He already has traditional learning under his belt, now we had better teach him some English, though not at the cost of losing tradition.' That was why I was put in private education."

Hearing Tripathi speak, I was reminded of the strange symmetry of our situations. I had been a private student of Sanskrit; I, too, had felt the need to play a Sisyphean game of catch-up. But whereas Tripathi had gone in one direction, toward the West, I had felt the need to go in the other, toward India. Tripathi recalled his friendship with a boy his age, who became a physics professor in Allahabad.

"We used to play together, and because he had gone into modern education, he would say that our epics were false, that Ram was a *mythical character*—not a *historical personage*—that all this was *mythical history*. I would say, 'No; he was historical, not mythical. These are not lies. How can they be lies? The Mahabharata is not a lie; it is true.' And we would argue like this throughout the day."

They were children's arguments, but as is so often the case, they revealed a deeper tension. Tripathi's Brahmin family had come into the bright light of a world that had already made all kinds of judgments about them, but they for the most part had nothing to say back; they had prepared no counterargument.

"I was reading world history for the first time," Tripathi said. "I was beginning to understand that it was not just India that possessed history and culture, but other places, too, that there was a world elsewhere. At the same time, I could not tolerate anybody casting *doubt* on the *authenticity* of my own history."

*Doubt,* a word for which this strategic bilingualist switched to English, assailed him more profoundly in the years to come. The lines of stress that had become visible in childhood and adolescence acquired a political dimension. He would come to see that what had felt like one man's experience was, in fact, the experience of an entire country. On leaving high school, Tripathi went to Allahabad University and, as he said, "straight into modern education."

The search for the guru in traditional India—"that special relationship of disciple and master," as Coomaraswamy says, "which belongs to Indian education in all its phases"—is a religious search. It has been likened to the search of the soul for its appointed body. It is meant to contain an element of strife, of looking without finding, of a time spent in the wilderness. The search ideally ends in a mystical meeting, and like all things worth obtaining, it is extremely difficult at first, then extremely easy. What ensues is a relationship akin to that of a father and son, but is even deeper, for whereas the one is granted by birth, the other is part of one's spiritual progress on earth. A young Brahmin I met later, a student of classical grammar with a diamantine mind, said, "The student is like the guru's son. It is written." Then, quoting Panini from memory, he added, "'Lineages are of two kinds. Those of birth, and those of knowledge.'"

Tripathi grafted this idea of the guru onto the modern university. The expectation might well have ended in disappointment. But, happily, it did not: Tripathi found his man.

"Professor K. Chattopadhyay." Then, as if the Western title didn't capture his stature, Tripathi added, "Pandit Chattopadhyay." *Pandit,* learned or wise, was like those other words of Indian learning—*guru, Brahmin, swami*—that have mysteriously, and with some slight alteration, made their way into English.

Tripathi now spoke of Chattopadhyay, a Bengali, with a great reverence. It was as if he were speaking of a sage in the epics. Chattopadhyay was skilled in the Vedas. He had mastered Indian philosophy and history. He knew Pali, Prakrit, Apabhramsha, Persian, and the old Persian of the Zend-Avesta; Punjabi, Hindi, Bengali, of course; and in addition to the Indian languages, he knew Greek and Latin, German, French, and Russian.

"When he spoke English," Tripathi said, "it was Oxonian English. When a visitor came from abroad, it was not the English professor who was called to greet him, but Chattopadhyay." When the great Basham came to their university, it was Tripathi's guru who welcomed the author of *The Wonder That Was India*. "That is the kind of man he was, my guru. He taught me the Vedas, and history, and languages."

This description of the guru was too pious to be taken seriously, but even here, a modern story intruded, undoing the stylized portrait.

"The most important thing about Chattopadhyay was that he had been a classmate of the freedom fighter Subhash Chandra Bose." The two Bengalis—Bose and Tripathi's teacher—had done their M.A.'s together. "Bose went on to join the Indian Civil Service in England, while Chattopadhyay came to Allahabad, via Benares, to learn Sanskrit. Then, something interesting happened.

"Bose, after going off to England, grew *disillusioned* with the ICS. At that point he wrote a letter to my guru. 'Chattopadhyay,' he said in his letter, 'I have resolved to dedicate my life to the freedom of India and I want you to join me.' My guru replied, 'Subhash, you have chosen your path. I, too, have chosen mine: I'm going to dedicate my life to providing an absolutely correct understanding of Indian and

Vedic culture. British scholars have distorted it. I must answer these distortions. I will study the Veda and work on my culture. You fight for the political freedom of the country; I will fight for its cultural freedom.'"

Chattopadhyay was echoing a sentiment that had wide currency at the time of Indian independence, namely that an India that was politically free but, as Coomaraswamy wrote, "subdued by Europe in her inmost soul" was not worth fighting for, let alone dying for. Some, such as Sarojini Naidu and Bose in this story, believed that once the British were pushed out, their influence would end too. Others, such as Coomaraswamy and Alice, sensed that it was after the British had left that India's true reckoning would begin. The brutality of the colonial enterprise had made it easy to dismiss the appeal of the West. After colonization, India, like many other postcolonial countries, would be forced to contend with what was attractive about the other civilization, as well as confront the weaknesses of one's own.

"So," Tripathi said, picking up the thread of his story within a story, "Bose writes again. He says, 'Chattopadhyay, once the country becomes free, and an independent nation is born, there will be several Chattopadhyays. Come with me!' My guru replied, 'Subhash, take this from me in writing: the fight for a country's political freedom must run parallel to its fight for cultural freedom; the two must go together; one does not precede the other.'

"I am the student of such a guru," Tripathi said. "It is at the feet of this very great man that I have received my training."

Tripathi was a young man when he had an epiphany that mirrored mine at the Abhinavagupta Library. It happened during a performance of *Oedipus Rex* in Allahabad.

In the mid-1950s, when Tripathi was still at university in Allahabad, he came into contact with a journalist who had been a general secretary of the All India Congress Committee, as well as a student at Banaras Hindu University. At an anniversary celebration for Pandit Madan Mohan Malaviya, the journalist, an older man, was in the chair. Tripathi, a student in the Sanskrit department, had written some verses in praise of Malaviya. Once he recited them, the journalist offered him a prize of five rupees. But the journalist didn't give Tripathi the money immediately. Instead, he invited Tripathi to the offices of the newspaper where he worked. There, over tea and samosas, the two men got talking. Tripathi's father—the man who had been so instrumental to his education—had died that year, in 1955, and Tripathi was perhaps in search of a mentoring figure. In their conversations, the journalist learned that Tripathi's brother had been killed in 1942, at a rally in which the journalist had also taken part.

It was a tense year. Gandhi had watched with anguish as the British retreated from Burma and the Japanese stood poised on the borders of India. "Here is a mantra," Gandhi said, addressing the All India Congress Committee in Bombay. "A short one that I give you; you may imprint it in your hearts and let every breath of yours give expression to it. The mantra is, 'Do or die.' We shall either free India or die in the attempt. We shall not live to see the perpetuation of slavery." Later that day the "Quit India" resolution was passed, and within twenty-four hours the senior leadership of the freedom movement, including Gandhi and Nehru, was jailed. The arrests unleashed civil disobedience throughout the country. The British administration regarded the Indian protests during wartime as treasonous, and Lord Linlithgow, the viceroy, put them down with brutal force. There were mass arrests, the burning of villages, and the use of machine guns by low-flying aircraft. The situation in Allahabad, where the Nehrus came from, and where his daughter, Indira, was courting arrest, was especially bad.

When Tripathi's new friend learned that Tripathi's brother had been killed in the same movement, his affection for this young man grew immeasurably. "After that," Tripathi said, "he would call me over many times, and when he learned that I was working on Sanskrit theater, it was he who first urged me to do Sanskrit theater in *contemporary* and *modern* ways."

Modernity, I realized, did not then have the connotation that it has today. It was not another wave of cultural domination flowing out of the West, nor a synonym for the westernized classes in India. Modernity represented a fresh start: the possibility of something culturally neutral after colonial rule. Modernity was Le Corbusier and Picasso, Nehru and socialism; it was the life of the kibbutz and Tel Aviv. It spoke of fresh beginnings.

Tripathi, studying under Chattopadhyay, was immersed in Sanskrit theater, working on Kalidasa in particular. It was a vibrant time for theater, and some of the great personalities of the Calcutta stage would come through Allahabad, such as Utpal Dutt and Sombhu Mitra. "Top-rate people." Tripathi said. "Dutt was a Marxist, and let me tell you—I've seen Sir Laurence Olivier play Othello, and Utpal Dutt, actor to actor, was hardly less than him."

The year was 1962. Tripathi's journalist friend had heard that *Oedipus Rex* was to be performed in Allahabad, with Sombhu Mitra himself playing Oedipus, and his wife, Tripti Mitra, in the role of Jocasta. The journalist got hold of some tickets and took his protégé to see the play. For the young Tripathi, it was life-altering.

He paused. His voice trailed off, and his eyes grew large in frank amazement as he recalled the night at the theater.

"What *impact*," he muttered. "Overpowering! I was completely lost in the world of the theater, in Sophocles' world.

"After watching that play, we walked for almost a kilometer in total silence. We didn't say one word to each other. We walked like this for a long time, and then my mentor turned to me and said, 'Is there anything in your tradition to parallel *Oedipus Rex*?'

"I stopped to think; he pressed me for an answer. 'No, no. Tell me. Tell me now.'

"I said, 'Yes, the *Shakuntala* of Kalidasa.'"

Sanskrit drama was a sister of the Greek. The English philologist William Jones had been the first to notice a resemblance between the two languages that could not be accidental. Jones, a contemporary of the British governor-general Warren Hastings's, had gone as a jurist to Calcutta at the end of the eighteenth century. There, he founded the Asiatic Society and first posited the "common source" for Indo-European languages that became the basis for the study of modern linguistics. No doubt with the European Renaissance in mind, Jones wrote:

> To what shall I compare my literary pursuits in India? Suppose Greek literature to be known in modern Greece only, and there to be in the hands of priests and philosophers; and suppose them to be still worshippers of Jupiter and Apollo: suppose Greece to have been conquered successively by Goths, Huns, Vandals, Tartars, and lastly by the English; then suppose a court of judicature to be established by the British parliament, at Athens, and an inquisitive Englishman to be one of the judges; suppose him to learn Greek there, which none of his countrymen knew, and to read Homer, Pindar, Plato, which no other Europeans had even heard of. Such am I in this country: substituting Sanscrit for Greek, the *Brahmans*, for the priests of *Jupiter*, and *Vālmic, Vyāsa, Cālīdāsa*, for Homer, Plato, Pindar.

Jones introduced Sanskrit drama to the West. He had heard of the *natakas*, but he did not know what they were. The Brahmins deliberately misled him. They told him that they were "works full of fables" and consisted "of conversations in prose and verse, held before ancient Rājās in their publick assemblies, on an infinite variety of subjects, and in various dialects of India." Then one day a "very sensible Brāhmen" explained to him that these natakas were rather a lot like the productions the British put on during the cold season in Calcutta that went by the name of plays.

Thus Jones discovered Sanskrit drama. He read and translated *Shakuntala,* a play that suited the mood of eighteenth-century Europe and whose fame grew far and wide. Goethe came to hear of it and fell in love: "Wouldst thou the earth and heaven itself in one sole name combine? I name thee, O Sakuntala!"

Tripathi, once again coming from the opposite direction to me, needed no introduction to *Shakuntala,* but his first taste of Greek drama, a classical culture consanguine with his—at once utterly familiar and utterly distinct—was electrifying. He was immediately able to see in the one ancient culture a shade of his own, but he could not enjoy the feeling free of anxiety. Goethe and Jones had been able to reach into Sanskrit culture, secure about the place of their own culture in their own countries: the Sanskrit drama that had come from half a world away was no threat to their own. This was not true of Tripathi's India.

This anxiety was what lay behind Tripathi's mentor's question. Tripathi had barely been able to digest the impact of this wonderful new experience before he was confronted by a simple and brutal question: Do you have anything as good as this?

"Can you put it on?" the mentor asked.

"I absolutely can," the young Tripathi replied. "But I have only one condition. I must find my Shakuntala."

It was a turning point. From then on, coincidences attached themselves to the moment of intellectual discovery. In a popular weekly column in a Bombay tabloid called *Blitz,* the screenwriter K. A. Abbas recounted the story of a Soviet delegation that had recently arrived in India. They were asked what they would like to see and do during their stay. They instantly replied that they wanted to see a performance of Kalidasa's great play. The Indian side balked and fell silent. The Soviet delegates did not know what to make of their hosts' strange behavior. They thought perhaps that the play was not running, and that they were too embarrassed to say so. "If it's a question of waiting," the Soviets said at last, "we're happy to wait. But we must absolutely see Kalidasa's *Shakuntala* before returning to the U.S.S.R."

"They had to be told," Tripathi said with a wry smile, "that *Shakuntala* was not staged in India." Not in the way the Soviets, who took literature seriously enough to fear it, would have expected. They could wait a lifetime and never see a professional production of the play.

"All this," Tripathi said, "was recounted in great detail in K. A. Abbas's column." Tripathi's journalist friend knew Abbas, and as the column had appeared at the same time as the search for Shakuntala, the journalist wrote to Abbas, asking that he send an actress from Bombay to play Shakuntala. "Why are you searching for Shakuntala in Bombay?" Abbas wrote back. "Surely, she is to be found in the valleys of the Ganges. Go, look for her there!"

"That opened our eyes," Tripathi said. Not long after, they discovered a young girl of classical Indian features who was ideal for the role, even though she knew little to no Sanskrit. "I spent two to three months teaching her Sanskrit," Tripathi said. "She was a very good actress. I played the role of Dushyant myself. We rehearsed for many weeks. And then the play was staged."

It was a resounding success. Tripathi may have been too late for the Soviet delegation, but his production of Kalidasa's play found many eager audiences at home. Other people put up the money for further productions, now a Muslim tobacco magnate, now the bishop of the Allahabad diocese. Famous actors from the Calcutta stage gave guest appearances. It was the beginning of Tripathi's long career as an academic and impresario. But, as I listened, an overwhelming sadness rose in me. The air in the small government office was full of elegy.

"My target," Tripathi was saying, "was *Shakuntala* for contemporary audiences. I needed to show people that their cultural inheritance, when compared with Sophocles and Euripides, was no less a thing. Western literature, for me, was like a torch by whose light I could see my own. I was a man of classical tradition, of classical thought and art form. I felt we should strengthen this. What are our classics? Everyone has their own. What are ours? What is the meaning of contemporaneity for us? These were the questions that I was trying by my own lights to answer."

I felt my interest flag. Tripathi's voice had a note of desperation. I liked his story so long as it was a story about a young man coming to terms with where he, and his culture, stood in relation to the tremendous power of the West; but as the problem gave way to glib solutions, I thought Tripathi sounded unconvincing. He had at every stage been forced into a defensive stance. He was making a case for his culture, and in doing so he was undermining what his story was evidence of: that it was not culture, but confidence, that mattered. What was it about the meeting of India and Europe that had shattered India's confidence?

"Somewhere I had this consciousness of there being a kind of colonial hangover, and I thought we must overcome this," Tripathi said. "Slowly we were becoming alienated from our tradition. In the fifties and sixties, there was not the alienation there is today. But what I feared then has slowly proved true. And there is a great gulf now, especially where the urban middle class is concerned."

Tripathi was referring to the colonization of India by the Indians themselves, finishing off the job the British had begun. In many ways, they had been more successful. Their success was the reason why today this great cultural distance existed between Tripathi and me.

Tripathi's early and violent contact with the West produced in him a need to defend a culture of which he was still in possession.

Subsequent generations would be far less intact and would have to make a gargantuan effort to regain culture—something like what Mapu had done. It would never be complete; nor, indeed, could it be asked of everybody. Life is hard enough without having to fight a crusade on behalf of one's culture. And to what end? It is easier just to let it all go.

Tripathi anticipated me. He now said, "To know the meaning of *contemporaneity* in the Indian context, this has always been my endeavor. Sanskrit for me was this force. It gave me a direction. It was a path, a beautiful path, by which I could understand myself, and the world, and the people of the world. It lighted the way; that is why I value it. I think of it as valid even today. If tomorrow it is no longer valid..." His voice trailed off. It was a prospect too terrible to consider. "But for now, in my view, at least, it is still *valid*."

But what did it mean to be contemporary? And what did it mean for an ancient language that nobody spoke to be contemporary?

"To be contemporary," Tripathi said, "is to understand all of one's past, all of one's inheritance, *and*, while joining this to the present, to look toward the future. This is what it is to be contemporary. It has no political meaning for me."

Since he mentioned politics, I asked him about the election outside, which seemed to encapsulate so many of the historical and cultural tensions Tripathi had gestured to. Tripathi had spoken of cultural death. What did he think of Modi's politics of revival?

"I don't know," he said, "I honestly don't know. What I can say is that there is already a change in Modi over these past four months—a change in speech, in body language?"

"How do you mean?"

"What we are on the inside will always show on the outside. We can hide nothing. It will always show on our faces. And if I am filled with hatred, that will show too. This is why I say that the external and internal—mind and body, thought and action—are one."

A Hindu answer, if ever there was one! But did he mean that he thought Modi now seemed less full of hatred?

"I see a change. And let me tell you, anyone who wants to use the religion for irreligious purposes—to target minorities, say—will not survive."

I had one last question for him: "You said earlier that art saved you. What do you mean by that? What did it save you from? How did it save you?"

Tripathi looked hard at me. "There are some caves not far from here. They are some twenty-two centuries old. In one of them is an inscription—it is still there today; it is by Sutanuka. She was a..." He struggled to find the right word, settling finally on the French *danseuse*. "She was a great beauty of the time. And she was in love with an actor from Benares called Devadatta. In a gesture of her love, she built him an auditorium, cut from the rock; it is very beautiful. The inscription reads, 'I, Sutanuka, a devadasi, here build for my lover, an actor or *artiste*, Devadatta by name, this auditorium. Let poets come here, let artists come...'

"Everything is broken," Tripathi said, raising the ghost of Ozymandias. "It is from the second century B.C...." He paused. "I have written a poem in Sanskrit. It is called 'Sutanuka.' It is in free verse, and it is unlike any of the standard Sanskrit forms. In it, I say, 'You forever make me new, Sutanuka ... I was fossilized. But you touched me. And now I'm not fossilized. I am vibrating. I struggle, I fall; but I always stand up. This is not me, this is you.'

"Sutanuka is a metaphor for this whole art, this whole culture. There are many moments when I forsake all hope. I begin to feel I cannot accomplish anything. I become dull, dead, insentient. But, Sutanuka, you make me conscious again. You bear me along..."

Before I could say anything, Tripathi quickly added, "There is a second poem. It is to Europa. 'I have dwelt with you too,' I say. 'I have seen those same things in you. Where you are, the world is one. I call to you too, Europa.' Sutanuka and Europa, one myth, one reality. Sutanuka is the Indian reality; Europa, Greek myth. I speak to them both. From both I draw sustenance. This is what I mean when I say that culture can make a man whole. But it must never be a narrow thing. The moment it narrows, it is lost. It has to have fullness; it has to contain past, present, and future..."

Tripathi picked up a sheet of paper from the government-issue desk in front of him. He began to draw a diagram, a single point around which he made concentric circles, a pictorial representation of the telescoping that was a part of his daily practice. This space-time awareness was central to his organization of the world: to know where you are is to know who you are.

"There is this point," he said. "If we go a little wider, there is my village. Wider still, my state. My country, the world. There is no conflict between me and the world. It is but an enlargement of me. And that whole world can be collapsed back into this single point: me. This is our symbolism, this is what we call the mandala. It comes of use to us in our prayers. Every day we meditate on this idea. This is what spirituality can do, and this is what art can do..." It can make you whole, I thought he was going to say, but he stopped short. He was a theater man; he knew about leaving things unsaid.

"It is not my job to convert anyone," he added, "just to share my experience. If you like it, then well and good. If you don't, then strive to find your own truth; but make your truth manifest and move on."

We were at the end. Observing the effect of his words on me—I was seduced—he said, with only a touch of intellectual vanity, "Is that enough for today?"

**IT WAS EVENING WHEN I** walked back to the Alice Boner House. The dome of heat had lifted, and the town exhaled. The disorder did not seem so oppressive now. I was painfully aware on that walk of a great gap between the physical ugliness of India and the fineness of its internal life. I felt I was in a place where a vital connection between internal and external realities had been severed. People did not match their surroundings, just as Tripathi, working on an ancient text of Indian poetics, did not match the dreary government office where he spent his days.

Everywhere one saw signs of beauty, such as talent and genius, fighting their way out from an encroaching ugliness: a shade-giving peepal tree, its trunk bandaged in red religious threads, evoked the memory of something old and attractive, even as it was engulfed in brown smoke and traffic; a temple tank, its litter-strewn surface a deep inviting green, sought to bring tranquillity to the slum neighborhood that had sprung up around it; a woman in a shimmering sari of pink and gold, dripping with bangles and jewelry, stood in open slippers in a verge of wet black mud. Then there was the riverfront itself, where amid the palaces and steeples, there rose a pink sewage pumping station, its cylindrical surface ornamented with a crudely painted mural of Shiva. The ugliness of modern India, standing in juxtaposition with the beauty of what history had bequeathed, was enough to make one believe in the intangible India of mind and spirit that people here so often spoke about. It was the only way to justify a present that dishonors the memory of the past.

# 5

# THE CONQUEROR OF DESTINY

**THE ELECTION DREW TO ITS** protracted climax in the middle of May 2014. Voting occurred in nine excruciating phases, staggered over several weeks. Benares was among the last to go to the polls.

My final week in the city was unendurable. The white skies had arrived; the afternoons burned; the river in the evenings was swampy. The atmosphere was tense with the heavy presence of commandos and intelligence agents who patrolled the streets with sniffer Alsatians. One night, returning home, I came upon a street full of policemen and journalists.

The electricity had gone out and the street was under a cloak of smoky summer darkness. In the revolving blue light of a police vehicle and the halogen white of a TV camera, I saw the bloodied face of a party worker who claimed to have been beaten up by members of a right-wing Hindu group a few hours before.

I had not gone to Benares for politics, but politics intruded on my time there. It was present in the obvious form of a general election, which I wrote about in a weekly dispatch from Benares for a Delhi political magazine. But what interested me more than electoral politics was the underlying cultural crisis that was feeding the politics. Modi, for millions, represented a moment of awakening. People spoke of a second independence, in which Hindu India would shrug off the legacy of foreign rule, and the true soul of the country would find utterance. I wondered if the decay of old ways had brought forth this politics of revival, and I was interested in meeting someone in whom the mechanism could be observed.

I first met Anand Mohan Jha on the riverside one afternoon in early April. He was with a boatman I knew. We got talking about the election, and the boatman, a wild wheeling figure who wore a red bandana and heavily tinted glasses, reminding me of the Dennis Hopper character in *Apocalypse Now*, said, "When Modi comes to power, we will send this government of the English packing, and everything will become Hindi."

Anand watched our exchange from an anchored boat nearby. He lay like a Hindi movie hero with his hands behind his head. He was dressed in tatty stonewashed jeans and a checked shirt. His arms were thin, his face small, dark, and impish. A pubescent mustache was shaved strategically around a mouth of large tobacco-encrusted teeth. He had a bit of sandalwood paste on his throat and a dot of orange on his forehead. He now rose, and enjoying the effect of his words, he said that if India was not careful, a new era of slavery would soon be upon her. This was the perennial fear of the Hindu right: the return of foreign rule over a weak and divided country. Anand said that it was here already, in a covert sense; soon it would be out in the open.

"Why do you think that?"

"Why?" he repeated excitedly. "I'll tell you why: because people are selling out the country for material gain. Our culture is being decimated. Many in my family have received degrees in commerce; but I chose to be nearer my culture. A great civilization, like ours, cannot be subdued without the complicity of men on the inside, working against us. Someone—I cannot say who—is controlling us, and there is but the difference of a syllable between *vikas* [development] and *vinasha* [ruin]."

Anand was hard to place. His rag-doll appearance and his being in the company of the boatman, whom I knew to be part of a lower-caste community, made me think he was of the same background. But when he extended his hand and gave me his full name—Anand Mohan Jha—he could only have been a Brahmin from the neighboring state of Bihar.

His talk against development, which was Modi's slogan in the election, made me think he was not a supporter. I was soon to learn that he was not merely a supporter, but a card-carrying member of the Hindu right. Anand belonged to the Akhil Bharatiya Vidyarthi Parishad (ABVP), which was the most powerful Hindu nationalist youth organization in the country. The ABVP, like its fountainhead, the Rashtriya Swayamsevak Sangh (RSS), sought to weaponize Hinduism to bring about a cultural renaissance. For these groups, politics was not an end in itself, but a way to conduct the cultural struggle by other means.

As the election picked up pace, corresponding day by day to the onset of exquisite heat, Anand and I encountered each other more frequently. He seemed to become more and more embroiled in the election's frenzy, here participating in passionate political conversations in tea shops, there handing out flyers for "cultural events" that were thinly veiled conduits for whipping up support for Modi. On the day Modi came to Benares to file his nomination papers, Anand was delirious with excitement. As a student in the Sanskrit department at BHU, he had been charged with showering Modi with flowers upon his arrival on campus. When he saw me hanging about, he exhorted me to come with him and join the *jansailab:* the deluge of humanity. The election provided a kind of release for Anand. I imagined him as one of the many young men who now roamed the riverside in the evenings wearing cardboard Modi masks, the eyes cut out in almond-shaped hollows.

Anand made me nervous. I did not think I would speak to him at any length. I feared that to do so was to let myself in for erratic ruminations about the evil West and the virtues of Hindu tradition. He must have sensed my reluctance to speak to him, for one evening as I was packing to leave, he showed up uninvited at the Alice Boner House.

It was the first week of May. The broad leafy avenues of BHU were alight with the burnt orange of gulmohars in bloom. A hot desert wind called the *loo* had begun to blow out of the west, bringing with it the full blast of stupefying heat. It robbed the sky of pigment and reduced the clouds to veined outlines. The wind emptied the city's streets for most of the day and feathered the surface of the river with whitecaps.

We sat downstairs on the veranda in the fluctuating light with nothing to keep us cool but a white pedestal fan. Truth be told, I hardly noticed the heat. I was in thrall to Anand's story. He began to speak at sunset and spoke continuously for ninety minutes. When he was done, it was dark outside.

"My name," he said, "means 'joy.'" It was given to him by his grandfather. Anand was born on the fifth day of the lunar month of Chaitra, which is auspicious; his birth came after a long period of adversity in his family. There were court cases, land disputes, an uncle with four girls and no boys. But soon after Anand was born, the cases were resolved in the family's favor. A son was born to his uncle, and his grandfather, believing Anand to be the cause of this good luck, said, "He came and brought joy, so we will call him Anand."

Anand's grandfather had two brothers. The younger had made good on the dream of an earlier time: he had secured a government job with the Railway Police and built a house of brick and mortar; he had raised his position in society and, with his deeds—his karma—improved his bloodline. He was one kind of model for Anand.

The older brother was another, but he represented a more cautionary tale. He had become a bandit in Nepal, just across the border from their village in Bihar. He was said to have locked a police officer in his station and set the station alight. Anand, trying to elevate the older brother's image in my eyes, described him as a Robin Hood figure: "He would steal from the rich and give to the poor. He was a great devotee of Mother Durga."

But the stain remained, and Anand lived with the specter of further degrading his bloodline, especially because as he grew up, he found himself attracted to disreputable characters.

"Astrologers believe that each person is the product of thirty bloodlines," Anand said. "There are fourteen familial bloodlines that come through each parent; fourteen and fourteen, that makes twenty-eight; the individual parents add two, so thirty in total."

The idea of blood redeemed or degraded through deeds had a biological reality for Anand. When he spoke to me of more illustrious ancestors, such as a decorated musician who had performed before Nehru, or a famous astrologer, he was trying to improve my impression of his lineage.

"We had once been an aristocratic family. We had land, and money, and jewels. There was only one other family—the Thakurs, I believe, was their name—who were our equals in the whole district. It was us, and them, and nobody else."

Anand's village was organized along caste lines. "Our house is right in the front with the other Brahmin houses, almost as soon as you enter the village." Then, stratum by stratum, Anand rattled off all the other castes and trades: from land-owning Brahmins to washermen, barbers, weavers, and oil pressers, the caste to which Modi belonged. "Right at the end, some four or five kilometers from our house, come the Muslims. Some ten or twenty houses, and that's plenty, if you ask me."

The village was more than a place where people lived: it was a physical manifestation of caste. Hearing Anand speak, I thought I could hear the echo of voices older than his own. Recent events seemed to recede into a folkloric darkness.

As time went on, Anand said, "a mountain of poverty" descended upon his family. The Jhas were forced to sell their land as others, less highborn, moved in. The family jewels were stolen in a robbery. Before long, this Brahmin family, which had once owned land and horses, was reduced to penury. "Things became so bad," Anand said, referring to a time before his birth, "that for three and four days at a time there would be no food cooked in our house. It was a terrible burden on my grandfather."

Anand's father, who had dropped out of school after tenth grade, was unmarried. The atmosphere at home was tense. Anand's grandfather locked Anand's father in the house with the intention of pressuring him into marrying against his will. Anand's father escaped and ran away. He thought he could make good on his own.

The old caste-based society of India was changing. Brahmins could do certain forms of work, such as government jobs, teaching, joining the civil service, that were almost like modern iterations of their old vocation. But work in India is never just work; marriage never just marriage; every element of how you live, down to what and with whom you eat, is informed by the imperative of caste.

Tradition could allow for incremental change, but it could never have permitted the debasing work that Anand's father in his despair ended up doing: he went to Bhimnagar, on the Koshi River, and washed buses for a Muslim proprietor. "And," Anand said pointedly, "he lived with him in his house."

"Despite being a Brahmin?" I said.

"Yes, yes," Anand said, grateful that I had understood the implication.

Anand's father earned one rupee a day. Of that money, he spent twenty-five paise on a bag of roasted gram flour, which was all he ate; the remaining seventy-five paise he sent home, and there would be food in Anand's house.

I had just been in Patna, the capital of Bihar, and under its overpasses, which cast long shadows over the low-lying sprawl, I had seen vendors selling the conical tubes of newspaper containing the roasted gram flour that Anand described. It was meager sustenance. Patna had presented a frightening vision of urban decay. The streets were strewn with dust and bits of paper; open gutters ran alongside them, choked with blackish liquid and plastic bags in blues and pinks and whites. The one image that redeemed the city was the soaring spectacle of silk-cotton trees in flower: their fleshy coral blossoms as large as fruit lay in blankets on the street, rotting in the spring sun. I looked again at Anand's physique: the delicate bones of his face, the skin stretched taut like parchment, the knotty joints, the thin arms and wrists. A history of real physical hunger lay behind Anand's hunger now, his hunger for the world.

Anand brought his story out of the darkness of a parable into the hard bright light of Indian poverty, garish and detailed. Nothing made his descriptions more real than his uncanny ability to remember monetary values, every penny earned and spent by either him or his father.

Anand's father didn't come home for fourteen years. "He learnt drivery," Anand said. "He was employed after much struggle as a bus driver by the Bihar government. He drove on a contractual basis, and for every kilometer he drove, he received thirty paise." A stamp, a piece of fruit: that was what thirty paise bought you.

Anand's father went back and forth from Patna to a town seventy kilometers away, earning between forty and fifty rupees for the two-hour journey. Eventually he earned enough money to marry. His dream was to land a government job, and the woman who became his wife—Anand's mother—chided him for this fixation, which, though it offered security, must have seemed more trouble than it was worth. "I have waited so long," he told her, "I have borne so much; sooner or later, I'm sure the government will reward me."

And so it did: he received a three-year contract with a regular monthly income. He was made "fix," Anand said, using the English word to mean that his father, after years of uncertainty, had found some modicum of stability.

The story until now—about Anand's father, his grandfather, the distant but illustrious ancestors—had been a prelude to his own. He wanted me to see the loss of prestige against the background of what had been. Without that, it would not be possible to understand what it meant to fall; nor indeed what it was to pick yourself up again. And it was only about now—fifteen or twenty minutes into our conversation—that I made a quick note:

> At first I could not tell what his story was about. But soon it became clear it was a story about dharma lost and regained, all embodied in a journey from a roguish and poor past to Banaras Hindu University here, at this ancient seat of learning.

Anand was born on April 1, 1994, but he gave even this recent date a mythical cast, so that it seemed it could hardly have been the year of Kurt Cobain's suicide, or of the release of *Pulp Fiction*.

"I was born in the same month as Lord Ram, and as I grew up, it became clear to my parents that this tongue of mine, with which I'm speaking to you now, and speaking *frank*"—Anand used the English word—"would not descend. My parents grew worried. The doctor said, 'This boy may never speak.' So, I had to have an operation, and only after that was I able to speak. My first school was a convent in the village, a private school. I will tell you all that I remember," he said, embarrassed suddenly by the breadth of detail he had supplied. "I have forgotten a great deal too."

The words he used for forgetting and remembering—*asmarana* and *smarana*—are beautiful. They share a root with the English word "memory." Anand's language, in general, was refined. He spoke a Sanskritized Hindi, which from a less deft speaker might have seemed cumbersome and haughty, but with him was fluid and natural. My language, in comparison, was inferior. Here, in India, the modern had yet to surpass the classical. If the cities of the West nurtured sophistication and education, the pockets of urban anglophone life in India had nothing to compare with the cultural richness of the old country.

With the full resources of his language at his fingertips, Anand used a Sanskrit word of great charm to describe himself as a child. He said he was a "chanchal-type" person; it meant "unsteady, inconstant, movable." I had seen this instability in him, and it had perturbed me. Now, by identifying it himself, he seemed in some way to neutralize it.

His fierce intelligence, raw, prehensile, equipped with a photographic memory, was visible even in boyhood. In speaking of his astonishing recall, he said, "I would see something, and it would go straight into my..." He tapped his forehead. "In the third grade, I came first out of seven schools. I was publicly honored by the elected head of the village. I still have the certificate," he said with a trace of sadness.

A self-destructiveness was evident in Anand even at an early age. His chanchal quality grew into something more sinister. What began as the normal antics of a naughty child—pushing his chair back in class, stealing the lunch of another child—had by the fifth grade already acquired something of the air of criminality that was prevalent in Bihar at the time. A few years before Anand was born, the state had elected a thuggish peasant as its chief minister. By 2004, around the time Anand was ten, *The Economist* reported that "Bihar [had] become a byword for the worst of India: of widespread and inescapable poverty; of corrupt politicians indistinguishable from the mafia dons they patronise; of a caste-ridden social order that has retained the worst feudal cruelties."

Anand and his best friend, Rahul, must have imbibed something of this atmosphere. They were both denied a TC—a transfer certificate required for them to go from primary school to secondary school. The denial was not for academic reasons; they were both, as Anand put it, "toppers."

"Then why were you denied it?"

"We beat someone up," Anand said, sheepish still after all these years. Referring to his lady teacher, Anand said, "Madam would not give us our TCs. She said, 'You have to call your guardian, or your parents, first.' Naturally we did not want to do that, so this Rahul, who was a pretty rough guy and used to carry a knife around with him, pulled it on Madam. He planted it squarely into her desk and just left it there. 'If you don't give us our TCs,' he told her, 'I'm going to kill you. Understand?' Madam got frightened. She said, 'Obviously you won't listen to reason. So I had better just do what you want.'

"She gave it"—Anand smirked—"and we took it!"

It was the first of many such moments when Anand had fallen prey to his environment. He even came to look fondly on the legacy of his bandit great-uncle.

"At least he made a name! I feel I've got to do something with this life of mine. I've got to become something."

The stories that most enchanted Anand were tales of affluence. He told me of one uncle who had fallen into bad ways. The son of the most esteemed Jha brother, the Railway Police officer, got himself thrown out of the house and ran away to Ayodhya in Uttar Pradesh. But there he did not fail. He made a love marriage with a woman who was a Ph.D. from a university in Faizabad. They bought a large house and a car. "And that same man who could not do without guns, booze, and meat," Anand said, referring to a triune of sins that exists only in India, "is now totally reformed."

I suspected Anand wanted something similar to happen to him. He would have liked nothing better than to make good somewhere, by whatever means, and to thumb his nose at the pious fools in his village who were convinced that the bad blood of his uncle and great-uncle was reasserting itself in Anand.

The village was rife with malicious rumors that Anand was on the path to ruin. His father, trying to save Anand from himself, sought his father-in-law's advice. The boy was sent to a Sanskrit school forty or fifty kilometers from the village. It recreated the ancient pastoral of Brahmin boys learning the scriptures by the banks of a river, and here Anand would be reformed.

"It was a beautiful place," Anand said, pointing outside, where the palpitating dusk had given the Ganges a granite hue.

There was a river; the living conditions were excellent; their temple housed a statue of Ram ornamented with a crown of solid gold. In the morning, the boys were fed a porridge of yogurt and sugar, which was known as "the children's breakfast." In the afternoon, there was "a royal repast." In the evenings, they took a ritual bath and cooked their own food. No one could eat until Lord Ram had been fed first.

Little Brahmin boys, cooking and cleaning for themselves, serving Lord Ram, devoting themselves to the study of Sanskrit and the scriptures—it was an idyll. But even here, Anand soon began to play what he called a "leadership" role.

"It took me six months to get the measure of the place." He meant it took him that long to sniff out the malefactors. He studied for six months with all his heart. His father had convinced him that there was something special about him, and he worked hard to live up to his potential. But then the chief priest of the school, who had a connection to Anand's village, showed up with the guns.

"Guns?" I said.

"Yes." Anand grinned. "He had a little trade in guns on the side and wanted me to perform a ceremony to bless them."

"How old were you?" I asked, astonished by this development.

"I must have been—what?—ten or eleven."

The chief priest kept his munitions in a cave, where he was also harboring a fugitive from justice. A "sooter," Anand said, and for a moment I didn't know what he meant.

"He was an excellent shot. He had amazing aim. People would hire him to kill other people."

"Ah."

"So, there I was: I had been sent to this place to be reformed, to learn Sanskrit, but I was soon living like a criminal."

The shooter, like many men of criminal backgrounds in Bihar, had political ambitions. By the summer, he was campaigning to be the chief elected official in Anand's village.

"We had holidays. There was a nice election mood heating up."

Anand's father was horrified to see his eleven-year-old son as a mascot in the shooter's campaign, riding about in an open jeep with a turban tied on his head. "How do you know this man?" Anand's father asked gravely. Anand had no reply, and his father saw that his worst fears had been confirmed: Anand had fallen into bad ways.

He was pulled out of the Sanskrit school and brought back to the village, but by then it was too late. Anand had developed a taste for the unsavory side of life. As he put it, "Whatever mold you cast the clay in, that is the pot you'll get." He became a "big boss" at school; he was elected monitor, he said, giving the English word a deep tilde, so that it sounded like "manyetor." He began once again to adopt a "leadership role." Teachers grew afraid of him. He cut class with impunity. He sat all day in a village shop, watching Bollywood films.

"And you know what kind of films I would watch?" he said with sudden urgency. "Those films in which the hero becomes a millionaire, films with strife and struggle in them. I would love all the adversity the hero had to endure before he became a big man. One film in particular was my favorite: *Muqaddar ka Sikandar*." The Conqueror of Destiny.

I knew the film. Bollywood was perhaps the only shared cultural point of reference left to us both, all the proof Anand and I had that we even lived in the same country, and that was now in jeopardy too: a new generation of Indians, educated abroad, found the films too operatic. The industry was increasingly run by native English-speakers. I had met many actors, producers, and directors from this world over the years, and the impression they gave me were of people guessing at the tastes and desires of a vast Hindi-speaking audience they were no longer culturally in touch with. Many, I suspected, would have preferred to make films that were more subtle and urban, less melodramatic, but those films did not speak to young men such as Anand. And it was interesting that the actors Anand described as his heroes, in that little shop in rural Bihar, had been my heroes, too, despite our fourteen-year age gap. Even this film Anand admired so much—The Conqueror of Destiny—had been made in 1978.

In the three years Anand spent in the village, he became a man of fashion. He adopted what he called an "espice" cut.

"What is a spice cut?"

"Hair forward"—he ran his fingers through his brilliantined hair—"and short at the back. That's the fashion I would keep. I wore colorful English-style T-shirts and torn jeans. My living style became Western. My own culture—our culture—began to change. And do you know how I paid for all this?"

"How?"

"I would perform religious ceremonies for people here and there. I'd studied Sanskrit for two years, and so I could get by, and I'd earn some two or three hundred rupees a pop."

I laughed out loud. "You would use your earnings as a Brahmin to pay for your Western fashions?"

"Yes." He grinned broadly.

An idea of the West, even if only as a source of technology and fashion, had reached Anand in his little village in Bihar. The priestly work of his ancestors became less an exalted duty and more a way for a young man to fund his growing taste for a Western lifestyle. Anand's predicament—which was the predicament of so many young men—crystallized in a very real way in his life: a choice.

He'd done badly in his tenth-grade examinations. He'd earned a third division: "I didn't study at all." The only subject he'd done passably well in was mathematics, in which he got 66 percent. He wanted to study commerce. He had a natural head for business and thought it was a field in which he might amount to something. He was desperate to make a name for himself. He filled out the application form, paid his fees, and secured a place to study business administration in one of the top government colleges in Muzaffarpur.

His name was already on the list of students when something put Anand on an altogether different course. At a wedding at the house of one of his maternal uncles, a guru, versed in the scriptures and in astrology, came to perform the rites. As the guru recited various mantras during the marriage ceremony, Anand began reciting alongside him in the background. The guru heard Anand and was impressed. He said to his father, with the special authority of a clairvoyant, "Give this boy an education in Sanskrit. It will be good for him. His future is very bright."

As I heard this, I felt something of the dread we feel in certain books and films when we desperately want a character to go one way, and they go inexorably another. Commerce was an excellent choice for Anand. It represented a kind of shorthand in his mind for modernity, and his desire for material wealth ought to have been given a proper outlet. Anand was intelligent, but did not strike me as an intellectual. I felt he was especially unsuited to the pieties of a traditional education in Sanskrit. He would surely revolt and feel guilty. It was a pattern that had already done him considerable harm. The idea of dharma had calcified over time: it could no longer serve as a guide for self-realization. Commerce was much nearer Anand's real dharma. He had tremendous energy, which, unharnessed, would fester and become the cause of a greater disturbance.

But Anand's father—the man who had waited a lifetime for a contract to drive buses for the Bihar government—found it difficult to refuse the revered elder figure of the astrologer-priest. Mr. Jha, though poorly educated, was in the end a Brahmin. A man far grander than himself had seen promise in his son and was telling him to initiate the boy in the ancient rites of their caste. How could Mr. Jha refuse him? Anand had his heart set on commerce, but he could not, in turn, refuse his father. Anand said, "If it's something you want me to do, then it must be good, and I'll do it." His father replied, "It's you who has to study. Not me."

Father and son—under the sway of the prophetic visitor—together arrived at a place of perfect misunderstanding. The dream of commerce was abandoned, and Anand was sent to yet another Sanskrit school. He tried again to correct course, tried once more to alter his nature to fit the pieties of his vocation. Once again, his intelligence and charm earned him the affection of people around him—most notably a Brahmin Sanskrit teacher called Madam Veena—and yet his chanchal disposition landed him in trouble.

Madam Veena was a dwarfish woman with a searing intellect. She taught the boys at the school some twenty-five verses of Sanskrit a week. She took a close interest in Anand and gave him some useful advice: "If only you would put one iota of the energy that you put into life into your studies, you would go very far."

"She really believed in me," Anand said. Almost as an elegy for Madam Veena's trust in him, he now recited some verses of Sanskrit that she had taught him that he still remembered. They were from the invocation of *Karnabharam* (Karna's Burden), a play by the Sanskrit dramatist Bhasa, who lived some fifteen centuries ago.

The Sanskrit sounded out into the courtyard of Alice's house, where the lights had come on. Anand recited the verses hurriedly, as if the practice of committing them to memory was still fresh. He enjoyed how easily they came back.

I put my notebook down. I had in my travels through the Muslim world seen young boys who knew the Koran by heart. But Bhasa was not religion; Bhasa was literature; and though Anand was not an impressive figure, not a learned Brahmin, it was as if this twenty-something waif, with his threadbare appearance, were saying, *I am still part of an aristocracy of the mind.*

Anand left the second Sanskrit school in ignominy. He clashed with a senior, a Ph.D. student, who told him to wash his dishes. Anand refused outright. There was a stand-off, and Anand was called into the office of the man who had foreseen a bright future for him in Sanskrit, the guru from the wedding. When this venerable figure questioned him, Anand replied with a defiance that would have been shocking. He said, "I'm not a eunuch. I'm no less a man than you, from no less a family. My blood runs hot too."

The guru balked. "Anand, if you can speak to me like this, I can only imagine how you must have spoken to that senior."

Anand was told to take some time off. He had blown too many chances with too many people. Then, in the midst of his despair, he was thrown the kind of lifeline that only those who have been in disasters of their own making can ever really appreciate: a few older friends told him about the Banaras Hindu University, a seat of learning that had been founded in Benares a century before with the express hope of resurrecting the glory of the Hindu past.

"You're wasted where you are," they told him. "That place is too small for you."

Anand took their advice and applied to BHU. He had nothing to lose. His father didn't even know that Anand had applied and was surprised when a "call letter" arrived—the arrival of a letter in a village is always an event!—requesting Anand's presence in Benares for an entrance exam.

It was a Friday. Anand was not in the village. He was 120 kilometers away, performing a religious ceremony. He was dressed in a dhoti and kurta, but didn't even have time to come home and change. He got his father to give his "admit card" to the stationmaster at Muzaffarpur station. When Anand got there, the man handed it to Anand. He changed out of his traditional clothes, and into Western clothes. "I was dressed in jeans," he said proudly, "when I first arrived at BHU."

He had no idea what to expect. He thought the great university was yet another Sanskrit school. He arrived at the cantonment at 1:00 a.m. and spent the night at the station itself.

In the morning, Anand saw from the vast crowd that had gathered at the station that this BHU, which he had thought was another piddling Sanskrit school, could not be so small an affair after all. He took a Tempo, a kind of open truck, the ten kilometers into town.

Anand arrived at the great arch, pale yellow and red and ornamented with the features of Hindu temple architecture, and stood there for many minutes. There was a statue of the founder of the university at the center of a roundabout, where a drab blue-tiled fountain occasionally played. Anand still didn't understand. He hadn't realized what this place was—that here every subject under the sun was taught.

At the end of April, when Anand came for his entrance exam, he felt the temperature fall by a few noticeable degrees upon entering the sylvan sprawl of BHU. He had left traffic, noise, and smoke behind him. The big umbrageous trees of the north flanked the wide streets, scalloping them with pools of shade. The gulmohar, with its terraced canopy of ferns, would have been coming into bloom, and the laburnum, with its restless plumes of solid gold, stirring in the hot wind, would have given the heat and dazzle of the day a bewitching quality.

Anand would have passed by the university's many faculties, which are European in their use of mass, space, and proportion; but where there might have been a cupola or a Corinthian column, there appeared soaring shikhars with notched capping stones, sloping chhajjas, and ornamental chhatris with sweeping arcades of bracketed Hindu arches. Sanskrit and Ayurveda sat alongside Chemistry and Computer Science. The buildings were the expression of the idea upon which the university had been founded a hundred years before: the idea of synthesis.

The Brahmin glory may have run thin in Anand's village in rural Bihar; but here, in BHU, on exam day, it was on full display. "I couldn't believe what I was seeing," Anand said, "vast foreheads ornamented with sprawling caste marks; great big shikhas, oiled and combed; everyone dressed in dhotis with huge brocade borders. And there I was, a ragamuffin, in jeans and shirt. I tell you, my mind short-circuited. I thought, 'What is going to become of me in this crowd? I, who know nothing except how to perform the odd little religious ceremony?' I had to tell myself, 'Listen, Anand, it's Shiva who's brought you this far—he must have done it for a reason. Now go in, do your exam, write whatever you know, and leave the rest to Him.' And that is just what I did."

That evening, after his exam, Anand hit the town. He saw the Dashashwamedh Ghat, where the worship of the Ganges was performed every night; he tried (and failed) to give offerings of flowers and holy water at the Kashi Vishwanath Temple. "The crowd was huge, and I don't believe in this form of prayer. I pray through my heart, and I said to Baba Vishwanath, Lord of All, 'Please. I want to come and live in this town of Yours, which I love very much. But I'm from a poor family, and only You can make this possible.' A voice came up from within me that said, 'If Baba wills it, you will be permanent here.'" *Permanent!* It was Anand's word for an infinite security, and it had run right through his story.

Anand's father did not know that Anand had applied to BHU, let alone visited Benares and sat an entrance exam. When he was admitted, his father was not sure what BHU was, or how hard it was to get into, especially for someone such as Anand, who was the first in his family to be admitted to a university of this caliber. Mr. Jha wanted to be happy for his son, but needed to call a more cosmopolitan relation in Patna to confirm the meaning of the news.

"This man went berserk," Anand said. "He told my father that BHU was a huge deal; they would teach me—really educate me—my entire future would change. When my father heard all this, he short-circuited too. He couldn't believe that his son, the son of a bus driver for the Bihar government, had been selected for this great honor. He said fearfully, 'How much is it going to be, son? You know what I earn. How will we send you there?' I said, 'Baba has made all this possible. He has put down my name for this. He will find a solution.'"

Anand had tended throughout his story to let the certitudes of a pastoral past intrude upon the hard reality of his life. And he was doing it again. This business about God and fate may have consoled his father, but I knew it did not console Anand. Certain beliefs that had solaced an earlier generation—his father, his grandfather—had died in Anand, and I was pretty sure that he believed this life to be the only life. In fact he was in the grip of an extremely modern anxiety about what to do next, and how to pay his way. He had come this far, but he had no idea how he would go any further. His Sanskrit education was of no use to him. He had no real academic interest, and he had stumbled into a thesis on Buddhist India. "I don't have the intellect to be a professor," he said with desperation. "I don't have the money to sit around. I don't know what I'm going to do." He was due to leave BHU the following year; he had no career prospects, and in his confusion, he had strayed into the world of Hindu nationalism, which promised to restore the glories of his past.

Anand took his phone out of his pocket and said, "Look at this." It seemed just like any other phone. But then he removed the red rubber band that held it together, and the whole instrument—dial pad, battery, screen, and cover—came apart in his hands.

Anand put the pieces back together carefully. "This is my story," he said. "I've told it to you. And perhaps, after you, no one will ever hear it again."

That was May 2014. Ten days later, in the last phase of voting, the sacred city went to the polls. I was back in Delhi when I saw that Modi had been elected by the largest mandate the country had seen in thirty years. Anand was ecstatic. He sent me a text message, saying he had danced in the streets of Benares until dawn. "If only you'd seen the deluge of humanity!"

# 6

# THE MODERN TRADITIONALIST

**IT WAS TRIPATHI WHO SUGGESTED** I meet P. K. Mukhopadhyay. "He is a profound scholar," he said, "representing the Brahminic tradition of Bengal on the one hand, and totally versed in modern European philosophy on the other. You will enjoy speaking to him in English. His English is excellent."

As a young man in Bengal, Mukhopadhyay resolved that when his time at Jadavpur University in Calcutta was over, he would spend his final years in Benares. In 2003, after some forty years of teaching, he left his post as head of the philosophy department and made good on his vow.

One hot afternoon in May, as my time in Benares was nearing an end, I went to see Mukhopadhyay in his small flat on a desolate intersection, a short distance inland from the Alice Boner House. I had called ahead, and Mukhopadhyay gave the auto-rickshaw driver clear directions. The congestion around the river soon gave way to a treeless stretch of road. We took a right after the Durgakund Temple, with its tank of still green water, the surface litter strewn. We came to a roundabout—the Gurudham Intersection—on whose raised platform a solitary black bull lay in the dust. Political posters quivered in the hot wind; a large metal billboard advertised a preschool. Mukhopadhyay lived above a shop that sold Exide car batteries. An underpass led into a petrol-stained courtyard, where a few scooters and motorbikes were parked.

I climbed an open-air staircase that led up to Mukhopadhyay's flat and stopped at the landing to look out at Gurudham Park, with its balding patches of grass, lined with hulking ashoka trees, a ragged palm or two, and bushes of flowering oleander. The blazing summer day fell at a slant over the park.

A young Brahmin boy answered the door and led me into an anteroom of sorts. There was a small porcelain sink, a desk, and a low, heavily varnished bench with thin cushions in an ugly checked pattern, all reddish brown. Other doors gave onto other rooms: a bathroom, a prayer room, a kitchen in the distance, where I could make out a stove and red gas cylinder. A smoked-glass window, partly open, overlooked an interior courtyard. A calendar of the Bengali freedom fighter Chittaranjan Das gazed down at me from the yellow walls.

Soon P. K. Mukhopadhyay appeared, a small man dressed in a short-sleeved kurta that left his pale hairless arms exposed. He wore a white dhoti with an attractive indigo border. His skin was sallow and veined blue; there was the faintest trace of sandalwood on his forehead. His garland of rudraksh and sacred thread was visible. His face was stern and tremulous, with piercing eyes, but it was also somehow boyish and elfin, with short blunt teeth that turned inward at the middle. The soft folds around his eyes gave an impression both of ill health and sagacity.

We sat down by the window. I was at a hard angle to Mukhopadhyay, and this fitted the mood of our early conversation, which was stilted and difficult. I found the Bengali Brahmin tetchy, defensive, and keen to shock. He wanted me to know that he was extremely conservative, and he illustrated his point with an anecdote.

"Some time back, I was asked by a colleague of mine ..." He paused. "He is a man of a different caste, and there is a deep-rooted intellectual and scholarly difference between us. I was very friendly, but he always took the opportunity to poke me on this point: 'Ah, you are a Brahmin, and all that.' One day it so happened that he said, 'Professor Mukhopadhyay, many people tell me that you are very strict in your food habits; but, at the same time, you love to feed people. So, what would you do if I was to come into the room while you were eating and sit down across the table from you?'"

Mukhopadhyay, reliving his shock, flared his eyes. "'How dare you say that? You will not be permitted.'"

"Not permitted?" I asked.

"The question does not arise. How do you permit it?"

I was not yet sure if he was teasing me.

"I had a student of a low-caste background. He stayed in my home. I maintained him. I fed him. I taught him. He was a boy of a very poor family. And because he could not cook for me, I had to cook and feed him. I was happy to do it, but if he takes food in my house, he will clean the place. He will clean the utensils."

This was no ordinary cleaning. Nor were the dishes dirty in a mere physical way. They were contaminated. The deeds of a past life had left the young man Mukhopadhyay spoke of, his student, spiritually unclean. A vessel that has come into contact with saliva can only be handled by someone inferior in rank, or equal, to the eater. Mukhopadhyay could not touch the vessel his student had eaten from, so the "cleaning" he described was a kind of purification.

Mukhopadhyay tried to make it seem like a simple matter of doing the dishes. He wanted to show me how easy it was to accommodate his belief that human beings were inherently inferior or superior. But as with other carefully crafted race laws, this attempt to domesticate the alarming belief only enlarged my horror at what was implied.

Nor was Mukhopadhyay acting out the unconsidered continuities of an ancient tradition. "All the beliefs that I have now," he told me, "all the pride I take in being a Hindu, an Indian, a Brahmin—all this I developed myself after studying and thinking. I never inherited any of these things nor accepted them blindly."

Mukhopadhyay had also made a journey back, "a return to self," of which he was profoundly aware. "How would you describe what we are discussing?" he asked after we had spent many hours together, stretched out over multiple days.

I said, "An experience of cultural loss, and the journey you made back to a place of wholeness ... ?"

"In my opinion," he cut me short, "it is just the birth of a modern traditionalist."

Some thirty years before Mukhopadhyay was born, in 1910, the great Bengali writer Rabindranath Tagore published a novel called *Gora*. The eponymous hero of *Gora*—the word means "fair-skinned" or "white"—is an Irish orphan adopted by a Brahmin family in Bengal. He grows up believing himself to be Brahmin, but his orthodox father knows better and, ritually cleansed from a morning bath in the Ganges, he avoids Gora's touch before his prayers. The novel is set in the world of the educated classes in Bengal as they negotiate the transition between tradition and modernity. It is a world suffused with the atmosphere of Hindu reform movements. The Tagore family had played a key role in the development of the Brahmo Samaj in Bengal, a monotheistic reformation of Hinduism that thrived during the Bengal Renaissance. Tagore throughout his life faced tremendous pushback for what was seen as an attack on Hinduism. Gora is an embodiment of that reaction. He rejects the reformist movements altogether and ardently believes that modern India can only be rescued if she returns to her roots in strict orthodox Hinduism. "Take it from me in writing," he says early on in the novel, "India has her own very special makeup, her own special strength, her own special truth, and it is only by developing these that we can succeed, and save ourselves."

Gora argues tirelessly with his reformist best friend; he denies his feelings for a girl of a reformist family, upholds the traditional role of women in Hindu society, and punishes his mother for her lax attitude to the food prohibitions that underpin caste. At the end of the novel he discovers the truth of his birth, and it shatters his belief in his religion and caste.

The problem *Gora* dramatizes is an old one. The spirit of reform has not arisen organically, but is the product of contact with another civilization, namely Europe's. How do you give autonomy to what began with assimilating the criticism of others? This anxiety is a theme that recurs again and again in Dostoyevsky. Yevgeny Pavlovitch Radomsky's "extraordinary fact" in *The Idiot* is that Russian liberalism is not a critique of Russia's social and economic structures, but an attack on Russia itself. "There cannot be such a liberal anywhere else who would hate his very fatherland," says Radomsky. His explanation for why such a man should exist in Russia is that he isn't in fact a Russian yet, but the embodiment of an alien criticism.

*Gora,* too, addresses this question of authenticity, presenting it as a matter of survival. "If you think that by uprooting our ancient practices, and destroying our traditions, the nation will become one," Gora tells the chief proponent of liberal Hinduism early on in the novel, "well then you may as well drain the ocean in order to cross it ... The cause of rot might be air; but so long as we are alive we survive; if we die, we rot ..."

The world Mukhopadhyay was born into—Bengal at the end of two centuries of British rule—was similar to the world of *Gora.*

The Mukhopadhyays were Brahmins, but in name only. They did not read their scriptures; the majority of their rites and rituals had lapsed. The thread ceremony, which marked initiation, was still performed, but more as a matter of course than a sacred duty. The family, Mukhopadhyay explained, were typical of a period of liberal Hinduism in Bengal.

The forces of Hindu nationalism were on the rise now, but in Mukhopadhyay's day the greater danger seemed to come from liberal Hindus, who dominated the discourse. Mukhopadhyay, by nature a contrarian, might always have rejected any form of received wisdom. "But," he said, "since, at that time, the practices and beliefs in the society were being governed by the ideas of liberal Hinduism, it was the only thing I had to object to."

What bothered him most was the unthinking quality of his world. There was, on the one hand, a total absence of "commitment," a word Mukhopadhyay seemed to use as a substitute for "dharma"; on the other, there was an unwillingness to make any sacrifice for one's beliefs or ideals. "A culture," Mukhopadhyay said, "is the projection of the image its people have and bear about themselves." But the culture he grew up in had grown unsure of itself. His people were not ashamed of being Brahmin; they were in fact quite proud of it; but he found to his dismay that they were neither willing to deny nor defend their beliefs. If there was a shared experience of being Brahmin at all, Mukhopadhyay said, "it was in the absence of Brahminism, rather than in its presence."

The village Mukhopadhyay grew up in was scarcely fourteen miles from Calcutta. Half its residents were daily commuters to the city. It had been founded in the early nineteenth century—the foundation stone was laid by the British governor-general Lord Bentinck himself—and it had an old public library. Intellectual life was vibrant enough for one of the residents to write a two-volume history of the village. Mukhopadhyay drew this portrait of the place where he grew up to make a more general point about Bengal: that it was "far more socially advanced" than any other part of India.

"They were very educated," Mukhopadhyay said of his people. "During my forefathers' time, the Mahabharata was already being translated for the European people into English."

If Bengal was as socially and intellectually developed as it was, it was because Bengal of any place in India had had the longest sustained contact with the new learning out of Europe. The Bengal Renaissance, of whose fruits Mukhopadhyay was justly proud—the library, the translations, the men who wrote two-volume histories of villages—was the result of an intercultural meeting with Europe, and nowhere did India come closer to "digesting the West'" than in Bengal. Yet Mukhopadhyay felt that the relationship with the West had done more harm than good. Why?

"We all wanted, we young boys, to be modern, to be viewed as modern, to talk modern, to be recognized as modern; but a large part of what we understood of modernity was a negative concept, the critique of what has gone before." To be modern, Mukhopadhyay said, was simply to turn one's back on old India. "It had no positive meaning."

"I narrate one incident: When I was a student of the first year of college, one of my friends came and told me that a friend we had in common had thrown away his sacred thread. When I heard it—something must have been building in me—I just met that boy and said, 'What have you done? Thrown away your sacred thread?'

"He said, 'Yes. So?'

"'And you are proud of it?'

"'Yes.'

"'Why did you do it? Because you think to be modern you have to do it?'

"'Yes.'

"I said, 'Then what is the good of being modern? Modernity then is very old. If now you are to be modern, then you must be *extra*modern.'

"'What do you mean?' the boy said.

"'Challenge this modernity and wear this thread! If throwing away the thread is modernity, then to wear it morally, consciously, aggressively, will be even more modern.'"

As a young man, Mukhopadhyay found himself caught between those who blindly adhered to tradition and those who were apologetic of Hinduism, men such as Tagore and Vivekananda, who had, Mukhopadhyay felt, internalized a foreign criticism of their culture and pretended it was their own. "The West's India," he said, "became our India." Mukhopadhyay craved intellectual autonomy. There was something demoralizing in forever feeling acted upon, in forever taking one's cues from a foreign culture.

"I think I can now reconstruct what I was feeling," Mukhopadhyay said. "What pained me was that people took things in an oversimplistic way." The sacred thread was the symbol of an ancient organization of life. It could not be treated as if it were a mere garment, to be put on or discarded on a whim. "Whether you become a Brahmin, or not a Brahmin, you should be very serious about it. This is what I felt."

The young Mukhopadhyay struck me as so serious that I felt obliged to ask him how old he was at the time. He replied that he would have been around nineteen or twenty.

I now understood something he had said earlier. In describing his numerous troubles with his teachers as a young man, he had said that "99.9 percent" of those teachers had developed a great love for him, though they disagreed with him. The statement had struck me as odd because Mukhopadhyay seemed so prickly and difficult, so painfully oversensitive; he seemed like a hard person to love at first. But now, as I began to discern the intellectual integrity that underlay the irascibility of this Bengali Brahmin, I understood what someone would later say to me about Mukhopadhyay: "He is a very fine man. His mind, his words, his deeds, are totally transparent. There is no gap."

Bengal's universities in those decades following Indian independence were convulsed with strikes and boycotts. Every form of protest was rife on campus. There were Maoist rebellions and student-led insurgencies. It was easy to be co-opted into a system of thought, and Mukhopadhyay seems to have guarded his intellectual independence by resurrecting the idea of dharma. When the Marxists came calling, urging him to strike, he told them that he rejected what he saw as a borrowed form of protest. It was for the union or factory worker to strike, not the student. "They have their way," he told them, "you should have your way."

Small and testy as these early assertions of dharma were, they spoke to something deeper. The Brahmin was the eternal student. It may even be said that, of the four great stages of Hindu life—student, householder, retiree, and renunciant—the second, householder, the man who goes out into the world to earn a living and build a family, was but an interlude for the Brahmin between his young years as a student and the time when, as an old man, he would once again be permitted to give up the world and return to a life of study and contemplation. The Brahmin's prerogative was to have his actions comport with his dharma. If Mukhopadhyay found himself at odds with the world around him, it was because he was trying to reorder the confusions of modern India through a strict adherence to dharma.

"There was this mixture of confidence," he said of his young self, "expressing itself as the desire to say something new, to express a new way of thinking, to respond, to not just accept everything..."

Even as Mukhopadhyay was full of these feelings, his intellectual journey was stalled. His family had fallen on hard times, and it was almost impossible for him to continue his education. He only just about managed to pass his school examinations. But there was no money for him to go to college. He had wanted, as a young boy, to be a professor of English literature at Presidency College in Calcutta. These plans had now to be abandoned. "My intellectual ambitions," he said with a wry smile, "were about to be nipped in the bud." It was thought that Mukhopadhyay should go into "service" of some kind to support his family. "But I did not give up, and more importantly my father did not give up."

The poverty of the Brahmin family became a test of their commitment to the life of the mind. Mukhopadhyay's father told the rest of his household, "If all the family is to go hungry and starve, then so be it. Since he has the desire for studying, let him study."

Knowledge for knowledge's sake was the creed of the Brahmin. Power in India, Mukhopadhyay had said earlier, was of two types: the power that comes out of *tyaga*, "renunciation," is called Brahminic power, and then there is martial power, or brute strength. The Indian scriptures had made it clear, through a contest between two sages, that the former was superior. "To be Brahmin means certain things," Mukhopadhyay said with frustration, "certain virtues and qualities—it has nothing to do with being a dominant caste. This sort of verbal jugglery was very cleverly done for many years by the Western interests."

The ideal of the Brahmin is expressed in *Gora* too:

> If other countries yearn for generals like Wellington, or scientists like Newton, rich men like Rothschild, our country yearns for the Brahmin—such a Brahmin who is without fear, who detests greed, who has attained victory over sorrow, and who worries not for scarcity, for his mind is conjoined with the Supreme Self. He who is steadfast, calm, self-realized; India has a deep yearning for such a Brahmin. Indeed, her independence depends on her ability to throw up such a man, for in every section of our society, in everything we do, the Brahmin is there to remind us of the need to remain free.

When I mentioned Tagore to Mukhopadhyay, he said waspishly, "Rabindranath was of that group of people who could not so much as drink a drop of water without abusing Hinduism."

But Mukhopadhyay emphatically agreed that the source of the Brahmin's prestige in society, though he lacks financial and physical strength, is his autonomy. Though not always true in practice, he said that in Bengal, a Brahmin family that accepted a donation or a gift was considered to be lower in rank, whereas one that did not accept any such gift or donation was ranked very highly. "These people were not greedy," Mukhopadhyay said, "not hankering after fame, not after money, or favor. This was their strength."

Mukhopadhyay's father, after his wife died, lived with Mukhopadhyay for fourteen years, "He was alone with me, and I had the opportunity to observe him closely. He really had very little desire, or demand, for anything. He did not ask for any service, any help, any care."

This was the man who had stepped in to reassert the Brahmin ideal of learning above all else when his son's university education was imperiled. No sooner had Mukhopadhyay entered higher education than he embarked upon the quest to find his second father—his guru—and it was even more intense than Tripathi's had been, every bit an intellectual romance. Mukhopadhyay's future guru had taught him philosophy as an undergraduate and had impressed the young Mukhopadhyay with his confidence. "He was the only one who did not ask me to take his subject as my major," Mukhopadhyay said. And this more than anything else, if only out of childish pride, won Mukhopadhyay over. "It was how I came to philosophy," he said with a girlish laugh. For his M.A., Mukhopadhyay thought, "Enough is enough: I'll take my admission in English literature." Destiny had decreed otherwise, but before the mystical union between disciple and master could happen, there were crossed wires and missed meetings, hurt feelings and chance encounters. Mukhopadhyay nearly enrolled as an English student at the University of Calcutta. By a stroke of pure luck, like a man narrowly prevented from marrying the wrong woman, Mukhopadhyay got his future guru on the phone that day. The young Mukhopadhyay was instructed to come down to the recently established Jadavpur University; he did as he was told, and there his guru was waiting for him.

"When I went there," Mukhopadhyay said, "he just took me with him, straight to the administrative building, met the registrar, and said, 'I want this boy to be a student of philosophy in this university. Arrange everything. It may not be possible for him to pay immediately the fees or admission.' I returned back home a student of the M.A. class in philosophy. All Providence!"

It was amazing to see a transformation in Mukhopadhyay as he spoke. For a moment, the stern moralist became giddy with excitement. "I didn't know it at the time, but I had found my teacher. That was the turning point in my whole life. He made me whatever I am. When I published my first book, I dedicated it to him. One has many teachers, but I say, 'No, I *studied* under them; they are not my teacher; my teacher is this one person alone.'"

Just then, the doorbell rang and the green metal door of Mukhopadhyay's small flat swung open to reveal two young men dressed in full saffron robes. At the sight of Mukhopadhyay, they fell to their knees; each placed his right forearm on the floor, palm up, crossed it with his left, then touched his forehead to the ground before him. I was stunned. Who were these young men? What connection did they have to Mukhopadhyay?

He was a specialist, he explained, in ancient Indian logic, and these young men of peasant backgrounds came to see him most afternoons for instruction in logic. This was the life Mukhopadhyay had vowed to live when his time at the modern university in Calcutta was over. I was entranced at first, perhaps for no other reason than the thrill of seeing the antique figure of the monk as a scholar still alive in India. But as I talked to these two young men—one from Bihar, the other from the eastern state of Orissa—I began to see that their idea of scholarship was very different from my own. We encountered some of the same problems I had faced in speaking to Pavan Kumar Mishra a few weeks before.

Why had they come to Benares?

To study, they said in one voice, using a Sanskrit word that suggested a ritualized form of scholarship rather than intellectual curiosity.

Why did they want to study?

Because these were the values and traditions of their forefathers, they replied.

My interest waned; later Mukhopadhyay confessed that this kind of student had little to say for himself. The "studying" was almost a form of piety, one not driven by any spirit of inquiry. These young men, unlike their teacher, were still *within* tradition; they had not had their world shaken up by the bracing contact with modernity. Their idea of learning seemed to me to be exactly the kind of thing Mukhopadhyay disdained. It made me wonder if these young men were not attractive to him for the same sentimental reason they had been attractive to me: they represented continuity for men in whom a break had occurred.

**MUKHOPADHYAY AND I HAD AGREED** early on to avoid abstractions and to speak in specifics about his life and experience. He eventually gave in, but at first he was appalled by this request:

"You want me to speak about myself? But ahamkara [ego] is the most serious of all evils."

We moved chronologically, covering boyhood, adolescence, education, the search for the guru, and Mukhopadhyay's first teaching job in the philosophy department at Jadavpur University. But something peculiar began to happen. As I listened, I grew worried about the direction of our conversation. The life we were discussing seemed to occur in a void. I could not follow its development: there were no landmarks, no milestones, no contours. There were, to be sure, intellectual thrills and battles; there were more vows, such as

Mukhopadhyay's vow never to go abroad. "I will go when it becomes as easy for an Indian to get an invitation there as it is easy for a European to get an invitation here," he said archly.

What I was looking for from Mukhopadhyay was something far more prosaic: love, marriage, children, career changes—those basic things that give a householder's life shape. But try as I might, I could not extract any information of this kind. I began to lose all sense of time, and at last, just in the hope of reestablishing a basic chronology, I stopped Mukhopadhyay midsentence:

"Are we still in your twenties?"

"No, no," he replied with irritation.

He had mentioned turning points earlier. I now asked him for others.

"Nothing other than this! What I've already narrated. There is nothing in my life which I can narrate that is of more importance. I live 90 percent of life mentally. I hardly mix with any people. I have never been a member of any clubs and societies, never had any affiliation to political parties, nor any literary group. I am very much a lonely individual. Very much. And most of the people are very uncomfortable with me, in my presence."

I thought he must have misunderstood my question, and asked again for a simple chronology.

"I can give it to you, but this chronology I distrust most. Time gets its value from the event that occurs there. Otherwise, time is the same. It is what happens that makes the time specific."

"Until now I had some sense of your childhood, of the search for the teacher, of certain discoveries you made. What happens in the following years? Where did you live? What did you do?"

He used to live in the teachers' quarter, and he taught. "Outside teaching and study, hardly I had any life at all."

"And you taught in Jadavpur University for ... ?"

"The entire period," he said, by which he meant his entire life.

"You were in Jadavpur until you came to Benares?"

"Yes. In April 2003, my service was over. In May, I came here." Because, he reminded me, he had made a vow to come to Benares forty years before. "And I did it. It was God's wish that I could do it."

"Did you have a family?"

"Yes. In the Hindu sense, I had a family. My father, my mother. That's it. In the European sense, wife and children, no."

"You committed yourself entirely to intellectual life?"

"It was so engrossing and time-consuming. I had little time to do anything else."

It was a devastating moment. I had not realized until then how austere his life had been. It did not merely *seem* featureless; it *was* featureless. The second of the Hindu stages of life—that of the householder—had been neatly removed. Mukhopadhyay went straight from student to renunciant, and I began to see that the turning point he had spoken of earlier was the only turning point. From there on, he had waited out the clock. When it was time to retire, he came to Benares to die, as he had resolved to do four decades before. It was terrifyingly bleak, but there was a kind of severe beauty about his life. It had special meaning for the Brahmin because, as Mukhopadhyay himself said, "One of the unique features of Indian culture is that here, for the first and perhaps last time, the quest for spirituality developed and flourished alongside the intellectual quest."

As much as I admired Mukhopadhyay's fortitude and discipline, his resolve to live what he believed, I now doubted his understanding of the world beyond the confines of this small flat. He began to tell me a story from real life, which was meant to illustrate the principle of tyaga, at work. It was on one level a classic boy-meets-girl tale of two students who met in his class, fell in love, and married; but this was not at all the story Mukhopadhyay meant to tell.

The boy in the story was Brahmin and seriously bright—"proud, pampered, overconfident." He belonged to an orthodox sect of

Brahmins in Mukhopadhyay's village. The boy was initiated, like the rest of his family, at an early age. Their teacher believed in certain orthodoxies and practiced them. For example, he did not allow Brahmins to eat in the company of non-Brahmins. The guru and his followers went around the village chanting and singing, and for this they were ridiculed. Mukhopadhyay did not admire the boy's guru, but Mukhopadhyay's own guru had, and so Mukhopadhyay was prepared to believe there was some good in the man. Mukhopadhyay acknowledged this boy was talented, but restless. He had enrolled in Jadavpur, where he wanted, in part because of his religious background, to study Vedanta, one of the six branches of Hindu philosophy, known for its strict monism. One day at the university, the boy confronted Mukhopadhyay, asking him why he didn't teach the subject.

"Because I'm teaching logic," Mukhopadhyay replied. "I cannot teach all the subjects. And besides, the department has not allotted it to me."

The boy said, "I have a great desire to study Vedanta. But I won't study Vedanta with the teacher who is teaching it. He is not a Brahmin; and as such, he has no right to teach Vedanta."

So this boy ended up in Mukhopadhyay's class, where he became a thesis student. There he met a girl, also a good student, shy and self-effacing and not Brahmin, nor even Bengali. Mukhopadhyay had taken a keen interest in the girl as well because he feared that unless she studied harder, she was not going to do well in the examination.

"I used to call her occasionally and give her instruction," Mukhopadhyay said. "Study this, study that, do not leave any question unanswered. So much so"—he chuckled—"that she used to tell others, 'Even in my dreams P. K. comes to chastise me.'"

One day, after passing the examination, she came to Mukhopadhyay's house. She had an opportunity to study in America on a scholarship. She wanted to know from her guru whether she should accept.

Mukhopadhyay said no, she should not. And that was that: she did not go to America. But some time passed and the opportunity arose again. Again, the girl sought Mukhopadhyay's counsel. This time he said, "Go."

The girl was taken aback. "Sir, I thought you alone would rescue me. I thought you'd say no, and then I would have a reason not to go to America. I would tell my family that my teacher does not wish it. That is why I cannot go."

Mukhopadhyay now explained—such are the circles the guru runs around the unsuspecting disciple!—"That is exactly why I told you to go. There is a desire in you to go, and you are using me as an excuse not to, but you are not convinced."

Mukhopadhyay now gave his consent, but with two pieces of advice about how the girl was to conduct herself abroad. She was to try to learn about the people and culture she was going among, and not to confine herself to her own group, and she was never under any circumstances to speak of India abroad.

The first bit of advice seemed unobjectionable, but why the second?

"The reason," Mukhopadhyay informed her, "is that you are an Indian. And the West has not brought you over to hear about their philosophy. They do not depend on you to promote their philosophy. But it is natural that they would expect you to know your own and to teach them. But as you and I well know, you do not know Indian philosophy. You do not know your country; you never cared to know your country; but the moment you go there, you will be expected to, and you will make a fool both of yourself and your country.'"

The girl accepted this brutal bit of advice without question and left for America.

In the meantime, the boy, who was a few months into his time at Jadavpur University, came to see Mukhopadhyay to tell him that he was also leaving.

"Why?" Mukhopadhyay asked.

"It's not for me to study here."

"Why? What is the problem?"

The boy said the coeducational environment in the college was disagreeable to him: "Mixing with ladies is not good for me because I'm a *brahmachari*." That is, he was a traditional student, vowed to celibacy.

"Good. That is a good decision. But may I ask you one question: What is your idea of being a brahmachari? Is it living with that clan of yours in the ashram?"

"Exactly."

"Then you're making a very wrong decision. You are not made for that."

But the boy did not take Mukhopadhyay's advice. He went away and became an ascetic, donning the saffron cloth and wearing his hair in matted locks. Occasionally Mukhopadhyay ran into the boy in his ascetic's robes and told him again that he was making a grave mistake: "Asceticism is not for you. Your approach is very emotional."

"Why do you say that, sir?"

"You are overrun by love and affection for your guru. But your guru will not be in his physical body long. He is already quite aged. Do you think you will find enough of your type in the ashram? You'll simply go mad. You'll have to leave that ashram."

Mukhopadhyay confided to me, "It was not at all suited for him. And besides, I knew that this boy had a great desire for fame and recognition. Which"—Mukhopadhyay laughed wickedly—"does not make one a very good ascetic, does it?"

"No," I said, in thrall to this strange story and unsure of where it was headed.

After some time, the boy came back, in his saffron robes, and joined the University of Calcutta, where, once again in a coeducational environment, he completed the master's degree he had abandoned and started teaching.

The story had been presented to me as a lesson in the principle of tyaga, but so far there seemed to be nothing to renounce.

Now, Mukhopadhyay said, almost as an afterthought, that the boy had also left India for the West; and there, presumably after his flirtation with asceticism was over, he had reconnected with the girl from Mukhopadhyay's class, and before long the two were married.

After the marriage, both of them returned to India many times. On one occasion, the first after their marriage, the girl asked if she might be permitted to visit Mukhopadhyay in his house.

"You can come," Mukhopadhyay replied pointedly, "but not your husband. Your husband is not permitted."

Why the one and not the other?

"Her husband had enough learning and caution. So, if he had committed a wrong, then that wrong was done in complete knowledge. If this lady has done something wrong, for which she fears that she may not be able to come to my house, then he is responsible for that mistake, not her."

"The mistake being the intercaste marriage?"

"Yes," Mukhopadhyay said gravely, "the mistake was the intercaste marriage."

Mukhopadhyay had meant for the story to be a thought experiment of sorts. He felt an obvious and simple solution existed for the moral predicament the couple found themselves in—a solution, he described, that would "add glory" to each of their lives and glory to the system of which they were a part, and from which they had broken because of their unlawful marriage. Mukhopadhyay would have the couple announce before all that they were in love, but that as their "system" would not allow for its consecration, they had decided to forsake their romantic happiness and respectfully part. After all, life was short. Some thirty years or so had already passed; another twenty of youth and vigor remained; was it necessary to spend them enjoying the charm of an illicit union? Surely it was more honorable to sacrifice one's selfish happiness for the endurance of the system one's ancestors had devised.

I was staggered.

It was not merely the awfulness of what was suggested, but that Mukhopadhyay, the logician, seemed to have made an obvious error in logic. Did he not see that the "system" he wished to preserve was encircled by another, one that did not demand the sacrifice of personal happiness, but encouraged people to make the pursuit of that happiness the foundation of their lives? Would it not be better to acknowledge the limitations of one's system than for these two young people to stop their ears to the obvious appeal of the other?

Mukhopadhyay said, "The point is that they are taking refuge in another system of morality. Their sense of morality is just a negative one. It is a system based on what it is not. Do they have any well-developed system? Have they any tradition? Have they ever thought about it? Have they lived it? Were they born into it? They are constructing a system that is purely negative. It is that which is not Hinduism.

"You cannot first fall in love, and then because you find the system does not allow it, you deem it bad and reject it."

But you can, I wanted badly to say. That is exactly what the young couple had done.

In his quest for autonomy, Mukhopadhyay refused to acknowledge that the shake-up of old ways had been a direct result of contact with the West. That contact could not now be wished away. In his desire for agency to be restored to India, Mukhopadhyay was prepared to defend all that Hinduism had not independently criticized about itself. But he was missing something important, for, as Sucharita, the female protagonist of *Gora*, points out, if Hinduism was "going to change by itself, then why hasn't it changed until now?"

The mood in the room grew somber. Mukhopadhyay could sense my disappointment. It was true: I was disappointed. His wish to damage the happiness of the two young people diminished him in my eyes. He seemed like a man with nothing to offer the world but the joyless severity of his dharma. Earlier, he had spoken of how Europe had misconstrued India by labeling it an exclusively spiritual culture, while claiming for itself a monopoly on science. "It was a left-handed compliment," Mukhopadhyay said acidly. "They said, 'No, no. India is a very great culture, but in a *spiritual* way.' What they were really saying was, 'You have no claim on scientific culture, you have no claim on rational culture. You're a dreamy, irrational, spiritual people.' And it was not true," Mukhopadhyay cried. "We were, like any great culture, a total culture."

It was a valid point. But as much as the West had reduced India to a spiritual culture, India was also guilty of seeing the West as nothing but the source of material comfort. Mukhopadhyay had seen in the motives of Indians who went abroad to study something "insincere, dishonest, and extra-academic." By this he meant they were attracted to the comforts of the West—"the glamour, the money, the ease of life. Only this and nothing else," he said derisively. In a place such as India, where even the most basic amenities—of clean air, green space, a modicum of peace and quiet—were hard to come by, it was not difficult to see why people would be attracted to these things. But even if we were to follow Mukhopadhyay's severe criteria, putting all thought of comfort out of our minds, his comprehension of what lay behind the appeal of the West was fatally limited. He saw it as a force that had remade his culture, robbing it of autonomy, but he was no closer to seeing why it had been able to exert such power. His own story, had he only been more open, might have provided him with an important clue. "This idea of the pursuit of happiness is at the heart of the attractiveness of the civilization to so many outside it or on its periphery," V. S. Naipaul said in a 1990 lecture entitled "Our Universal Civilization." He went on:

> I find it marvelous to contemplate to what an extent, after two centuries, and after the terrible history of the earlier part of this century, the idea has come to a kind of fruition. It is an elastic

> idea; it fits all men. It implies a certain kind of society, a certain kind of awakened spirit. I don't imagine my father's parents would have been able to understand the idea. So much is contained in it: the idea of the individual, responsibility, choice, the life of the intellect, the idea of vocation and perfectibility and achievement. It is an immense human idea. It cannot be reduced to a fixed system. It cannot generate fanaticism. But it is known to exist; and because of that, other more rigid systems in the end blow away.

The knowledge of the existence of another system had reached the two young students in Mukhopadhyay's class, even before they had left India. It was what allowed them to walk away from their own system—the system in which Mukhopadhyay would see them imprisoned.

"We should wrap up," Mukhopadhyay said. "I've already taken up so much of your time." He meant, I think, that I had taken up too much of his.

I got up to leave.

"I am always ready to enter into all sorts of dialogues and discussions," he said, "but I am not ready to let anyone walk over Hindu culture and society."

The green metal door closed behind me with a clamor and a sharp squeak of the bolt. Just before it shut, I heard Mukhopadhyay softly say, "I don't think I was of much help. I am a very conservative man."

**LEAVING MUKHOPADHYAY'S HOUSE, I COULD** think only of something he had said early on in our conversation. He had brought up Tagore's play *Achalayatan* (The Petrified Place). It was a metaphor for the rigidity of Hindu society and the ossified world of tradition. "It is a place, a house, a system, which is unmoving for a long time, dead,"

Mukhopadhyay said. "Fixed, rigid, static ... This is how Tagore saw Hinduism."

Mukhopadhyay felt that even in delivering this searing indictment of Hindu society, Tagore could not help but acknowledge Brahmin glory. At the end of the play, when the lower castes tear down the entire structure of Hindu society, and all the priests have fled the petrified house, the head priest—named Mahapanchak—remains. He sits at the entrance of the house, a symbol of immovability. The others come and ask, "Who is this man? Let us remove him, let us kill him." But the guru says, "Where he sits, you cannot even touch."

"He was so very firm," Mukhopadhyay said, beaming with pride. "That itself is a glory, that itself is a beauty."

Mukhopadhyay, like Mahapanchak, had sought salvation in rigidity. As much as I admired Mukhopadhyay's steadfastness—that iron resolve to make the word flesh—I felt he had tried to banish the threat to his culture by delegitimizing the appeal of the other culture. It was an act of sophistry—"verbal jugglery," to use his own phrase—and it made him seem like a man afraid of life. When I asked him about the Modi election, and the spirit of revivalism that was sweeping through Hinduism, Mukhopadhyay gave me an evasive answer, seeming to imply that while he endorsed the new assertiveness that had come to Hinduism, he could not go along with the hate. He said, "It is my ambition to be a Hindu, without vengeance, and without apology."

# WINTER

# 7

# THE REVOLUTIONARY BRAHMIN

**EIGHTEEN MONTHS HAD GONE BY.**

We flew through a thin light-suffused mist. The land below was parceled out into small holdings—the dun quilt of India, with its furrows like the channels in a piece of brown corduroy. I glanced at IndiGo's in-flight magazine, called *Hello 6E*. Sweetie, the air hostess, handed me a junglee chicken sandwich. She was dressed in dark blue, with a matching slim leather belt and pillbox hat; a pin on her sleeve said GIRL POWER.

A golden oval of winter sunlight swept searchingly over the cabin. We landed among mustard fields, whose little yellow flowers were attractive against the pink and white of the airport's boundary wall.

The studied cool of IndiGo airlines had enforced a civility on the passengers, suppressed certain instincts that, now that we were on the ground and close to disembarking, returned with force. There was a small stampede at the front and loud talking on mobile phones. The South Koreans on our flight, who had come to Benares as part of a Buddhist pilgrimage to Sarnath, retreated in the face of these rough manners. I was reminded of an episode a few hours ago, on the ground in Delhi. A Frenchman had pushed past me in the line for the security check.

"Are you going to cut ahead?" I said. "Would you do this in France?"

He gave me a Gallic shrug, a tant pis of such contempt as only the French are capable.

"You're very bad mannered."

"Don't teach me. These are Indian manners!" he said and vanished ahead into the crowd.

Manners were the least of India's problems. There was a deeper reckoning that had to be made. In Delhi, a few days before, I witnessed this scene:

A fashionable woman, lunching at a new restaurant in a mall, found her pasta was not al dente. She called over the waiter. He was happy to replace it, but she stopped him. It was not enough that he replace her pasta. Did he understand, she wanted to know, the meaning of the phrase "al dente"?

He reached in again for her plate. No, she said, her cruelty now sublimated into gentleness. She wanted him to learn. Did he even know the meaning of the phrase "al dente"? No, he confessed.

The waiter, for a moment, believed the scolding was about the food. Now he saw what was really happening. He could smell the woman's wish to diminish him. Otherwise why ask what village he was from, what his training consisted of, whether he was qualified to be serving this food? The woman had seized on the phrase "al dente"—no doubt picked up on a holiday abroad—to crush him: to expose him for the servant she knew him to be.

Mukhopadhyay was right: to be modern was to renounce India. The transition stripped uncolonized India of its confidence, as it stripped this waiter of his. It created a new class of interpreters, comprising people such as this woman, who were ready to impose a new tyranny of borrowed artifacts, a club to which ordinary Indians could only hope to belong if they left behind much of what was dear to them, from language and dress to culture and worship. The relationship between old and new had been severed: to be modern was to come empty-handed into an unfamiliar world.

**THE HERMETICALLY SEALED, BLUE-GLASS** world of the airport fell away. The car sped out into sugarcane and mustard fields. There were clay houses with red-tiled roofs and low redbrick walls that enclosed empty plots of overgrown land. The walls were covered in advertisements for mobile phones and soft drinks, for bootleg educational courses and aphrodisiacs. A line of single-story shops selling streaming bright packets of pan masala and potato crisps appeared along the edge of a thinly tarred road.

The fields gave way to a drab urban sprawl, then Benares thickened around us. There were open drains and paper kites wheeling against a polluted gray sky. The shops sold cheap clothes and kitchen things. A barrow with a pyramid of red gas cylinders blocked our way. The infrastructure crumbled; political posters and religious flags hung limp on that windless December day.

We crossed a black-watered drain, garbage eddying out in a paisley shape. Degraded as it was, it was a sacred boundary: the Varuna River.

Near the Taj Hotel the congestion eased. We entered an area of heavy trees and boulevards, bungalows and churches. This was the cantonment—an aloof and scolding memory of the British presence.

A statue of Vivekananda was painted a garish copper color. In 1893, representing Hinduism at the Parliament of the World's Religions in Chicago, Vivekananda had roused the West to the power of India's greatest export: spirituality.

The statue of Vivekananda was one point in a constellation of statues that Modi had visited on his way to filing his nomination papers eighteen months before. It was a blistering morning of soaring white skies, and I remember him moving slowly through the city. Benares appeared deserted. The shopfronts were shuttered. I rode pillion on my friend Vishal's motorbike. Only at intersections could I see the crowds snaking their way to where Modi was. Later, when people asked me how many people had been there, I found it impossible to say. The city did not have vistas enough for me to gauge the numbers; it was as if all of Benares had come to see Modi.

We now passed another statue that Modi had honored. It was of Sardar Patel—India's first home minister, recently repurposed as a Hindu nationalist alternative to Nehru, less colonized, more muscular. A wreath of marigolds still hung from his neck. The flowers were shriveled, the petals a deep burnt red, a memory of heat and the passage of time.

"Are the good days here?" I said to my driver. "Good days are coming" was Modi's campaign slogan.

"It will take time," the driver replied, his mouth swollen with the thick granular remains of a betel chew.

The old city, the maze of shaded streets through which arteries had been forced, now began to close around us. We passed an old house whose façade had been ripped right off, and a full cross section of the house, with its many floors, its whitewashed walls, and its high-pointed alcoves—one with a clay urn still inside—was visible. A line of destruction, jagged and red, rose from the street and ran several stories high; it exposed a slim premodern brick that gave an idea of the building's antiquity. In another country, one would almost think the city had been bombed, but these were the peacetime ravages of modern India—the handiwork of the Varanasi Development Authority.

Soon there would be a view of the water. During my months away in New York, I had spent hours looking out of my window imagining that first glimpse of the Ganges. The riverfront had been built over many times, but it enshrined the spirit of old India and spoke through the overlay of centuries. The city looked across the river into an empty sandbank, and I could not help but feel that only a civilization that gave the world the zero—*shunya*: the mathematical symbol for the presence of absence—would have shaped negative space in this way, erecting a city that gazed for eternity into a void.

The car turned a corner and stopped outside Alice's house. I got out and walked some distance in anticipation of the famous view. To be back in Benares was to feel the full sensual power of my attachment to India. Soon, as with certain bad relationships, one's reasons for leaving would return too; but in that moment, the intensity of the bond was what I felt most. I approached the vista, ready for it to go through me.

That December afternoon there was nothing for me to see. The view was shrouded in a thick fog, and the Ganges flowed tranquil and somber into a blinding wall of white.

**I WOKE BEFORE DAWN TO** the loud pealing of a bell. A solid one-note toll at 4:00 a.m., without let-up. I didn't mind. It is the hour of Brahma, an hour conducive to those engaged in intellectual work. Despite the hour, and the cold of the December morning, the continuous sound of footsteps came from outside my window: people were making their way down to the river.

The breath of the river, which was just beyond, could always be felt pressing against Alice's house. It was heaviest at this hour. A sluggish cross-weave of ripples ran over the water. The brightening of day corresponded to a quickening of activity on the riverfront. The first flecks of pink in the dark oily water brought the first bathers. The river, like the city, was endowed with mythical power—it ran between this world and the next—but its true power, for me, was in seeing how it threaded the sacred through the daily life of the city. There was something marvelous in the sight of one grown man losing himself in the sanctity of the river. Arms spreadeagled, he splashed it repeatedly, as if preparing it for his ablutions. Then he dunked himself and pirouetted with his hands raised. He dug at the water with folded palms and pushed it away from him. He scuttled off to the bank and returned with a small clay lamp in his hands. He turned and turned clockwise, the smoky flame trailing after him. When his compact with the river was complete, he left the lamp burning in the dark earth, a testament to the vows he had made: a small perishable memorial to how one ordinary man began an ordinary day.

The air was soon reverberating with the sound of bells and conches. A film song, crackling and morose, carried from a radio. The day did not so much brighten as it exposed. At the first sight of squalor, I felt something of the dismay of waking up in a house where a party has been held the night before. The squalor was so pervasive, so all-encompassing, that it seemed as sourceless and inevitable as the broadening of day itself. A mangy bitch, with flapping udders, licked clean the yellow remains of potato curry from a heap of used leaf-plates. White and pink plastic bags, like dead jellyfish, collected at the edge of the water.

**THE ENGLISH-SPEAKING CLASS IN** India is small, powerful, and easily identifiable by its wealth, its speech, and what seem almost like racial differences. As Aldous Huxley once wrote of the British in India, they "are accepted much as paper money is accepted, because there is a general belief that [they] are worth something." But were the currency to lose its value, then the Indian, "without any violence, merely by quietly refusing to accept" westernized India at its own valuation, could reduce the power of that class to impotence.

A few weeks before my return to Benares, the Supreme Court of Pakistan upheld the capital sentence handed down to my father's killer. It was meant to be good news, a sign of the hardening resolve of the Pakistani state, but I could think only of the testimony my father's killer gave the court, which had been translated into tortured English:

> On the faithful day, I being member of Elite Force I was deployed as one of the member of Escort Guard of Salman Taseer, the Governor Punjab. In Koh-i-Sar Market, the Governor with another after having lunch in a restaurant walked to his vehicle. In adjoining mosque I went for urinating in the washroom and for making ablution. When I came out with my gun, I came across Salman Taseer. Then I had the occasion to address him, "Your honour being the Governor had remarked about blasphemy law as black law, if so it was unbecoming of you." Upon this he suddenly shouted and said, "Not only that it is black law, but also it is my shit." Being a Muslim I lost control and under grave and suddenly provocation, I pressed the trigger and he lay dead in front of me. I have no repentance and I did it for "Tahafuz-i-Namoos-i-Rasool" [protection of the honour of the Prophet]. Salman offered me grave and sudden provocation. I was justified to kill him kindly see my accompanying written statement U/s 265(F)(5) of Cr. P. C.

Pakistan was not India. India was a democracy. There was a credible state in India that had not been undermined by military coups every decade; India had a long tradition of press freedoms and the peaceful transfer of power. Hinduism, with its great pluralism, and none of the doctrinal strictness of the monotheistic faiths, could never serve the needs of politics the way Islam could. Yet the underlying shape of society was the same. Both places had the same class of interpreters; both had a new middle class—untouched by colonization, but not spared globalization—that had awoken, as if out of a sleep, to the discovery that all power and wealth was concentrated in the hands of a godless, deracinated few. They awoke with rage to a world they had no hand in making, with a profound sense in both countries of being trifled with—a belief that Western ideas and norms had been used against them to maintain the power of a ruling class that was as good as foreign.

In the schism between the "real" India and the India of urban elites, the two sides were sometimes referred to as Bharat and India. The distinction was not unlike that of red and blue America, but in India added tension came because these divisions, which exist everywhere, were further imbricated by the legacy of foreign rule. *Bharat* was the Sanskrit word for India, and the name by which India knew herself at home, in her own languages, free from the gaze of outsiders. *India* was Latin, and the etymology revealed a long history of being under Western eyes: *indos* is the Greek word for the Indus River, which is in turn derived from the ancient Persian *hindu*, and *hindu* is a corruption of the Sanskrit word for river, *sindhu*.

*India* and *Bharat*. The one implied an accretion of foreign influence over the ages, the other a pure mythical India, untainted by the historical present. These were the battle lines along which the culture wars were being fought, and they surfaced everywhere, from ideas of history to sexual mores to even how the society judged violence. Consider the epidemic of rape that was sweeping the country. Rape, it is often said, is not about sex but power. Modernity is power; and to men who feel disempowered by it, rape can become a crude assertion of power over a victim who is physically weaker, yet threatening for being modern. That is not how the head of the RSS—the fountainhead of Hindu nationalism—regards India's problem with rape; he recasts it instead as yet another dramatization of the conflict between India and Bharat. When asked about an unspeakably brutal assault—a twenty-three-year-old medical student was gang-raped in Delhi in 2012 and later died of her injuries—he says, "Such crimes won't happen in Bharat or the rural areas of the country ... Where Bharat becomes India with the influence of Western culture, these types of incidents happen."

**ONE EVENING, A FEW DAYS** into my return to Benares, I was given a first-hand example of how the Modi election had brought some of India's oldest tensions to the surface.

Below the Alice Boner House was a wonderful bookshop. The owner, Rakesh, and I soon became friends. He was a treasure of a man who joked of the good old days in Benares when there were just "buffaloes and anthropologists," and not the present influx of tourists and pilgrims. His bookshop, Harmony Books, was an extravagant and impractical undertaking. It would be too rarefied in Brooklyn. Literature was on the left, the likes of Czesław Miłosz and Magda Szabó; art books were on the right; academic tomes in the back; and Sanskrit in a farther room. Watching my eye fasten on *The Teleology of Poetics in Medieval Kashmir*, Rakesh smiled and said, "They'll sell one day."

During what had become our usual end-of-day banter, a large man burst in through the double doors of the shop. The sight of Tiwari, the travel agent, brought an expression of dread to Rakesh's face.

Tiwari was the kind of man the election had empowered. He was a loping mountainous figure, long armed and prognathous, and dressed in jeans and a green waterproof jacket. Rakesh's shop, with its wide selection of imported books and daily stream of foreign visitors, was at once repellent and attractive to Tiwari. The two men were divided by politics and education, temperament and sensibility, but they were roughly of the same class. Tiwari was also a Brahmin, which still meant something in small-town India. He now entered Rakesh's shop full of a story that was sending him into transports of rage and joy.

For many days now, a rumor had been circulating about two Muslim boys being beaten up on the riverside. They had apparently showed up with Pakistani flags on their bikes. If so, they were inviting trouble, but it was unlikely. Pakistani flags were not common in the Muslim neighborhoods of Benares. Now we were given a detailed account from one who had seen it all:

Tiwari had been running down to the ghat to see Brad Pitt. The actor was in town and, as Tiwari said, "I am, you see, a great fan of Brad Pitt. It was my dream to see him in person." On the way, Tiwari passed the bikes—and, yes, the flags looked odd to him—but he didn't think anything of them at the time. His head was full of worries related to an insurance claim. Besides, he was in a hurry to see Brad Pitt. Only on the way back from the river did he see Radhe, the wrestler, in a confrontation with two Muslim boys.

I had seen Radhe on the ghat. He was a friend of Vishal's, a burly figure in a tight T-shirt. He was part of a group of young men who worked out at the nearby Chitvan gym. The mania for building bodies had come to India; gyms had sprung up in places that lacked even basic amenities. The new love of physicality, especially in this country that had historically prized the attainments of the mind over the body, was in part a simple assertion of crude strength, in part a nation shrugging off the depredations of socialism and Gandhism and partaking in the joys of the flesh. Radhe was forever making crude jokes to Vishal about the dim prospects of their getting laid.

"So, there is Radhe," Tiwari explained, "standing next to the bikes. And he has broken the flags on the bikes. There is an altercation going on between him and these two Muslim boys. 'What?! You live in India,' he is saying, 'and you dare to put Pakistani flags on your bikes?' The boys do not seem to know that the flags are Pakistani. They try to tell Radhe that their madrassa, which was promoting an Islamic conference, had asked they put them up."

"What did the flags look like?" Rakesh discreetly inquired.

"They were red or something."

Rakesh tried to point out that in that case—even if they had "only a little bit of red on them"—they could not be Pakistani.

"Whatever they were, they were certainly not Indian." Tiwari continued, "These boys, they fought back hard. They were demanding to know why the flags had been broken. It was their bikes, they said, and they could carry whatever flags they liked. 'Why are you getting so hot under the collar?' Radhe said back."

Tiwari, now full of animation, came over to me. The memory of violence excited him. He grabbed me under the arms and lifted me up, to show me what Radhe had done to the boys. Then he made to throw me to the ground. Laughter bubbled up in him. "The dispute was growing hotter," he said. There was a mention of police. A crowd assembled around Radhe, threatening the boys with inciting communal tension, a bookable crime in India. Tiwari, by his own proud admission, now exhorted the crowd to beat the boys for what they had done. Then, before another word could be said, the first blow fell. Radhe, with his open-palmed broad wrestler's hand, slapped one of them. Tiwari, the fingers of his own large hand splayed, showed me how. *Phataaak!* It split one of the boys' lips in two. Blood was everywhere.

The boys were Muslim, and, significantly, of low-caste backgrounds. Everyone, regardless of whether they were Hindu or not, retained an idea of caste in India. The Syrian Christians of Kerala, among the oldest Christian communities in the world, still regarded themselves as upper-caste converts, while in Pakistan, which had had no contact with Hindu society for over seventy years, notions of caste, and even untouchability, still prevailed. The two Muslim boys worked for Sulabh, a nonprofit organization committed to the "Gandhian ideology of emancipation of scavengers." Sulabh had tried to give Untouchables, who still did the majority of cleaning work in India, a modicum of humanity by providing its employees with bright orange uniforms and modern cleaning implements.

Sulabh's good work had won it the contract to clean the stretch of riverside where Tiwari runs his travel agency. The two Muslim boys, in protest of the unwarranted violence against them, decided to go on strike.

Tiwari now told us how he brought their protest to an end. "I summoned them and told them that if they did not start working in one hour flat, I would call the police and register a complaint against them for spreading communal tension." The boys took fright. "I give you one hour," Tiwari had said. He knew that the police, if they came, would be sympathetic to him. He chortled at the memory of the boys' fear. Then, he did an imitation of them groveling before him and hurrying back to their work of sweeping the street that ran in front of his shop.

> It is the caste system which cuts human beings off from each other by denying to them the possibilities of connubial and commensal intimacy and a more basic affinity as moral entities. It is the caste system which helps deaden the imagination to the state of mind of other human beings. It is the caste system, perhaps even more than the other factors like poverty and the crushing ubiquity of other human beings, which makes the upper-caste Hindus, from whose circles most Indian intellectuals are recruited, fundamentally and humanly insensate to the mass of the population who belong to the lower castes.

These sentences were written by the American sociologist Edward Shils in the late 1950s. Shils's basic assumption still held: for those who grow up in India, caste either directly or indirectly creeps into the treatment of other human beings in ways that are almost so deep as to be unknowable.

Modernity should be the natural enemy of caste. Urban life, apartment buildings, restaurants, even something as simple as municipal water and housing, has the power to erase the connubial and commensal restrictions upon which caste rules depend. Democracy, too, ought to be the natural enemy of caste. The Shudras and the Untouchables, together, form a significant voting bloc. They cannot be ignored by any politician hoping for success at the ballot box. The subject of their number is so sensitive that the most transparent survey of caste that we have still dates from 1931, when the British conducted one and found that Brahmins accounted for only 6.4 percent of the population. The other lower castes, together, constituted an overwhelming majority.

Modernity and democracy undermined caste, but they also exacerbated old tensions by upsetting traditional hierarchies and making people aware of one another as never before. The higher castes, whose numbers were small, became insecure about their place in the world. So, the spread of modernity in India threatened caste but also made the need to assert it more vehement; and the unfolding story was not of the disappearance of caste, but of its surprising resilience. Brahmins continued to exert an outsize influence over intellectual life; the armed forces were still dominated by the martial castes; a majority of rich businessmen and industrialists still belonged to the mercantile castes; and the lower castes still did the most wretched work.

Caste had the power to hide in other forms of distinction, such as class, race, education, and privilege. But deeper than the manifestations of caste was that basic grounding in the intrinsic inequality of human beings that had been bred into the Indian psyche. It was the society's deepest affinity, stunting the ability of people to transcend their group. Caste, secreted away in the Indian soul, prevented men from seeing in the experience of others a shade of their own. It abolished birth as a shared point of origin, leaving it instead as a spiritual stain.

Caste would have informed the behavior of the woman at the Italian restaurant. It was what made a relation of mine in Delhi say to me, "This is the only country in the world where one person can look at another and say, 'Oh, he looks like a servant.'" Tiwari, too, was acting out of caste hatred. He might have resented English-speaking India, he might actively have loathed Muslim India, but it was for those who had been excluded by the Hindu caste system, the Untouchables, and whom even a change of religion could not save, that he reserved a bottomless contempt. They were scarcely human to him. He could never join hands with them socially or politically; the sight of them in orange jumpsuits with modern cleaning implements, refusing to make a spectacle of their degradation, filled him with distaste. The active ingredient in caste violence is not so much a hatred of the inferior caste, but a horror of transgression. The man who steps out of the place society has designated for him and who has the audacity to believe that religious conversion will save him from degradation attracts the ire of an attacker. Too often I am asked abroad why India was spared an all-out class revolution, though outwardly the conditions are so opportune. My answer every time is caste.

**ANAND INTRODUCED SHIVAM TRIPATHI TO** me one evening on the riverside with the words, "He is a revolutionary Brahmin."

Shivam was dressed in a saffron lungi with a saffron scarf—saffron was the color of Hindu nationalism. He was slightly built, with dark piercing eyes. His face was downed in a growth of light brown hair; his intensity was feral. I could feel the force of his gaze on me, before it shifted to Anand, whom he eyed with disapproval.

The two men could not have been more different. Anand was in the grip of that fatal instability—the chanchal side of his nature—that had always been his downfall. One minute, he was singing Bollywood songs, the next he was frenziedly talking politics. His support for Modi, the source of such delirium eighteen months before, had lapsed. "The mood has gone cold," he informed me. A few months ago, in Anand's home state of Bihar, Modi had suffered his first serious electoral setback since he swept to power. Anand had no love for the winning side, but he was elated by the drama of the result. Politics for him was less an expression of ideology than a vessel into which he channeled his restlessness.

"Have you ever seen such a thing?" he trilled. "A prime minister, making some twenty-odd speeches in a single state election, and losing! Now Modi has learned that we Biharis, we have our own way!"

Shivam, though I did not know it at the time, was also a member of the Hindu nationalist ABVP. He watched Anand's performance with displeasure, perhaps as much because of its wild, erratic quality as for what was being expressed. He was reserved and watchful, but I sensed that beneath the calm on the surface was a cauldron of passion. When Anand explained why I was in Benares—"He is writing about the conflict between tradition and modernity"—Shivam could not restrain himself:

"The conflict is not between tradition and modernity. It is between modernity and spirituality." The word Shivam used, *adhyatmikta,* was important; it was derived from *atman,* which meant "self," both in the sense of the personal self and the Hindu idea of the Supreme Self, or soul. In old India, *atmanam viddhi*—"know thyself"—was the great message of the Upanishads. It was thought that the personal self could serve as a site for the discovery of the Supreme Self, making it possible to transcend the illusion of individuality. "The *Atman* is impartite," writes Coomaraswamy, "but it is apparently divided and identified into variety by the differing forms of its vehicles, mouse or man, just as space within a jar is apparently signate and distinguishable from space without it."

No sooner had Shivam set me straight than he wanted urgently to show me something. I recoiled from the force of his personality, but he had an integrity that I was powerless to resist. I had not told him much about my journey, but he seemed quickly to have grasped what was at stake. In appropriating my reasons for traveling, he gave me the surest indication I had thus far received that my line of inquiry was important not merely to me, but to those I found myself among.

Before Shivam and I could do another thing, Anand begged five minutes of us. He, too, wanted to show me something.

"Five minutes!" Shivam said sternly.

"Five minutes," Anand said.

Then we were off, racing up the steps of the ghat; we passed an assemblage of small squat temples, covered in thick orange paint, each with a border of silver. We turned around and went up another flight of stairs. Some Bengali writing was on the wall. All the while Anand was saying, "You know how I don't like the girls of today. I hate all that lip gloss and high heels and jeans. I've fallen in love with a very different kind of girl. She lives in this ashram that I'm taking you to. She's very pure, like the women of classical India. Pure inside, pure outside. She spends her days lost in prayer, in her studies, in classical song and dance. She thinks only of God and passes her hours in contemplation of the Ganges. She's like someone out of Kalidasa's *Shakuntala*, and she has tremendous internal power. I did not think it possible that such girls could still exist."

We came onto a beautiful balcony, set deep within a bend of the Ganges. The river sprawled below, fading into violet darkness. At our back was a building with loggias. An ashram of sorts, it was set around a courtyard, and the rooms were reminiscent of the small monkish cells found in Buddhist ruins.

Anand took me to the end of the balcony, where a shrine lay beyond a shuttered gate. It contained a large picture of a beautiful woman with prominent rounded cheekbones. Her eyes were vast pools of melancholy and inner calm, and she wore her long black hair loose. This arresting face, though I did not know it at the time, was of Anandamayi Ma, a famous twentieth-century saint whose advice was sought by Indira Gandhi and of whom we have not one, but two, literary portraits, from Arthur Koestler and Octavio Paz.

"Her husband never enjoyed her," Anand said of Anandamayi. "He loved her like a mother. He let her fulfill her dreams and do something for the girls of Kashi."

We stood at a balustrade overlooking a grove of frangipani trees. Across from us, and deliberately kept out of view, was a cream-colored building with pale blue jalousies. "The girls are never exposed to men," Anand said. "They never leave this place, except under the surveillance of a guard."

Then, suddenly, Anand gestured across the courtyard to a roof terrace, where through the gaps in the thick balustrade a few figures were dimly visible. "There she is. Now she's gone. There she is again." For a second I saw her: a fearful-looking slight girl, with dark skin and attractive features. A green shawl was draped over her head. She looked piercingly at us, then was ushered away. Anand, overflowing with romance, said, "What a life I could have with someone like that! None of this awful modern stuff. What our society would be if we could depend on the strength of women like that—women possessed of knowledge and ascetic power, the secret of the sages."

The glimpse of the young girls, with cropped hair, looking like child widows, was depressing. And when I tried to square it with the society that I knew to be a furnace of sexual desire—in which men, who were unable to converse with women, were nonetheless avid consumers of pornography, and where rapes happened only in India, not in Bharat—it was more than depressing; it was alarming. Anand, more than he realized, was part of the collapse of old ways. It fed his fantasies of a return to a golden age when women were pure. I did not believe he could sentimentalize tradition in this way if tradition were still intact in him. And the sentiment was not benign, for underlying the wish to bring back an irrecoverable past was a more violent impulse to undo the present.

We were still in the ashram when Shivam burst in on us in a rage.

"This is your five minutes?"

Anand recoiled.

Seeing him shrink from his temper, Shivam softened. "Do you want to come with us?"

"No," Anand said, perhaps fearing that his frivolity would land him in more trouble. He looked long at me and said, "You'll be all right with him."

Then Shivam and I were off again, at a fast pace, through the network of winding streets. They were flanked by seventeenth- and eighteenth-century buildings whose narrow balconies were open to thin strips of sky. Paper kites flew overhead and flocks of pigeons burst out of the shady depths of the streets. The setting sun showed like a wan sickle at the edge of the rooftops. We passed bulls and ascetics, bent-over old crones with staffs and spruce young grooms with brides bedecked in silk and brocade following blindly behind them. I was dimly aware of passing mosques with enclosed gardens, where the azan now sounded. Through the iron bars of little alcove temples a smoky yellow light wafted out. I had not yet acquired the local talent of walking without stepping into something dreadful. My eyes were fixed on the paving stones, which were now wet with paan spittle bleeding into puddles—bits of Styrofoam floating in the reddish water—now smeared with cow shit; they were also covered in urine stains, large and brown and frilled, like great wilted carnations. The air stank, and then with that Indian genius for contraries it was overwhelmed by cloying waves of jasmine.

The scene around us was changing fast. The temples were suddenly garish; I caught a glimpse of the curls and sharp angles of Tamil script, impenetrable as a line of riot policemen. Shivam explained that we were entering the South Indian quarter of the city. The increase in human traffic, and the appearance of souvenir shops and flower sellers, made it clear that we were approaching a major temple. The evening tide of worshippers swept us along. Shivam's roommate, Rohit, a student of classical grammar, had joined us. The temple appeared at the end of a long bulb-lit street.

In the interior courtyard, the cold marble floor was marked with the black impressions of wet bare feet. Rohit and Shivam pressed their heads against the keystone of the temple and entered with the ease and familiarity of people entering their own home. We passed many smoke-blackened subsidiary shrines before coming to a statue of Kali. The two Brahmins, wrapping one leg around the other, while holding the lobes of their ears in a gesture of reverence, squatted low before the dread goddess. Shivam took me into the central sanctum to see the great scarified head of the Kedareshwar linga. It sat in a brass casement and was among this city's most powerful representations of its ruling deity, Shiva. It was not smooth and polished like the others, but dark and rutted, a domed outthrust of rock with a single white line running through it. The linga was ringed with cloudy water and strewn with leaves, marigolds, and tiny white flowers. Shivam sank to his haunches and drank the water with his cupped hands. I gingerly touched my head to the linga. Before I could look up, Shivam had smeared my forehead with cool streaks of sandalwood paste. It was a gesture of warmth and spontaneity, designed to bring me out of myself.

Unspoken between us was the understanding that I was to try to apprehend what was happening here, in the sanctum, by using my intuition, rather than my intellect. It was as if Shivam could tell that I had been too long in my head and had failed to see—or, rather, *feel*—something important. So when, midway, I stopped to ask him the name of the leaves on the linga, he looked at me with annoyance. He told me they were bilva leaves and supplied the verses from scripture, which said that they were dear to Shiva, but I was missing the point. Faith functioned by an internal logic; it was its own means of knowing, and one knew by feeling, not by asking questions.

As if wanting me to recognize this, Shivam now threw his head back, closed his eyes, and began to sing. He sang beautifully, in praise of the goddess Durga, bringing the song to an end with, "Shiva, Lord of

All, who abides in Kashi, on the banks of the Ganges." Then he recited a verse in Sanskrit, the meter sounding out like shot in the sanctum.

Afterward, Shivam led me out from the back of the temple into the open night air. The steps going down to the river were bathed in white from floodlights. A pilgrim boat was arriving, full of middle-aged women who came onshore, hitched up their saris, and began to trudge up the steep stairs. Behind us some teenage girls, in jeans and pink socks, with busy designs on their sweaters, were taking selfies, screaming and giggling. Shivam turned to me and said with disdain, "Look, that is our modernity." Then, pointing down the steps toward the river, he said, "And that is our spirituality." On the edge of the Ganges where a few lamps floated, I could make out the figure of a man meditating. He sat with his back to us, draped in wet saffron, still as a rock.

"Either we throw ourselves into this modernity," Shivam said almost hatefully, "or we go back to what we were. What is intolerable is this limbo, this middle condition, for in the end"—he pointed down the dark arc of the river—"the truth is only that." Through the thick murk of a December evening, the roaring orange fires of the cremation ghats were visible.

**THAT NIGHT, LYING AWAKE IN** Alice's room, I began to feel that even those who seemed most at home in India, most at home in a place such as Benares, were increasingly living in a world grown strange—a place they called home but no longer recognized. It was as if homelessness itself had become a political force in our time, and the promise of greatness restored, which every politician from Delhi to Washington was now peddling, was the fantasy of a homecoming—a promise to those who felt powerless in the world beyond the security of home.

Eighteen months after Modi's election, India was on the edge of mass hysteria. In October, two months before my arrival in Benares, a Muslim man had been lynched on the outskirts of Delhi for allegedly possessing beef. The cow was sacred to Hindus, the consumption of beef forbidden. During the election, Modi whipped crowds at his rallies into a frenzy over a "pink revolution," an alleged conspiracy by his political opponents to promote the slaughter of cows. "We've heard of the Green Revolution," he thundered. "We've heard of the White Revolution, but today's Delhi government wants neither. They've taken up arms for a Pink Revolution," he said, referring to the color of beef. "Do you want to support people who want to bring about a Pink Revolution?"

The cow had been carefully chosen as a symbol in the culture war. Modi knew that the English-speaking elite did not have the same regard for the animal as his religious base did. He knew, too, that the meat industry was predominantly run by Muslims and that the consumption of beef was not forbidden in Islam. The cow was a way both to inflame the passions of the base and settle the scores of the past. After the first lynching, Modi, normally a voluble man, was silent. It was seen as a signal, and the killings continued.

Caste, class, religion: all the ancient fractures were bristling. That old lie of India, the nonviolent country, was steadily being undone. A deep historical violence had been awakened. Shivam himself had been swept up. When Anand had said that Shivam was a "revolutionary Brahmin," Anand was referring to a student protest in which Shivam had taken a bullet. The protest was ostensibly for a student council, but it had turned into a show of strength for the ABVP, part of the group's growing clout on campus. Before falling asleep, I googled Shivam.

> BHU STUDENTS' STIR TURNS VIOLENT: One student was injured in the melee, although reports that he had been shot at were categorically denied by the police and the university administration. The student, Shivam Tripathi, was reported to be out of danger.
>
> —*THE INDIAN EXPRESS*, NOVEMBER 21, 2014

# 8

# THE COMMUNITY OF DEATH

**TO DIE IN BENARES IS** to break free of the cycle of rebirth. That is Shiva's promise, and that is why death here is not a fearful thing. But there was another kind of death taking place in the city that was less easy to confront. Old India itself was dying.

It was Shivam who first made me see cultural death against the backdrop of this city of death. Shivam had come to Benares as an eight-year-old from a small Brahmin village in central India to learn the Veda. That rite of young Brahmin boys coming to Benares to learn their scriptures was so old that it had become a little bit of theater in the lives of those who would never actually undertake the journey.

"The boy makes as though he were about to start on a long journey," Mrs. Sinclair Stevenson tells us in *The Rites of the Twice-Born*, "and, as provision for the way, he takes in his hand a ball of sweet-stuff tied in a piece of cloth. Sometimes a copy of the Vedas is also wrapped in cloth and tied to his bamboo, and, with this bundle on his right shoulder, he leaves the house as though 'off to Philadelphia in the morning…'" But his maternal uncle has gone on ahead and, apprehending him before he goes too far, brings him straight home.

What was merely a comedy in the lives of other Brahmin boys had been the real lived experience of Shivam. He had done what most only made to do. He had spent time, money, and labor studying what was valueless in modern India. He was of a poor family and could not afford to be romantic about the beauty and antiquity of his education. Nor was he insulated by the unthinking continuities of tradition. He could see his situation clearly. The questions that he asked himself, and which had inspired his political awakening, were: What would become of young men such as him, traditional students of Sanskrit? What would become of the sacred language itself in this country where it had flowered? And since he was using the language as a metonym for the life of tradition itself, the real question was whether modern India would move into the future with no thought to her past. Would old India simply be forsaken? If so, what would the future look like?

We sat in his tiny room, which he shared with two other students. The floors were strewn with rugs and mattresses. On a low table to the side, bound cheaply in red, were the great books of classical India: grammars, treatises, epics, the Vedas. They were some of the oldest books in the world, and the room, with its air of medieval scholarship, was like a scene out of Chaucer. I could not help but think that this was what an Indian education in the humanities might look like if only some distance could be created, if only Shivam could come to this learning not from a spirit of piety, but of intellectual curiosity and inquiry.

In the corner was a picture of Kali, red-tongued and fierce, with a small linga in front of it. As few were fit to cook for them, the Brahmin students did all their own cooking, and there were little plastic jars of spices, a small gas stove, a rolling pin, some dry flour. In the courtyard outside, a great tree had died, the same tree that gave us the bilva leaves that were so dear to Shiva. Its branches cast long shadows over the powder-blue walls of the house. The courtyard was overrun with weeds, and half-hidden in the undergrowth was the carcass of a uniquely Indian contraption called a desert cooler. Its screens of matting were punched out and the broad blades of its fan rusted in the night air.

Shivam wanted me to come with him to his village: "If you want to see living Indian culture, you must come home with me." It was not the vitality of the old country that he wanted me to see, but rather a place in its death throes. He wanted me to meet young people crushed by the conflict between modernity and adhyatmikta. "Let them meet someone like you, who is modern through and through. Then they will understand this terrible middle state they're in."

**I WAS IN A MIDDLE** state of my own. In the intervening months, between the summer election in Benares, and now this winter, eighteen months later, I had met someone, married, and moved from Delhi to New York.

Everything about my husband's and my meeting—from the way we met to the life we cobbled together—was a repudiation of my life in India. We met through a dating app in New York. We had absolutely no one in common. He also came from a place—the American South—where religion and politics had formed a toxic amalgam. The shape of our lives—the single mother, the many half-siblings, the distant father—was uncannily similar. We were two individuals operating alone, with neither tribe nor tradition to serve as a guide.

We had come together out of an immense pool of humanity. It felt modern in the very real sense of being new, of being like nothing that had gone before. There was no other time in which we could have met; no world previous to ours that could have supported our union. We made a life in a small apartment on Manhattan's Upper West Side, and soon we had something else in common: the violent death of a father.

On a rainy November morning, a few weeks before I was to leave for this return journey to Benares, my husband received a Facebook message from his half-brother saying that their father was dead—shot in the back of the head at point-blank range by his nephew, their cousin.

My husband was estranged from his father, as I had been from mine. At the time of my husband's father's death they had not spoken in a decade. His father was living with his sister in Florida. He had an altercation one night with his nephew, a policeman.

"The uncle and the officer's mother had been embroiled in a rather heated argument," said the Volusia County Sheriff's Office. "The argument became physical ... The officer"—later exonerated—"attempted to break it up and separate them. He was unable to. That's when he made the decision to retrieve his gun."

The big Florida night; the heavy overhanging foliage, incongruous through the lens of a November night in New York; the little house on Tradewinds Drive, with its white louvered windows; the sheriff's yellow tape; the police car; the pretty Fox 35 reporter in red—the details made the violence more lurid, even as they made death more remote. I did not envy my husband's trying to make real the surreal, trying to find his father in the garish spectacle of the late-night news bulletin from Deltona, Florida.

We had only been married a few months, and many elements about my husband's father's death reminded me of my own father's killing: the violence; the not knowing what to do, or whom to call; the period of mourning conducted through YouTube and Facebook. But in my father's case there was an added element: his death was political.

It was inseparable from the shadow that was falling over Pakistan's old colonial elite.

When I was last in Benares, I had found the spectacle of death in the city distasteful. It was in part grotesque, in part too much a thing for tourists. There they were, on the Harishchandra Ghat, photographing the chaos: of corpses, doms, passers-by, and mourners in peaked white Nehru caps. Goats roamed about, looking like teenagers from the 1980s, in baggy T-shirts of sackcloth. A boy slapped the ribbed gray belly of a reposing cow. Through a wall of orange cremation fire, I could see women on the river shore, washing clothes on a smooth slab of red stone, twisting the cloth into what looked like thick colored strands of twine. The soap mixed with the ash; a mother or sister removed nits from the hair of a small child; birds wheeled over the river; and stony-faced ascetics sat on their haunches, watching the scene, like old park-benchers waiting for a game of chess. The blissful ease that surrounded the industry of death in Benares had seemed to me to dishonor the memory of the dead.

I felt differently now. The experience of the last few weeks in New York, of watching modern life consume the reality of death, had left me more open to the philosophical implications of a city that could look death in the face. The cremation ground in every other Indian city was profane, polluted, and placed outside the city limits. Not here; Benares was the supreme cremation ground. Here the cult of death, as Octavio Paz writes of Mexico, was a cult of life, "in the same way that love is a hunger for life and a longing for death."

Death, for my husband and me, was dull and anesthetizing, quietly bludgeoning. We did not weep; we carried on. My husband took the week off work because one had to, for the sake of others. But then he went back to work, and I sensed he was relieved to have the distraction, to be back in the society where death did not exist. Eventually there was a funeral, a brief affair. The deaths of our fathers had embarrassed us. Their violence made them too particular, too detailed, too ostentatious. It was harder for the society around us to forget and move on.

**IN BENARES, DEATH WAS NOT** merely to be endured; it was on occasion to be celebrated as an affirmation of life.

One foggy morning, a crowd gathered at the Tulsi Ghat, upriver from the Alice Boner House. Two boatfuls of people were waiting at the shore. At the center of a green-bottomed boat was an object that looked like a red box in a chair. It was covered in garlands of marigolds; men were dancing around it, crying, "*Hara hara Mahadev*" (Shiva, take away [my sins]). They had incense and drums. I asked someone standing next to me on the shore, a young man in track pants and blue rubber slippers, what was going on.

"*Baba hai,*" he said tersely: there was an old man, or ascetic. I tried to inquire further, but the young man slipped off.

The tempo aboard the two boats was picking up. Another young man, this one in a bright green jacket and jeans, appeared next to me.

"What is happening?"

"*Baba hai,*" he said.

"What are they going to do with the baba?" I said at last.

"We," the man said pointedly, though he had no more part in what was about to happen than I did, "are going to immerse him."

"He's dead?"

The man refused to dignify this with a response.

The crowd of young men began to dance around the red box, which I realized now was not a box at all, but a chair in which the dead ascetic sat. He was old, and so the death was not to be mourned. The crowd of young men knew exactly what to do; nobody needed to tell them. Custom contained belief; the belief was not so much held, or articulated, as it ran through action. It was manifest.

P. K. Mukhopadhyay had felt that it was precisely this instinctive aspect of tradition that made it ripe for destruction, for how could one defend what one did unthinkingly? He believed that for tradition to live again, to be relevant, it had to be able to speak to modernity. His view, like Coomaraswamy's, was that tradition suffered "from the inevitable consequences of all formulation. The formula, however admirable, is inherited rather than earned, it becomes an end instead of a means, and its meaning is forgotten, so that it is insecure." Yet to watch these young men dance around the dead ascetic was to feel the power of the unselfconscious. It was basic; it was tribal; it needed no explanation.

A few minutes later, the two boats set off through the fog. I followed them down the river past the bathers and the boatmen and knots of idle youth. I walked all the way to the Prabhu Ghat. Midriver, the cries of "*Hara hara Mahadev*" grew louder through a white fog. The *damru*, a small two-headed drum, struck by two beads fastened to two strings—this was the drum of Shiva, sharp, percussive, and stilling—reached a crescendo. The body had been thrown overboard, I thought to myself.

On my way home, the boats were returning, now without the red casket. The baba had been immersed; the revelers were quiet. All that could be heard was the steady chug of the motor, emitting little puffs of black smoke.

> Rama Nama Satya Hai! Ram's name is truth. This was the sound from the street! A corpse in white cloth, sprinkled with a few flowers, and rocking on the bier, carried on the shoulders of poor fellows dressed in soiled clothes and continuously shouting: Rama Nama Satya Hai! Innumerable corpses were carried over and cremated down below by the Ganges. How easy life and death are here. Everyone already knows how it will happen. There is no drama and no tragedy, because everything that happens is part of eternal becoming and passing away, endlessly repeated. Personal destiny is insignificant. That is why individual aspiration is so rare. That is why almost everyone

thinks, talks the same way, and that is why there is so little differentiated individuality. And yet there is no superficiality. It is a deep relation to the whole creation: Rama Nama Satya Hai!

—ALICE BONER DIARIES, JANUARY 27, 1936

**"THE CITY IS DYING," PINKU** said to me one morning. "If you come here in ten or twenty years, you won't see what we have now."

Pinku is Ajay Pandey. I had met him eighteen months before at the height of the Modi election. I had gone on one of his guided tours of the city, of which he possessed an encyclopedic knowledge. I was struck by his intelligence, his quiet self-effacing manner, and his beautiful literary Hindi, which had been his subject at university.

Pinku was a Brahmin, too, albeit a reluctant one. The family story followed a now-familiar pattern: a grandfather, lost to the mists of time, who was a priest in a royal household; a father who was a government servant; and Pinku, who, in this age of private enterprise, was his own man, half tourist guide, half something grander. He was tall, dark-skinned, and fine-featured; his large eyes conveyed fatigue and melancholy; he kept a Brahmin's shikha, but it was ragged and unkempt, more an afterthought than a gesture of self-regard. A single recessed tooth, stained brown, gave his otherwise pensive aspect a touch of humor. Pinku's vocation—his dharma—was his love of Benares, where he had lived all his life, and of which he had compiled a painstaking oral history of ruin and decay.

"If you spend too much time with me," he said as we set out one morning, "you will become despondent."

"Why?"

"Because I see this city, and I see the buildings that give it its distinctiveness and character, falling away before my eyes. When I look down this street"—he pointed to a faceless modern building that interrupted a line of fine blue-washed buildings with delicate tracery and wrought-iron balconies—"I cannot see Benares; I could be anywhere."

We came to a row of redbrick buildings with pale blue accents. Pinku pointed to the deep interior courtyard of one house where, through shadow, I caught a glimpse of mildewed walls bathed in sunlight.

"The hallmark of the Bengali style was the marrying of architectures," Pinku said, "the European with the traditional Indian."

Buildings cannot lie, and these buildings showed the creative potential of the contact between Bengal and Britain. It had produced an attractive synthesis—one of spirit, rather than of ornament—and it stood in marked contrast to the relationship with Western influence today, which was sterile at best, and corrosive at worst. The names on these buildings were the anglicized names of Bengali Brahmins: Mukherjee and Chatterjee standing in for the hard-to-pronounce Mukhopadhyay and Chattopadhyay. The houses built by the Bengali Brahmins reflected the depth of their engagement with the new culture of Europe. For a brief moment in the late-eighteenth century, Britain seemed to brighten India, and there was a hope that the meeting of the two cultures would be fertile.

"Look," Pinku said, with dismay. "It has come up in literally one year." He pointed to a five-story block of flats with undulating white balconies. It stood next to a slim tall building, in the Bengali style, from whose façade the playful parrot green of a Corinthian column had fallen away. The balcony was a shattered stump. A stunted forest of weeds grew up in an internal courtyard. The buildings formed a diptych: decay, with all its surprising beauty, acting as a preservative next to the clean effacement brought by change. Pinku, as he went about his tours and historical walks, lived in constant awareness of change as an agent of erasure. I had heard an American guide a few days before use the phrase "intangible culture." He was referring to a time in the not-too-distant future when India may live on in hearts and minds, but there would be nothing left of its spirit enshrined in stone. I could not help but think it was a fitting outcome for a culture that had historically held the material world in such low esteem.

As we approached the river, near the Dashashwamedh Ghat, Pinku showed me a family of bright orange stones.

They were planted along the edge of a road leading up from the river. One or two were housed in their own tiny temples, no bigger than coffee tables. On the surface of each stone were the carved figures of a man and a woman with rounded breasts.

"Sati stones," Pinku muttered.

He explained that the stones commemorated women who had committed sati, the Hindu rite by which widows immolated themselves on the pyres of their husbands. The practice had been outlawed by the British in the nineteenth century. But the stones remained, a reminder of the violence of the medieval world, no less real than its romance. Pinku pointed to a man asleep in one of the miniature temples. He clutched the sati stone as if it were a pillow.

Behind us, the Ganges glittered in the morning sun.

**PINKU WANTED TO GIVE ME** an oral history of Benares. He expertly threaded it into certain places where he brought me as if by chance. One morning we found ourselves at the Chet Singh Ghat, overlooking a dusty *maidan*, an open quadrangle streaked with long slim islands of grass. Some Brahmin boys with thick knotted shikhas were playing cricket to one side; card players gambled in a tight circle on the other. Around us, on all sides, were the age-blackened spires and domes of temples and palaces, whose rough, scarified surfaces were framed against the pale blue sky.

Pinku began to tell me of a pivotal moment in the eighteenth century. Muslim power was vanishing into a perfumed haze of over-refinement; the British were circling; Hindu India, after years of subjugation, was ascendant. The Muslim governor of Benares, Mir

Rustam Ali, fell in love with the city and devoted himself to its sensual pleasures. While he was distracted, a Hindu dynasty rose in cahoots with the British. "For the first time in over five hundred years," writes Diana Eck, "the city was under the jurisdiction of Hindu kings."

The first of those kings, Balwant Singh, belonged to a special class of land-owning Brahmins known as Bhumihars. He had no legitimate sons, so when he died, in 1770, his family tried to install a favorite nephew as king. But his illegitimate son Chet Singh staged a coup. "Even as his father's last rites were being performed on the Manikarnika Ghat, Chet Singh seized this palace and fort," said Pinku.

Soon, however, Chet Singh ran into trouble. He tried to get out of paying taxes to the British, whose protection he had invoked against the Nawab of Awadh, in the west. Warren Hastings, the British governor-general, was fighting a bellicose Muslim prince in the south, and he was under constant pressure to send money to the East India Company in Britain. "The English government now chose to wring money out of Cheyte Sing," Lord Macaulay writes in his great essay on Hastings. "It had formerly been convenient to treat him as a sovereign prince; it was now convenient to treat him as a subject."

The two men—Hastings and Chet Singh—confronted each other on this very maidan in 1781. "The national and religious prejudices with which the English were regarded throughout India were peculiarly intense in the metropolis of the Brahminical superstition," writes Macaulay. Chet Singh was popular, Hastings outnumbered. A crowd assembled in the streets surrounding the palace. "The tumult became a fight, and the fight a massacre." Three British officers and over a hundred sepoys were butchered.

Pinku now pointed out the little memorial to the soldiers on the far end of the maidan. In the confusion that ensued, Chet Singh, who had been held prisoner by the British, used a rope made of turbans to climb down the high embankment on which we sat, then took a boat to the opposite shore.

The rope of turbans finds mention in Macaulay's essay, too; but Macaulay tells a far sadder story, and it makes the history of this time hard to read. Chet Singh was doomed from the start; his autonomy was an illusion. Hastings had no intention of settling with him. "The plan was simply this, to demand larger and larger contributions till the Rajah should be driven to remonstrate, then to call his remonstrance a crime, and to punish him by confiscating all his possessions," Macaulay wrote.

Stories like this one abound in the history of India at this time. As Pinku retold it, I realized why this history was so difficult for me. It was because the people in the story for whom I had a natural affinity were not historical actors at all, but the playthings of history. They were men *acted upon*, and what made their situation more tragic was that they were unaware of the forces that encircled them. They protested; they revolted; they even seemed, at moments, to be winning a battle or two; but they never grasped the greater historical drama that enfolded them, which was the drama of the rise of Europe and the shattering of the old world everywhere. In this drama, India was but one theater. The Indian prince in the story is crushed, as were other local princes, in Africa, in Japan, in Persia. The British, though, were historical actors; they could see the whole picture. It gave their history a narrative drive, a seemingly unstoppable momentum.

Chet Singh developed illusions about the strength of his position. The country was in open revolt, as it would be again in the next century during the great revolt of 1857. But nothing would come of this revolt, just as nothing would come of 1857. Macaulay writes, "The tumultuary army of the Rajah was put to rout," his "fastnesses were stormed," and "the unhappy prince fled from his country for ever." A relation was appointed king, but henceforth the Raja of Benares, like the Nawab of Bengal—and many others to come—was to be "a mere pensioner."

History, it is said, is written by the victors; what we do not mention is how dull and shapeless the history of the vanquished can be. There is no arc, no larger theme, no internal life. It fails as a story even before it fails as history, and it is no surprise that it is excluded from textbooks. Pinku now provided an alternative theme, in which magic was used to explain away defeat. The British did not win because they were better or stronger or more organized: it was because Chet Singh was the victim of a curse.

He had insulted an Aghori—a member of a tribe of ascetics who worship Shiva, dress all in black, and perform rituals with the remains of the dead—who was drawn to the palace by music from an evening of revelry. The ascetic sought entry, but was blocked at the door. Chet Singh heard the ruckus and came out. When his doormen explained what was happening, Chet Singh turned to the ascetic and said mockingly, "What will you do with all these fine things?" He ordered his men to bring the ascetic a corpse. They pleaded with their master not to offend this fearsome devotee of Shiva, but Chet Singh would not hear reason. A dead body was brought into their midst. Even before the shroud was lifted, the ascetic had pronounced his curse on Chet Singh: "Your line will vanish with you."

The Chet Singh story was a prelude to what would happen all across India as British power expanded over the next 150 years. Macaulay, writing in the 1840s, could clearly see what was happening. But to read another kind of writer was to feel oneself engulfed by a folkloric darkness. Take the Hindi writer Jaishankar Prasad, for example; he was born and died in Benares and had the advantage of writing more than half a century after Macaulay, once British ascendancy was complete. In Prasad's famous story "Gunda," which is about the Chet Singh episode, the writer seems unable to see how the confrontation with Hastings fits into a larger pattern. In Prasad's account of the eighteenth century in Benares, we are simply told that Kashi is no longer the Kashi of ages past, no longer a place where scholars and men of learning gather, where Gautama Buddha and the Shankaracharya conducted their famous religious and philosophical disputes. The temples and monasteries are all broken, the ascetics scattered or dead, and the worship of Vishnu has fallen into occultism and black magic.

In the time that has elapsed since Chet Singh was removed and Prasad writes his story, British rule has come to encompass a fourth of the planet, but all Prasad has surmised of this period is that it is a dark time, in which knowledge is subservient to brute force, and hoodlums hold sway. It will be up to another kind of Indian, those made on the fault line of the contact between Britain and India, to give India a truer sense of what has happened to her. These other Indians—men such as Tagore, Gandhi, and Nehru—were part of the class of interpreters Macaulay had sought to create, and they were all in their own way beholden to the British for the insight that had come to them.

Clouds of dust blew over the maidan. It was the Prophet Muhammad's birthday. Some Muslim boys in white skullcaps wandered by, wearing pajamas that were cut off above the ankle, an expression of their religiosity.

We stayed a little longer, considering this place where history had done its work, then went to lunch at the Kerala Café. There, over a dosa and a soda, Pinku told me of his grandfather, who had been an important priest in the princely states of Chota Nagpur in eastern India. He wanted his youngest son, Pinku's uncle, to follow him into his line of work. But it could not be. Pinku, with uncharacteristic vagueness, perhaps concealing a family secret, said that his uncle "lost himself in the world of friends" and died an early death. Whether this was a euphemism for alcoholism, or just a failure to follow in the family tradition, was hard to tell. Pinku's father went into medicine, in an administrative capacity. Another son went to work for the government, and Pinku himself was "in private."

One morning, I saw clearly how the lines of transmission—*parampara*—can go dead from one generation to the next. Pinku picked me up outside Rakesh's shop on a battered motorcycle, and we made an unplanned stop outside what looked like the ruins of an old house. The body of the building had fallen away. All that remained was a blue-washed back wall with pretty pointed alcoves. It was open to sky, and grass grew in a neat rectangle at the center. Behind was a row of unvarnished wooden columns and a sloping ledge of corrugated iron, like a parody of that most beautiful of Indian architectural features: the *chhajja,* a deep overhanging eave that casts a precise and lustrous shadow. There sat, on one side of this ruined house, an old man in a beige monkey cap. He gazed out at the busy street and looked to me like a watchman of some sort. I hardly noticed him until Pinku beckoned me over.

He said, with an embarrassed smile, "My grandfather taught him Sanskrit."

The old man smiled back and chuckled. "And *his* great-grandfather studied under an ancestor of mine."

The two men paused at this enactment of parampara, the actual mechanism of transmission. It played out so literally as a sequence: one thing following the next, men doing what had always been done. But one day the line went dead; the sequence broke. It was so abrupt, both violent and involuntary, that a generation or two later those who were left holding the line, now Brahmin in name only, felt wonder at how it came to be that one was a tourist guide, and the other sat in a plastic chair, minding the ruins of his ancestral home.

"I didn't want to say it at the time," Pinku said later over the roar of his bike and the rush of cold air, "but his grandfather was a very famous commentator. He wrote extensive commentaries on the *Ramcharitmanas.*"

This was Tulsidas's epic poem, said to have been composed on the Tulsi Ghat, where I had seen the boats depart for the water burial.

A few days before, Pinku had taken me to see where Tulsidas supposedly lived. It was evening. The thick powdery walls of Tulsidas's house were pierced with grille windows that overlooked the darkening expanse of the river. On the smooth floor sat a man, with a copper vessel by his side that contained the sacred Ganges water. He was reading by the light of a clay lamp. An incense stick sent wreaths of smoke up into the darkness. Tulsidas's poem lay before him on a measure of red velvety cloth; he rocked slightly as he mouthed the words, and watching him, I could not help but feel that what he was doing was not so much reading as praying.

Tulsidas was an exact contemporary of Shakespeare's. His work, as often happens in India, had passed out of the realm of literature and become a sacred object. It could now only be approached through piety, even though in living memory, there had been men who had written commentaries on the poem. I had read commentaries like these in Sanskrit, and they came out of a close reading of text, with a special emphasis on literary devices and tropes. They were more technical than our modern criticism, but clearly the result of an intellectual engagement with a text. They could not be written anymore. It is hard to say why. "Modernity," writes Adam Kirsch, "cannot be identified with any particular technological or social breakthrough. Rather, it is a subjective condition, a feeling or an intuition that we are in some profound sense different from the people who lived before us." This intuition had taken hold in India. The door of tradition had closed. What lay behind, though not very old, was petrified, and Tulsidas was revered into silence, at once immortal and dead.

> Death in all aspects has been a constant preoccupation of my mind, particularly during this winter when working on my big Kali composition. It seemed to me that somehow, through this work the reality of death had almost become a familiar thought, almost like a friend. The terror of the utter loneliness of death had given place to the feeling of the great community of death, the only real community, the only condition in which all differences are obliterated and all are one, merged into the same substance.
>
> —ALICE BONER DIARIES, MAY 11, 1954

Death came in and out of focus in Benares—now metaphorical, now real. One afternoon, in a boat on the river, we drifted up to a corpse. I couldn't tell what it was at first, but Pinku knew immediately.

"*Shava,*" he said with distaste, using a Sanskrit word derived from the verb "to swell."

And this shava was indeed swollen, all gray and yellow, bobbing happily about in the river like a Dead Sea tourist. The afternoon sun struck the exposed head, knees, and feet. I could make out the tarsals and metatarsals, the interstices of the toes. As Pinku asked the boatman, who had until a moment ago been singing a boatman's song about the Ganges, to steer the boat away, I caught a glimpse of the face. Half of it had rotted away, and the half that remained bore a broad and mirthless smile.

Pinku explained that certain categories of corpses cannot be committed to fire. Fire was a deity, and sacred; therefore lepers, who are contaminated, cannot be cremated. Nor can ascetics, for they are symbolically already dead. The performance of their own death rites was a part of their initiation.

**THE KASHI LABH MUKTI BHAWAN** is a place where people come to die. One morning, Pinku showed me some pictures from this house of death. They were of what seemed like a living corpse, the skin stretched so thin over the bones of the face—teeth grotesquely enlarged, eyes vacant—that I could hardly tell if it was a man or a woman.

I was now less dismissive of death in Benares than when I had first arrived. The white man I carried on my shoulder at all times, at whose likes and dislikes I found myself guessing, had in part been silenced by my time in the West. I had been back in the West scarcely eighteen months, and already I had found myself craving India. It was not beauty, not charm, not home; it was a certain knowing quality about the people, a wisdom kept in trust among human beings and seemingly etched into the landscape. It was what Mark Twain, travelling through India in the nineteenth century for *Following the Equator,* had observed:

> You soon realize that India is not beautiful; still there is an enchantment about it that is beguiling, and which does not pall. You cannot tell just what it is that makes the spell, perhaps, but you feel it and confess it, nevertheless. Of course, at bottom, you know in a vague way that it is history; it is that that affects you, a haunting sense of the myriads of human lives that have blossomed, and withered, and perished here, repeating and repeating and repeating, century after century, and age after age, the barren and meaningless process; it is this sense that gives to this forlorn, uncomely land power to speak to the spirit and make friends with it...

"I want to go to this place," I said to Pinku.

"We can go," he said easily.

A few days later we sat in the winter sun outside the house of death. It was a lovely redbrick building with a deep porch and green jalousie windows.

The old Brahmin manager, Bhairav Nath Shukla, was dressed in a yellow woolen vest and a lungi. He sat at a wooden table in the driveway of the great house, reading a Hindi newspaper, over which lay a small red-lettered religious text. His gray hair was cropped short, his face unshaven; the skin sagged from his thin bare arms, which he rubbed from time to time as he spoke.

"There were once many such houses in Benares," he said, "all of Kashi was like this." Then, perhaps anticipating that we might find it an unpardonable act of blind faith for poor people to come to Benares to die in the vain hope of attaining nirvana, he quickly added, "It is a difficult road, and when it gets too hard, people get off and say it's all a fraud."

Shukla was the caricature of Brahmin prolixity. He ran circles around Pinku and me.

"What is this word 'life'?" he said, when I asked him about his. "It is nothing in itself. Nothing if not self-realization. If you can unite the individual self with the Supreme Self, then that is a life. Otherwise, nothing. What is this body? A garment? A thing of veins and nerves. I may have this life now, but my soul has been coming along through the ages. Who knows where it will go after this?"

I asked him for details: Where he was born? When he came to work at this house, and why?

He was put off by the egotism implicit in the questions and answered with scorn: he was born in Gorakhpur, near the Nepal border; he had been the manager of this house for forty-five years; he came to Benares to study.

He used an important word for "studying": *adhyayan*. Mukhopadhyay's students had used the same word. It provided the most basic description of a Brahmin's vocation. What does a Brahmin do? He does adhyayan.

I asked Shukla his age, but this was a step too far.

"This body"—he smiled contemptuously—"is some sixty-odd years old; but this soul, who can tell? Will it find freedom? Will it not? Who can say? I must stay on my path."

I closed my notebook and shooed off a mantle of sun-drunk flies.

The manager at the house of death felt himself encircled by an alien culture, whose power he thought emanated from science, medicine, and technology, and whose ultimate triumph would mean that every day fewer people would come to his house of death. "We are in a state akin to that of Trishanku," he said, referring to the mythical king who, caught between the power of two great sages, was doomed to forever hang upside down in the ether.

It was India's incomparable metaphor for liminality, and a nice image to come from a man who specialized in states of purgatory. The body, he had earlier said, was a vestment; he now reused the image in a more interesting way: "I can understand the need for doctors, and engineers. And where there is necessity, I can see why one would have to don a shirt and trousers. But why not leave it there? Why not come home and change back into one's Indian clothes? Why imitate their fashions? Why not be Indian at home, and Western outside?"

**INSIDE, A WOMAN LAY DYING.**

On the way in, Aryan Singh—"the outside guard" of many years—explained the rules of the place. He was not a Brahmin, and after Shukla's abstractions, it was a relief to be given a few hard details. Dressed in a red shirt and a saffron scarf, blue Bata slippers on his feet, Singh said, "People come here once medical science has given up on them, and they have stopped eating and drinking. They are allowed to stay for fifteen-day installments, after which extensions can be granted until death. It is imperative that they have no disease." He pointed to the rules and regulations, which were written in Hindi on a board fastened to the wall. I took a picture on my iPhone.

"Has it all come?" Singh asked in wonder.

"Yes," I replied, and we went in.

In a large room, dark, cold, and musty, my eyes tried to make sense of what the darkness revealed.

From a pale blue wall the god Ganesh peered down on a room strewn with empty bottles, cooking utensils, duffel bags, and newspapers. At the center of this tableau vivant was the dying woman. Her small nacreous eyes were visible over the top of a thick brown blanket, and despite their murk, the vacancy of ebbing life, they showed signs of recognition and curiosity, courage and fear.

The woman's son, a sixty-five-year-old science teacher from Bihar, sat by her side, reading to her from Tulsidas's poem. The old woman's hearing was gone, and the reading, like the small sips of water from the

Ganges that were poured down her open lips, was a ritual act. It had been this woman's long-standing wish to die in Benares; her son had made good on this wish. He had brought her here to die and be free. Her illnesses were over; she had stopped eating; only death awaited. What made the scene especially affecting, as Pinku pointed out, was that this man who loved his mother enough to do this great thing for her had now to welcome her death.

"Think how hard it must be," Pinku whispered in my ear, "to wish for the death of one's own mother."

We got up to go. The old woman's son began to cry. He said, "Give me your blessings, for I have no mother now."

Outside, the sun came in through the top of a courtyard, casting a pattern of dots and long bars across a whitewashed balustrade, mildewed and peeling in places. In a pretty semicircular transom, some colored glass pieces had fallen out. "*Hare Ram, Hare Lakshman*" played through the house.

# 9

# THE ISLE OF ROUGH MAGIC

**WE ENTERED THE DARKEST WEEK** of the year. The skies were ashen. A thin mantle of foul air prevented the rays of the sun from reaching the city; its disk hung over the river, wan and sickly at midday, no more a source of heat than the moon. The temperature was mild—no icy winds, no polar vortex, no bright blue frigid days—but this mealy-mouthed cold neither set in nor left you alone. There was no way to insulate against it. I found myself on many mornings fully dressed to go out, rattling about the house in search of a warm nook. But there was none. The only solution was to get back into bed, and I found myself doing this: spending long mornings, fully dressed under a heavy blanket of bloated cotton, mattress lumpy underneath, reading like an invalid until the town woke up, people were done with their prayers and ablutions, and it was warm enough to go outside.

I had been here too long, and it was beginning to affect me adversely. Many aspects of my New York self had quietly come under assault in Benares. My sense of time was only the first and most obvious thing to go. I arrived with New York time, which I retained for a while, grafting it onto Benares. I was busy, officious. I went from person to place, gathering my material with surgical precision, ready to go home and write it up. I ignored the smiles of the people I was moving among. For a while the trick worked. The days went by swiftly. New York's speed and industry stayed with me. But all the while a deep undertow of Benares time—languid, sluggish, miring—rose up from below. And one day, as if air brakes had been applied to me, my dizzying pace in the city came to a halt. I felt dangerously out of step with the place. Like a planet retrograding, my days grew larger and emptier; the hours dragged. New York time crumbled, and no matter what I did, I was not able to seize it again. It was like a tune that had gone out of my head. The emphasis in Benares on the timeless fact of death, a preparation for facing eternity, abolished the modern sense of time. It made daily life seem inconsequential; and in doing so, it created the conditions for an ahistorical society.

"My notions of time are confused," wrote Alice in 1934. "What happened yesterday, the day before, or today? Or this morning? Perhaps it has already happened? I'm now beginning to understand why no historical chronology is possible in this country. Time is suspended and the change from day to night has nothing to do with it. A calendar is a nonsensical thing here."

Outside, the calendar year was out. A stage was being prepared on the ghat for the New Year festivities. Music, choreographed dancing, a live band, patriotic songs. "Hello, hello. Check, check. Hello, checking," the sound engineer's voice boomed out over the river. A large sign in the colors of the Indian tricolor said INDIAN, LET THAT BE YOUR RELIGION.

That religion, Benares had shown me, was composed of more than its fair share of actual religion; what it meant to be Hindu and what it meant to be Indian unavoidably overlapped. The knowledge of caste was just one tenet in this welding of belief and nationality. But as time went on, I was made aware of a whole substratum of belief composed of magic and superstition that formed a part of the daily life of Benares. They were the vestiges of what must have constituted belief in all classical societies. This was still in many respects a world similar to the one Gibbon describes in his history of Rome, where it was "the fashion of the times to attribute every remarkable event to the particular will of the Deity," and where "the alterations of nature" were "connected, by an invisible chain, with the moral and metaphysical opinions of the human mind."

It was a world in which karmic law was still in force and the actions of the present were seen to exert an unearthly influence over the future. People looked to soothsayers and divines, palmists, witch doctors, astrologers, and exorcists. Many in Benares would sooner go to an astrologer than a doctor. Nobody would dream of performing an important ceremony or rite without first consulting one. Calendar time mattered only in that it was laced with a knowledge of the beneficence and malfeasance of the celestial world. It was unthinkable that any two people would marry without first matching their astrological charts, and if they did not match—or if one was deemed to be born under a dodgy star—the girl or boy would do better to marry an astrologically compatible stranger, rather than a life partner who might be compatible in every other way but this one supreme regard.

Magic, like death, was ever present in Benares. There was a whole climate of subtle influence, now darkened by the malice of a family member, now brightened by the beneficence of the stars. People confronted these influences directly. They were as real as weather in the West.

One morning, Pinku and I passed a witch doctor, brushing clean a toddler of the evil eye. This old man with white stubble sat on the dusty pavement in front of a green door. He wore a little Union Jack beanie and kept his spells in a yellow plastic bag. He pressed a pink-handled kitchen knife gently against the jugular of the toddler, muttering all the time. Then, banishing the evil eye with a swipe of the knife to both sides of the boy, he blew on him, brushed him with a whisk, and tied a black thread around his neck. A line of people stood waiting. One woman, in a blue sari covered in large green flowers and little red sequins, carried a small child in a zebra-striped sweater. The child had a black mark on his temple to ward off the evil eye. He was getting sick, and his mother feared that someone, in praising him, had secretly wished him harm. She had brought him to see the witch doctor to clear him of the special ill will that came in the guise of a compliment.

"These are our little consultants," Pinku said, and laughed. "They stand in for the psychologist and the doctor." Then he confessed that he sometimes brought his little nephew to have him brushed clean of the evil eye.

"Do you believe in all this?" I said, with perhaps some alarm in my voice.

"No, but my family does."

It was not just his family who believed; everyone did. The great majority of India operated out of a kind of double consciousness in which the laws of reason and the laws of magic, like Roman and common law in Britain, reached an easy harmony. Each person came to his or her own special composite; but few—no matter how urban or westernized—lived their lives without factoring in the pressures of the supernatural.

Golu, Mapu's guru's grandson, and the last in a long line of priests, was a master manipulator of these beliefs. He was as enterprising as a medieval friar and knew exactly how to prey on the fears of rich businessmen and industrialists. He came to see me one afternoon and regaled me with tales of his lucrative trade in banishing the malfeasance of the stars.

He was tall by Indian standards, dressed elegantly in brown corduroy trousers, a dark yellow kurta, and a gray waistcoat. His forehead was emblazoned with broad yellow streaks pierced with red. He was vain, acquisitive, and, I thought, a trifle irritated at having to conceal his materialism in a garb of religiosity. God and Mammon found a happy balance in Golu. The ringtone on his smartphone was a famous verse from the Gita: "Whenever and wherever, O son of Bharata, there is a fall in dharma, and the rise of adharma—I will create Myself [anew]." When Golu folded his hands in greeting, I noticed a large ring of hessonite for protection from the ill will of Rahu, the eclipser.

We went up to the roof, where Golu brought me up to date with his priestly work. He blessed private planes and helicopters; he procured astronomically priced corals to stave off the wrath of Mars. The stars and planets were his bread and butter, and only he and his team of Brahmins knew how to manage their adverse influences.

Consider the case of the chewing-tobacco magnate from Rajasthan. The tobacco magnate had only just heard the bad news that the Supreme Court would outlaw his chewing tobacco, which was known to cause oral cancer. "It would have ruined him," Golu said with feeling for the rich man's plight. Golu immediately ordered a sacrifice worth seventy lakhs, or roughly one hundred thousand dollars.

The ceremony began at 9:00 a.m., and almost as soon as it was over—"even before it was over," Golu emphasized—two important bits of news came through. The first was that the magnate's son, who had been trying to get out of his marriage, had been granted a divorce. The woman came around and gave it to him. (That divorce was not part of the

Hindu scheme, but a borrowed concept out of the West, did not trouble Golu.) Secondly, the Supreme Court issued a stay on the tobacco ban.

"Can you imagine?" said Golu. "Right then and there—this is Rajasthan in May—it began to rain. Rain, as you have never seen before. A downpour!

"So, you see, it is very important to keep this relationship"—here he used the English phrase—"of *give-and-take* going. The Ganges takes from us, but she also gives, doesn't she?

"There is a secret character to this city. You need to understand that." Before leaving, he invited me back to the temple, promising to perform a number of expensive prayers and ceremonies to ensure my well-being.

It felt almost like a threat.

At the Pishach Mochan temple and tank, on the western limits of the city, the spirits of the dead were liberated and exorcisms were performed. A gnarled old tree overlooked a large tank of green water. Pinku pointed to the nails that had been hammered into the tree: "They are basically guesthouses for the lost spirits of the dead."

Those who had more money made little cement mounds. Yellowish-white lines were drawn on the ground in a hopscotch pattern, with marigolds, cloves, and little smoking stumps of incense placed in the different squares and circles. The wandering spirit, Pinku told me, was caught in one of the circles, then forced into a clove, and the possessed person was freed.

The tank, with its greenish water, was meant to have special powers. Trash lapped up against its stone steps, where children were playing. A small boy defecated in the long grass behind me. "They're making fools of people," Pinku said. "Most of the so-called possessed people really just have psychological problems."

Pinku's commitment to science felt like a form of resistance in a place where even the most educated people retained a magical cast of mind.

At a multiday reading of a religious text, held in honor of BHU's centenary, the presiding Brahmin, who had taught at Harvard, interspersed his songs about the deeds of Krishna with sermons on modern society.

He lamented that while many Indians worked in the software industry, far fewer could be credited with inventing new software. I imagined we were in for a lecture on the damage Indian education, with its overemphasis on mathematics and science, had done to creativity; but, no, the Brahmin took a different line. "Our young girls and boys are serving the West," he said with anguish. "When will the day come that their boys and girls will serve us?

"We once had these technologies too. But over the course of a thousand years of slavery, we forgot them. Or, rather, we were *made* to forget them." Then, as if speaking of magical powers, he said, "We must awaken these practices among us again."

The Brahmin was not alone in his conflation of magic and science. Modi himself believed something similar. "We all read about Karna in the Mahabharata," he told a gathering of doctors and professionals at a hospital in Bombay in 2014. "If we think a little more, we realise that the Mahabharata says Karna was not born from his mother's womb. This means that genetic science was present at that time.

"We worship Lord Ganesh. There must have been some plastic surgeon at that time who got an elephant's head on the body of a human being and began the practice of plastic surgery."

The achievements of the scientific West rankled in India like nothing else. India could do without Western literature, art, civics, philosophy, and religion, but the fruits of technology, science, and medicine, India wanted. This was the West's "weapon of demoralizing superiority." Yet, as much as India coveted the feats of science, little acknowledgment was made of the mindset behind them, nor of the centuries it took for Europe to shrug off its own belief in magic and superstition. In this climate of material results admired and methods disdained, or treated with ambivalence at best, even the coveted achievements of Western science could be regarded as the product of an especially potent brand of magic.

**IN HIS QUEST TO LEAD** me deeper into the world of belief in Benares, Pinku took me to see a boy ascetic. His ashram was a vast concrete shed with rough squarish pillars. A midmorning gloom pervaded this hall of giants, which was dotted with greasy generators and motorbikes. Deep inside, on a little wooden perch, sat Balak Das. He was from bandit country in Madhya Pradesh, and no longer a boy. His features were dark and tribal, his face thin, his hair ragged and long. He was dressed in saffron robes; two mobile phones lay on a satin bolster next to him; he talked down to us from his eminence, wiggling his toes as he spoke. He was sometimes giddy and playful, sometimes solemn and self-regarding. He had left his home in the Chambal valley, he told me, when he was but a boy of six. He had performed severe austerities, *tapasya*. He sat for days with fires burning around him, unmoving, lost in meditation, gazing upon the peace of the abyss.

"Completely still," he said, evoking the image from the Gita of the ascetic "abiding alone in a secret place, without craving and without possessions ... senses held in check ... body, head, and neck maintained in perfect equipoise," still as a lamp in a windless place. He gained special tantric powers. He was versed in the black arts. He could, for instance, if he wanted, reduce me to ash with the fire of his inner concentration. Then suddenly a wave of hilarity came over Balak Das, and giggling, he said, "The only thing that ever defeated me was Pepsi." He recalled the scalding sensation of the fizz going down his throat—no one had told him to drink it slowly—and he thought he was going to die. He spat it out immediately. It had to be alcohol. Balak Das's guru, enjoying himself immensely at Balak Das's expense, told him that the drink cost five hundred rupees, and he would now have to compensate him for the waste. "Five hundred rupees!" Balak Das guffawed. "Five hundred rupees was all the money I had in the whole world."

Balak Das had risen; he had become a *mahant*, a head priest; he now had political ambitions. He said brazenly, "I have a desire—I've always had it—to be worshipped and honored."

Balak Das was a child of magic. No social or moral idea he could express would earn him more esteem in the eyes of his followers—one now sat on the floor at his feet, looking like an overgrown adolescent—than his ability to perform miracles: to tell the future, to incinerate his opponents, to accrue wealth and honor through those who flocked to him because of the magical power he had gained through his austerities. In his view, the power of the West could also be attributed to magic. But of rather an inferior sort. He spoke of missile technology with equal measures of wonder and disdain: "The weaponry in our scriptures is superior, you see. When we fired our great weapons, they came back into the hands of our warriors. Yours do not come back. They are single-use only."

We picked our way out through the darkness of that immense warehouse of an ashram. Outside, the boy ascetic's two SUVs were freshly washed and gleaming in the morning sunshine.

**ONE AFTERNOON, AT A LECTURE** on a sixteenth-century poet-saint called Surdas, Pinku pointed out Urmila Sharma.

She was stout, in her early seventies, dressed in a beautiful silk sari and sweater. A long thin streak of black on her forehead gave her otherwise grandmotherly aspect a touch of severity. Pinku said she was the sister of a famous musicologist, and very knowledgeable herself. So, as the lecture concluded, I approached. No sooner had I introduced myself than Urmila asked me if I was Indian.

"Yes."

"In that case, I would prefer we continue our conversation in an Indian language." Any would do. She had mastered half a dozen. But not English. "I made a vow as a young girl to only ever speak to an Indian in an Indian language."

I went to see her one rainy day in December. She lived in a charmless residential neighborhood on the edge of BHU's vast campus. A forest of weeds grew out of the deep drains; heaps of uncollected trash were on the street corners; eroded islands of tarmac streamed with water. Urmila met me at the door of a drab yellow bungalow, which was in total darkness. In one room, I could just about discern the spectral shape of a sitar on a platform. The house was freezing. We came out into the open briefly and climbed a concrete staircase. A garden was visible through the diamond-shaped openings in a plaster screen.

Urmila led me up to a pantry of sorts, illuminated by tube light. The walls were green and badly scuffed in places; yellowing books and dented plastic bottles were everywhere. The furniture and electronics were under dustcovers. The room had a heavy air of decay, and I found myself looking longingly through the begrimed gauze of a mesh screen at a grove of rain-drenched mango trees.

As I was taking in the room, Urmila asked that I wash my feet. The house was filthy, but that did not matter. The washing of a guest's feet was an ancient Indian act of welcome, documented in Sanskrit poetry and epics. It must once have existed alongside a wider concern for the cleanliness of one's surroundings, but now it occurred in a vacuum, with no thought to the sordid state of the house or the neighborhood beyond. I offered to remove my shoes, but as if to emphasize the purely ritual nature of the act, Urmila insisted I keep them on. Then she poured the water as I washed the soles of my sneakers, and from then on, the empty ritual was repeated every time I came to the house.

Urmila, who was born into a Brahmin family from Punjab in 1944, was an exception in the Hindu society of that time. Women traditionally did not receive a classical education. They were forbidden, no less than those of low-caste birth, from studying or chanting the

Veda. Urmila had lived the Brahmin's vocation to the fullest; she was initiated into the life of the mind, a twice-born woman.

"I decided at a very young age," she said, "never to have any worldly relations."

"Worldly relations?"

"Never to marry. I wanted to remain free to live the life of the mind."

"Wasn't there pressure on you to marry?"

"No. From the time I was a very young child, I outright refused to be sent to anybody's house."

"And your parents didn't object?"

"No, how could they? My elder sister had refused too. Sure, they poked fun at me. I was only a child after all. But they knew that I had come into the world to do something. They had faith. My father was an excellent astrologer, and he saw in my chart that I would never compromise with the truth. He said, 'Let her do what she wants, because if we force her into a marriage, she will break it immediately.' Marriage is full of compromises."

Instead, Urmila devoted herself to one of the great dual objectives of Indian life: she would study like crazy, and then she would meet God. With the double aim of developing both spirit and mind, Urmila left home as a young girl and came to Benares. She went to BHU, where she obtained degree after degree. She studied every branch of Indian learning, from linguistics to ayurveda, Sanskrit grammar, and the secrets of the Veda. But throughout this intellectual journey, one thing was clear:

"I knew right from the beginning that the West had nothing to give me. Their language seemed far more impoverished to me than our own. Their script was an unscientific hodgepodge."

It seemed like an oddly regressive position for an otherwise brave and daring woman. When I questioned her further, I saw that it was not so much that the West had nothing to offer her, but that she was reacting against its power over Indian society.

Urmila had begun our conversation by reading off her telephone a quote attributed to Macaulay. It was in wide circulation in India on WhatsApp and other social media platforms. The quote was fraudulent, but the emotion behind it was not: it was a perfect articulation of what India believed Britain had done to her.

"'I have traveled across the length and breadth of India,'" Urmila began, in halting English, "'and I have not seen one person who is a beggar, who is a thief. Such wealth I have seen in this country, such high moral values, people of such caliber, that I do not think we would ever conquer this country, unless we break the very backbone of this nation, which is her spiritual and cultural heritage, and therefore I propose we replace her old and ancient education systems, her *culture*'"—Urmila repeated this word three times, then concluded—"'for if the Indians think that all that is foreign and English is good, and greater than their own, they will lose their self-esteem, their native culture ... and they will become what we want them to be, a truly dominated nation.'"

Urmila blazed in the triumph of the apocryphal quote. It was painful to watch, in part because it was so crude a portrait of Macaulay, who was a gifted writer. But more than that, it seemed harmful to India to accept, 150 years on, so oversimplified a description of what the contact with Britain had amounted to.

"Was your turning away from Western learning, then, a way to protect yourself?" I asked.

"No." Urmila put her phone away. "There was no need to protect myself. I knew that what we had was much better. To study their things was a comedown; it was to diminish myself. Frankly, I felt sorry for them." She laughed, a bitter, disingenuous laugh, unbefitting a woman who refused to compromise with the truth. If Western learning was as trifling as Urmila made out, her aversion to it would not have been so intense. In reality it had been a shaping force on her world, and her response was to reject it with equal and opposite force.

We now came to the mistakes Urmila felt independent India had made: "It was Nehru. He cut us from our roots."

"Were you aware of this as you grew up?"

"No. Because things were not so bad then."

"When did you become aware that things were going wrong?"

"I think it must have been around the time of the war with China."

The war was in 1962. India had been independent for only fifteen years. It came at the end of Nehru's life, and some say it killed him. He had been devoted to friendship with China, and they rewarded his dreams of an Asia united against Europe and America with a stealthy incursion into Indian territory. India was completely unprepared; in the end, Nehru, who had disdained American friendship, was begging Kennedy to bomb China.

But Urmila had her own special complaint with Nehru:

"Once I got older, I began to see what Nehru was doing. I began to see that he was degrading our things, and elevating theirs, now encouraging cow slaughter, now diminishing ayurveda. At the time of the China war, there was a man called Narayana Swamy. He was a prince of Mysore, and a very brilliant engineer. But with age, his eyes began to fail. The doctors advised he stop reading and writing altogether, or he would go completely blind. He decided to leave his work and go into the hills." He went to Gangotri, the town at the source of the Ganges. "There, he began to meditate on the water of the Ganges. He used to wear these very thick glasses, and one day as he was gazing into the river, they fell in and were swept away. Now he thought to himself, 'Well, Mother Ganges, if you have taken these, then there is nothing for me to go back to. In fact, I cannot go back. My eyes are completely gone. But at least nothing now separates us.' So, he continued to gaze at the purifying water of the Ganges, and slowly, *very slowly*, his sight began to return. The vision that was gone came back! But since he had already left everything behind, he decided to go deeper into the mountains. There, from a spot at twelve thousand feet, he had a clear view into China. His sight in fact had become so sharp that he could see for miles and miles. Do you know what *trataka* is?"

I did not. But later I learned that it was a form of meditation whereby if one focuses on a single point, such as a black dot or a flame, the energy of the "third eye" can be released.

Swamy had inadvertently done trataka on the water of the Ganges. Now, with his third eye gently opening, he began to do trataka on the moon and the sun. His vision grew sharper; he acquired the gift of long-sightedness. He was able to look deep into China, Urmila said. There, hundreds of miles away, he could see the Chinese army plotting their incursion into Indian territory. In 1958, he wrote Nehru a letter, warning him about what was happening, and advising him to strengthen Indian positions at various points on the border. "But Nehru wouldn't listen!" Urmila cried.

In 1960, Swamy wrote again to say that the situation had deteriorated considerably, and that if something was not done now, it would be too late afterward. He wrote two, maybe three, letters. But Nehru ignored them all. "He was too obsessed with his own power," Urmila said, "and with saving face." Nehru had said India and China are brothers. He wasn't prepared to be proven wrong, especially not by some ascetic on a mountaintop who'd developed the gift of clairvoyance. "But had he listened," Urmila said, "we might have been able to stave off the Chinese aggression."

This was the reason Urmila had lost faith in Nehru: "I became aware of his total contempt for Indian culture and civilization."

Poor Nehru! He may well have disdained Hindu worship and ritual, but he cherished Indian civilization. And his fears for the scientific temper in India were real. He would have known that someone such as Urmila was by no means alone in her belief in magic, and that if India wanted the fruits of Western science, it would also have to assimilate the methods. He would also have been aware of a tendency in India to dismiss those methods and to falsely claim the discoveries of the modern scientific West as having already existed in premodern India. Aldous Huxley, traveling through India in the 1920s for *Jesting Pilate*, had been dismayed by the proliferation of a pseudoscientific literature. He saw intelligent men squander their time and energy on proving to the world that the ancient Hindus were superior in every regard. "Thus," he wrote, "each time the West has announced a new scientific discovery, misguided scholars have ransacked Sanskrit literature to find a phrase that might be interpreted as a Hindu anticipation of it."

Huxley felt that this literature was the direct result of British rule in India—"the melancholy product of a subject people's inferiority complex"—and that "free men would never dream of wasting their time and wit on such vanities." He was only half right. There was indeed a pathos in India wanting to appropriate the discoveries of the West, and it may well have sprung, as Mukhopadhyay pointed out, from the harm British rule had done India's self-image by labeling it an exclusively spiritual culture, but seventy years of freedom had not been enough to put an end to this baleful tendency. Under Modi, the pseudoscientific impulse had gained momentum, and serious scientific platforms were being overtaken by people wishing to prove that Shiva was the first environmentalist, that air travel had been mastered by the Indians seven thousand years before the Wright brothers, and that nuclear weapons had been in use at the time of the Indian epics. It would be easy to laugh except that beneath the boastfulness there lay real pain.

Magic, like madness, could insinuate itself into a recognizable reality—it was a *partial* distortion—and there was something arresting in watching magic at work. The longer I stayed talking to Urmila, the more magic seemed to remake our world. My breaking point came in the middle of a story about Urmila's guru, Vimala Thakar. She had been part of a famous land reform movement in the 1950s that was led by a disciple of Mahatma Gandhi's, Vinoba Bhave, who had walked the length and breadth of India appealing to landowners to voluntarily give up their land.

I had tried to sidestep the subject of magic until now, even though it had encroached many times. Urmila had told me of cows that adhered to the dietary restrictions of the strictest Brahmins: "If so much as the skin of an onion blew in from outside and landed in their food, they would immediately refuse the food."

I quailed, but she was indefatigable.

"On one occasion, a boy who worked for us brought them what we thought were perfectly clean rotis, but the cow refused them. We thought, 'That's strange!' But when we inquired further, we found that the boy who had brought them had recently had a death in the family."

I looked blankly back at her.

"Don't you see?" Urmila thundered. "That was why the cow refused them! An orthodox Brahmin cannot eat food from a house of grief. He has to wait until eighteen days have passed."

We carried on, despite that our hold on a mutually accepted view of reality was growing more tenuous by the minute. At last, Urmila delivered her coup de grâce. Telling me of her years of "spiritual enrichment," when she quit the world and went to live in the Rajasthani hill station of Mount Abu, Urmila let it slip that Vimala Thakar's grandfather had received initiation directly from Tulsidas.

"Who lived in the sixteenth century?"

"The very same! This is nothing special for us. This is something that happens all the time. It is written of in our texts."

"You saw it?"

"Vimala saw it, and as far as I'm concerned, that is good enough for me."

"What exactly did she see?"

"Her grandfather was a rich landlord. And he would often say, 'If I am ever to be initiated, I want to be initiated by Tulsidas.'"

"Did he mean it metaphorically?"

"Not metaphor," Urmila scolded. "Real!"

"As in physically?"

"Yes, physically! And so it was that one day he began to feel that the time for his initiation had arrived. He sent the four-year-old Vimala out of the room—"

"She was four?"

Vimala, as a girl, was always by her grandfather's side. So when, one day, he asked to be left alone, she grew curious. No sooner had she been sent out of the room than she pushed a table up to the locked door and peered through the transom. She saw her grandfather, dressed in brand-new clothes, seated in meditation by a sacrificial fire. A few moments later, another man appeared in the room, though all its doors were closed. He was a tall, fair Brahmin. On seeing him, Vimala's grandfather greeted him with full prostration. The Brahmin gave his blessings and the two men sat down in front of the sacrificial fire. The rite of initiation began. The man whispered something into Vimala's grandfather's ear. They sat like that for an hour, then Vimala's grandfather rose and thanked the Brahmin, who left the room as magically as he'd entered it.

No sooner was he gone, Urmila said, with girlish excitement, than Vimala rushed in, "like a little squirrel," and began to quiz her grandfather about the strange man. Vimala's grandfather was amazed that she had seen him and asked for a full description. He then showed her a number of pictures of different saints to see if she could recognize the man she purported to have seen. She rejected each one, but when they came to Tulsidas, she cried, "It's him! It's him." Her grandfather was delighted, Urmila said. "He always knew that there was something special about the girl."

I had believed until that moment that Urmila's lapses into magic could be controlled. I admired much about Urmila: her severity, her solitude, her vows of chastity, her utter commitment to the life of the mind. But now it was difficult to go on. Magic, like fiction, was a closed circle; it was true and consistent within its sphere, but to partake, one had to submit oneself to its laws, and I found myself unable to go the distance. It is easy to be indifferent to what doesn't threaten, but in these altered circumstances, in Benares and later in the open country, where the great majority of people believed a version of what Urmila believed, I found myself jealously guarding the worldview that had come down to me from the West. Perhaps, as Nehru was, I could be accused of displaying contempt for Indian culture and civilization. I don't believe I had any such contempt, but Urmila made me see the extent to which a break had occurred in me that was final, and that I could not accept India as a changeless emanation of the classical world. She showed me how much I valued what modernity had wrought.

Before I got up to leave Urmila's house for the last time, she asked whom else I had spoken to in Benares. I mentioned Kamlesh Dutt Tripathi and P. K. Mukhopadhyay. The first name brought an expression of distaste to Urmila's face, the second one of pure delight. "Kamlesh Dutt Tripathi is duplicitous," she said, "but P. K. Mukhopadhyay is a very fine man, absolutely transparent. A true Indian, very special."

I asked her to elaborate.

"Indian knowledge and learning is both manifest inside P. K. Mukhopadhyay as well as integrated into his life and action. He's a philosopher, but he also lives his philosophy. His mind, his words, his deeds, are totally transparent. There is no gap. If you've spoken to him, then you've done a very good thing. As for Kamlesh Dutt Tripathi, I know him inside out. He has lived with us, and that is why I have not the slightest bit of faith left in him. He is a theater man with a deeply flawed character. Anyway, let it go! Let him preserve his appearances. You've spoken to P. K. Mukhopadhyay, and that is what counts. Let us concentrate on the good and set aside the bad."

**MY DECADE-LONG STUDY OF** Sanskrit had given me an intellectual—I might even say theoretical—entry point into a culture whose reality colonization had set me at a distance from. I had not thought hard enough about the nature of that distance: of who I would be were it to collapse, and whether I wanted it gone at all. I had learned Sanskrit chiefly among people who regarded it as they might Latin or Greek, a dead language—an object of intellectual wonder, but not a sacred artifact in an unbroken continuum. All around me now were people who lived the Hindu continuum, and they helped me to recognize how much my distances were part of who, and what, I was. I wanted to be near India, but I did not want to surrender my distance. "The West's India became our India," Mukhopadhyay had said as a criticism of men such as Tagore. I saw now that I did not want to undo that refracted image of India—the country seen for millennia through other eyes. It was not just that I believed purity was illusory; it was that I believed in the creative possibilities—no less than the hurt—of seeing oneself as others see you.

There were certain things about Tripathi that I had not wanted to acknowledge. He seemed to privilege the exuberance of an idea, or the elegance of a phrase, over its veracity. His "solutions" to India's intellectual and spiritual crisis were glib. But my real concern about Tripathi was what the rise of Modi would do to him. I was afraid that he would conflate the politics of revival (and revenge) with his own heartfelt wish for a cultural renaissance in India. I was afraid he would throw in his lot with the forces of Hindu nationalism, and that he would come out a diminished figure as a result. It was one reason I had not sought him out on this return to Benares. In the end, I did go and see him, for in a journey of this kind, the traveler, like the novelist, has no right to be afraid of what he might find.

**THE DAWN OF THE MODI** era had brought material changes to Tripathi's life. He was no longer in that dilapidated bungalow by the side of a busy road. The new offices of the IGNCA were in a large compound shaded with mango trees. There were government-style buildings in BHU colors—yellow picked out in red—ranged around mossy pathways of brick in a herringbone pattern. In one corner of the compound, above a sign that read TAYLIT, a flight of open stairs led up to a large first-floor space, carved up with glass and aluminum partitions into many discrete units. In this bright busy place, drenched in fluorescent light, the only reminders of the dreary bungalow that housed the old offices were the government-issue chairs, with their white plastic weave, and the green metal cabinets that contained Sanskrit books.

I was kept waiting a few moments, then shown into a large office with an electrical heater and a garden view. Tripathi, dressed in a blue woolen kurta and waistcoat, a scarf around his neck, sat in a wicker chair, two acolytes by his side. He greeted me warmly with his smile of long, gapped teeth. His eyes were bright and luminescent as before, but when he began to speak, I was sad to see that an unfortunate change had come over the man I had known eighteen months before. Then, in the heat of that election summer, Tripathi had been full of humility and repose; he was frantic now, messianic, and distressingly pleased with himself.

"Exactly what I thought was going to happen is happening," he announced to the room. "We are in a state of confusion. Things are very unclear. It is too early to say where they will go. But, I have been given the green light by the new dispensation to do what had not been open to me to do before, and I am determined now to dedicate what remaining energy I have to strengthening our thought."

"How will you do that?" I asked.

He would tell me later, he said; the first order of business was to meet the West on equal footing. "These people who claim to defend freedom of thought are not allowing real freedom. They say their way is the only way, that the capitalist notion of development is the only model available to us."

"How do they do this?"

"Through their monetary system, of course, and the pressure of their multinational companies."

Tripathi said he had just read a fifty-page book on the monetary system, and he was appalled to learn of the methods of domination. He launched into a tirade on the harm Western civilization was doing the world through climate change and on the need for the Paris agreement. It was a cut-rate version of the banalities one hears every day on American college campuses and was not befitting a man of Tripathi's sophistication. It made me doubt if that sophistication had been real, or an extension of my romantic idea of Tripathi. He now offered the "Gandhian model," with its emphasis on village life as the model for social and economic organization, as an alternative to the domination of the West; but Gandhi's solutions to the problems of modernity even a century ago—even to Nehru—had seemed impractical and woolly-headed. "Few of us, I think," Nehru wrote in the 1930s, "accepted Gandhiji's old ideas about machinery and modern civilization. We thought that even he looked upon them as Utopian and largely inapplicable to modern conditions." Now, with the world as interconnected as it was, with Modi traveling the globe in search of foreign investment, Gandhi seemed less applicable than ever.

"He was the last original thinker in our history," Tripathi said. "After Gandhi we have had no thinkers, only borrowed thinkers."

It was a depressing thought, and Tripathi himself walked it back: "Sometimes I think that this fight that we are engaged in is one in which we are just going to keep losing. Maybe Heidegger was right, maybe the destiny of the world does lie in complete westernization."

The remark reminded me of what Shivam had said: "Either we throw ourselves into this modernity, or we go back to what we were; what is intolerable is this limbo, this middle condition."

Shivam, pointing at the death fires on the river, had said, "In the end the truth is only that." I had not thought too much about the comment at the time, but listening to Tripathi now, I wondered if Shivam had been applying the Hindu concept of creative destruction to the decayed state of Hinduism itself. When I mentioned to Tripathi what Shivam had said, his earlier glibness fell away, and he was once more the man I had spoken to eighteen months before.

With pure unbridled passion, he said, "This is the voice of India. What you heard this boy of twenty say, this is the voice of the coming generation of this country. Either we become fully westernized, or we find a way to come back into the sphere of Indian thought."

The last time Tripathi and I had met, he had shown me photographs of sixty-five little Brahmin boys being initiated into their vocation by a thread ceremony. They sat before sacrificial fires, each wearing two measures of yellow unstitched cloth, their heads tonsured, receiving their second birth.

"I, too, was once such a boy," Tripathi had said. "I sat there in the same way. I must have been even younger when the mantras were whispered in my ear."

One of the boys, a beautiful child with dark intent eyes, was to come and live with Tripathi to learn the Veda. Like all the other boys in the picture, he carried a little twig in his hands, a symbolic staff.

"What are these sticks they're carrying?" I asked Tripathi.

"The staff of palasha wood."

I was amazed. I was reading Kalidasa's *Kumarasambhavam* at the time, in which Shiva appeared to Parvati in the guise of a student, bearing the staff of palasha wood. It was one thing to be told of the survival of the classical past into the present; it was quite another to be confronted with an actual object as proof. And it was so unselfconscious. It gave India's history a unique character. India's buildings were not especially old; there were no ancient Indian historians, no equivalent of Herodotus or Polybius, or of China's *Spring and Autumn Annals*, but in parts of Hindu India, the miraculous vestiges of a living past, made up of custom and ritual, whose antiquity went back twenty-five centuries at the minimum, could still be observed. It was not so much written down as held in trust among ordinary people. These continuities would have solaced India through the centuries of invasion. As with the Chinese concept of *tongbian*—*tong* meaning a deep knowledge of past practice, and *bian*, a creative transformation of custom—there would have been a degree of novelty and invention within the construct of tradition, but the modern age, though less physically violent, had closed a circle around tradition itself. "The Muslim centuries were very violent," an old Brahmin who lived and worked in a tiny room near Alice's house once said to me. "They destroyed a great deal, but our spirit remained intact. What the British did was worse. They gave our very DNA an injection, and we were never the same again."

I now asked Tripathi about his young student.

"He left me. He went back to his parents. The pressures of his environment were too great; he couldn't tolerate it."

By "pressures" Tripathi meant the forces of the new global world with all its appetites and distractions. The rigors of the old way of instruction, which had survived so much, could not survive this.

"There are one point three billion people in this country," Tripathi said as I got up to leave. "I do not believe that such a vast country can be so easily subdued by an external or superficial force. It is a source of comfort to me that among this huge population there will be voices like that of this twenty-year-old boy you spoke of earlier. It is upon them that all my hope rests."

**THE STAGE WAS SET AND** draped in purple cloth. The microphones blared. On the ghat were bright halogen lights and crowds. It was the end of the year, and it was fitting that I should spend it at the nucleus of worship and belief that was the Kashi Vishwanath Temple. Golu had wanted me to witness the ceremony at the temple again, now that I knew the city better. We had arranged to meet at one of the checkpoints before the cordoned-off area surrounding the temple. From these enclosed streets, crammed with brassware and bangles, oblations and flowers, where knots of policemen stood as gatekeepers, he now appeared out of an alley, as if from the depths of an underworld.

On seeing that I was with Golu, the policemen waved me through. Golu was haughty and brusque, half priest, half mafioso. He cut through the torrent of believers, sluicing and eddying around us in a contrapuntal motion. I kept my eyes firmly planted on the back of

Golu's head, on his admirable shikha, plaited and oiled, as he led me through the streets where he had grown up, toward the linga he had handled all his life.

The worship of the linga was the supreme example in this city of that blend of magic and theater that was part of faith all over the classical world, and of which traces could still be found in the liturgy of the Catholic Church. The Brahmins were the magi, and it was no accident that that word is deeply linked, in etymology and meaning, to magic.

The crowd thickened in the precincts of the temple. Golu sat me down on a wooden bench at one of the entrances to the sanctum, where I was able to observe at my leisure what in the past I had been too overwhelmed to see: from a fat and gentle Shiva dancing on a marble keystone to a cheap modern clock mounted on the wall. A fluorescent coil illuminated the small sanctum. The linga, deep in its silver basin, was totally submerged. Bilva leaves and rose petals floated on the cloudy surface of the water. Then the basin was drained, and the linga greeted us in all its simplicity, a smooth, wet oblong stone standing in for the primordial. It reminded me of that other rock, half a world away in Mecca, which millions flocked to see, and which exuded a similar austere power.

The worshippers were ushered out, one by one; then, slowly, like chamber musicians taking their places, the priests entered the sanctum. One, looking exactly like an opera tenor, with a great dome of a head, a light beard, and sensual lips, bore five stripes of sandalwood paste across his forehead, a red circle smoldering at the center. There were streaks of white on his huge flabby arms. He was the chief officiant, and his smiling half-closed eyes radiated the contemptuous sagacity of the Buddha. Beside him sat a man with a thick black mustache and a huge necklace of rutted rudraksh seeds resting on a bed of dense black chest hair. His countenance was fierce, his wet long hair brushed back. Amid this assemblage of corpulent men with lowering expressions was a young boy, who played a central role in the chanting:

"*Shambho, shambho,*" he cried, addressing Shiva from the Samaveda.

The older priests answered back with something indecipherable, a harsh and inarticulate call that raised the temperature in the sanctum. A silver bucket arrived full of the utensils of worship: ladles, pouring vessels, Ganges water. The little sanctum was crammed full of offerings. The flowers were tossed in the back. Other offerings—sweets, clay pots of yogurt, butter, packets of bhang—came to the fore and were smeared on the linga. The opera tenor, whose great bulk should have rendered him immobile, moved swiftly about his tasks, seeming to take a sensual pleasure in rubbing the different substances over the smooth stone. The yogurt turned a cannabis green; then it was slopped up and smeared over the linga again. The cycles of smearing and cleaning continued.

"*Shambho,*" the boy cried, and the chanting quickened.

A five-headed silver cobra was brought into the sanctum. An altar of flowers rose over the linga. The dark dithyrambs of the Samaveda started to gather speed. A controlled movement of bells—a jerk, then a clapping shut—produced an abrupt percussive effect. A man behind me, a devotee, began to mutter deliriously in conjunction with the priests; his eyes were closed, but slits of white were visible. Small implosions of religious ecstasy occurred now all around me. A ranging animal energy took hold, and people were rapidly coming undone. Fire burned out of view, behind the cupped palms of priests, the glow reflected in their faces. Then they tore their hands away and honored the linga with a smoky five-tongued flame, which they swung through the air in a circular motion. The chief officiant had lit a thick bundle of incense sticks. He put out the fire with one swift movement of his wrist, as if flicking off something unclean or hot, and wreaths of smoke scattered everywhere. He distributed the burning sticks among the other Brahmins. The chanting was at a pitch now. Bells were smashing. The voices coalesced into a low choral bass, which rose around the chief officiant like a flood; it curled up around the tower of flowers, whose summit was lost in the smoke-filled darkness.

The officiant so far had been silent, like a key instrument awaiting its turn in a symphony. He now added his voice to the mix, and it sent the devotees into raptures. Everything was coming together: the smoke, the bells, the two strains of chanting, and the audience of devotees, agog with emotion. We had been worked into a frenzy, goaded up a precipice.

It had to break. A wave of anticlimax swept through the sanctum, and the devotees, elated and fatigued, began to file out of the enclosure of the temple.

**ILLUSION, *NOT* SIN, WAS THE** error old India sought to disabuse men of. The tower of flowers went up, only to come crashing down a moment later as a reminder of the impermanence of existence. Death was held close, so that no man ever forgot that it was not real. Benares looked into a void that was a metaphor for the Hindu concept of the abyss—for it was, as Coomaraswamy tells us, "by the fire of the idea of the abyss" that the factors that contributed to ego were destroyed beyond recovery.

But to rid men of illusion is not to comfort them. The energy of Benares is primal, cruel, full of laughter. It radiates right through the city and gives it its tamasic character. It may have offered a glimpse into the true nature of the universe, but the need for men to keep their gaze fixed on the abyss has passed out of modern religion. The world is so full. One can lose oneself in the stuff of existence and never have time to stop and wonder what comes next. The monotheistic faiths, especially, are more concerned with this world than the next. I suspected that in India, too, the day was not far off when the darkling energy raised here tonight, and the loss of control it implied, would be too frightening for modern man to enter into. Then the void would cease to speak, and Benares would be confronted with the altogether new silence of an empty sandbank, where, in a time long ago, arcane laws had forbidden construction in perpetuity.

# 10

# THE DHARMA OF PLACE

**SPIRITUALITY IS IN THE VERY** soil of India," Urmila had said; then she told me a story that was meant to demonstrate the spiritual richness of India; and, I suppose, as a corollary, the bankruptcy of the West. The story was of an American sociologist who apparently doubted the extent to which spirituality had seeped into the soil of rural India. He had come all the way to Mount Abu in Rajasthan, where Urmila's guru, Vimala Thakar, had her ashram. Thakar said, "I'm driving to Ahmedabad in Gujarat. There are many fields and villages along the way. Why don't you come with me and speak to anyone you like?" The American sociologist agreed. They left at 5:00 a.m.

and drove by jeep along dirt roads. Dawn broke, and they saw a poor farmer making his way through the fields. The sociologist wanted to stop and talk to him.

The sociologist asked the farmer if he believed in God. The farmer replied with great confidence—the sun was rising—"Do you need to believe in that? That is just there. As there is the sun, so there is God." The sociologist thought the farmer had misunderstood his question. He picked up some soil in his hand and questioned him as to its nature. The farmer caught the soil as it fell and said, "You have sprung from this, and it is to this that you will return. This is the mother of us all. This is the mother, and *that*"—the farmer pointed to the sun—"is the father. Together they make us what we are."

Shivam must also have had in mind this idea of a spiritualized landscape when he said, "If you want to see living Indian culture, you must come to my village." I knew I would go. The loss of an idea of home had become a political force in our time; I myself had keenly felt the loss. Now Shivam was inviting me into his home. It was not merely a home to him, but a sacralized way of life, which he felt was in danger.

**WE LEFT BENARES AT DAWN** on Makar Sankranti, a festival day in the Hindu calendar, when the sun begins its northern course. The December murk was gone. The mornings were sunny, the sky cloudless; the city reappeared out of the haze. Shivam's roommate, Rohit, came with us, on his way to Maihar, a place of pilgrimage not far from Satna, the town nearest Shivam's village. The two Brahmins were dressed in jeans and sneakers. Shivam wore a maroon-and-beige-checked jacket with some meaningless words on the back STYLE RIGHT, THESTEROS COPIC FEETING. It was a kind of disguise. Save for their shikhas, and the occasional glimpse of a sacred thread, nothing in their appearance spoke of their identity. In this sense, they really were part of a secret India, an older life that had been forced inward.

We were a group of four—Shivam, Rohit, myself, and our driver, Mukesh, an erratic young man from Bihar. After a brief salutation to Ganesh, we sped out of the old town, through the spillover city of redbrick and ruin, and into fields of young green wheat and yellow mustard. I had not expected to feel so elated to be in the country; to leave small-town India after a long period was to know what it must have been like in medieval Europe to leave an urban environment of poor sanitation and disease for the freshness of the open country. It was such a relief to be rid of the beeping of scooter horns and the cloying sweet smell of unaired winter clothes. I felt as if I had woken from a long illness and found I had untapped reserves of strength, energy, and optimism.

The plan was to get to Satna by lunchtime. We would stay there overnight, then go in the morning to see the famous grouping of tenth- and eleventh-century temples at Khajuraho, before making our way to Shivam's village. Rohit would leave us in Satna and go off on his pilgrimage. Telling me about this, he now asked, his tone solemn and serious, whether medical science had found an explanation for how a human tongue that had been sacrificed could grow back.

I said I didn't know what he meant.

"But I have seen it a hundred times," Rohit said. He described men who, in the grip of religious ecstasy—"coming into feeling," as he put it in Hindi—sliced off their tongues and threw them at the feet of the goddess. And lo! Two weeks later, sometimes that very afternoon, the tongues grew back.

Upon hearing this, Mukesh became so impassioned he could barely drive, and he launched into story after magical story. There was the village official who had embezzled the donation money for a Hanuman temple and been punished by being thrown into jail on a false charge of murder; then there was that time, on festival day in Benares, when Mukesh had received an order from the goddess Durga to come visit her. A throng stood outside the temple, and he thought he would have to wait for fourteen hours, but no sooner had he arrived than the crowd parted, and he found himself in the presence of the goddess. Speaking of her, he said, "We fight a lot. I sometimes ignore her for days and say in anger, 'Mother, I never do any harm to anyone, why do you let harm come to me?' But, in the end, it is a mother-son relationship, and when she calls me, I always go."

As Mukesh spoke, the two Brahmins caught my eye in the rearview mirror to make clear their scorn. One of the reasons for the Brahmin's high regard in Hindu society is his self-control. The Brahmin is *jitendriya*—he who has conquered the senses and is able to exert total control over every aspect of his life from his speech to his diet, his actions, his lust, his emotions. Mukesh was nothing if not uncontrolled.

But whatever differences there might have been between the three men, they were much nearer to one another in belief, in language, in their feeling for the land, than I was to any of them. Listening to them talking among themselves, exchanging stories of pilgrimage, and mapping out the entire country—which was a third of the size of the continental United States—through its holy places, each famous for a particular miracle ("proof" was the word Shivam used), I realized the extent to which English-speaking India was a caste unto itself, more isolated and unassimilable than any of Hindu India.

The land around us grew more beautiful. A thin mist hung over the fields. Occasionally there were islands of elephant grass, towering lines of violet-tinted eucalyptus, and growths of small purple wild flowers along the edges of the expanses of green. A tunnel of small bowed trees, with gnarled trunks, enclosed the road, which became more rural by the mile. We saw women working in the fields and the occasional whitewashed grave of a Muslim saint, all framed against acres of pale Indian winter sky.

Land to me was merely land. The knowledge of crossing a state border, or the nearness of a certain town, might give it some shape, but for the people I was traveling with, the land was marked by myth and history. It was incredible to watch Shivam and Rohit—with Mukesh making noisy interjections—graft episodes from the two Indian epics, and the lives of the gods, onto the moving terrain. Here was the place from the Mahabharata where the five heroes, the Pandavas, rested during their time in the forest. Or: "We are very near the place where Ram and Sita spent eleven and a half of their fourteen years in exile." It hardly mattered whether these events were part of a genuine recorded history, or whether they occurred in the places where the two Brahmins said they occurred; what mattered was the Indian genius for imbuing the land with meaning. To see the country transformed into a holy land, the length and breadth of which the two Brahmins carried in their heads, was to feel that no patriotism was deeper than Indian patriotism. The country was already an article of faith. The sixteenth-century Indian scholar Narayana Bhatta had written of the "dharma of place," and of how worship could still occur at a site that had been destroyed because its inner sanctity remained. I now saw that idea of the dharma of place extended to the country at large, and no wonder this natural worship of the land could be converted into a political ideology.

We stopped by the side of the road at a sweet shop that Mukesh explained "was famous on account of its purity." The shop overlooked a thin stretch of road that shook with the occasional thunder of buses and trucks. The mustard fields beyond were a pointillist yellow sprawl under a pallid sky. Woodsmoke rose from the thatch of a small hut and was slatted in the sunlight. The sweets were brownish-red blobs that lay flat against the convex surface of a blackened iron vessel. The owner of the shop peered out past a pyramid of clay cups at us. Soon we had sweets on dried-leaf plates, and hot tea in thimble-sized clay cups.

Mukesh was blabbing on about the erotic content of the Khajuraho temples. "Sex," he said, using the English word, "has been shown in all its shapes and forms." The Hindu time cycle is divided into four great epochs, each hundreds of thousands of years long, beginning with an age of truth and ending with one of vice, Kali Yuga. We were in the last of the four ages at present, and Mukesh said, "The energy of Kali Yuga is female. It is women who create illusion."

The two Brahmins were dismayed at the oversimplification. Shivam said, "In order for one to go before God, one must free oneself of the things of the world. If you go in a state of sexual excitation, then you will get no reward. You have to quench those thirsts beforehand. It is only then that you can enter into a state of true self-wardness." The temples, he explained, were a metaphor for the change we had to undergo to get spiritual reward. "But," he said, gesturing to Mukesh's ignorance, "the great majority of people go to Khajuraho in search of what is on the inside, but get stuck on what is on the outside."

"Yes!" Mukesh chimed in, excited by the bawdy suggestiveness of the remark. "They go for honeymoon."

"If there is no feeling, there can be no reward," Shivam said. "I know an old man who sits in Kashi and has seen it change over the years. I said to him: 'Are you happy, baba?' He said, 'Happy to see all the facilities, but sad to see the harm that has come to our culture, our beliefs, our way of life. Since the electric light has come, men have gone blind.'"

This simple image was important. In old India, the gift of true sight was an aspect of inner realization. It was never enough to see what the electric light could illuminate.

We drove on. Near the Madhya Pradesh border the earth grew redder, the land hilly and shrub-covered. We were near one of the seams of the earth where the landscape of the north—pale, flat, and melancholy, with its dark soil and long sunsets and mantle of haze—gave way to the glossy-leaved plants and the ferric red of the tropical south. Madhya Pradesh—*madhya* means "middle"—is a vast landlocked state, full of dark forests, silver rivers, and a large aboriginal population. No state feels older, none more primordial. It is the navel of India, the point where the country seems to draw into herself. It has neither the sea air of the maritime south, with its old trading routes that had stretched from Java to the east coast of Africa, nor the girdle of mountains through whose passes welcome and unwelcome visitors alike, from Alexander to Tamerlane, had always entered India.

No country is more dependent on visitors for historical information about itself than India. One forms an idea of India by balancing what India knows about herself with what outsiders, from Megasthenes and Fa-Hien to Al-Biruni and Niccolò de' Conti, have written about her. It makes the country ripe for being defined from the outside. "The West's India became our India," Mukhopadhyay had said, and I sometimes felt as if all India's troubles could be boiled down to the simple fact that its past was truly a foreign country. What India knew about herself was too speculative and abstract, too mystical, for outsiders to apprehend, and what visitors said about India could make Indians feel the visitors were talking about a country Indians did not recognize. The violence of being seen differently from how one saw oneself had been a constant theme in this journey, and it now resurfaced in Satna, a cement town of self-wounding ugliness.

The streets were treeless and bleak and choked with traffic. The town was shapeless, but for an overpass and a railway junction. The tracks ran over patches of pale burnt grass, hummocked in places, where a few blue and brown dusty carriages stood. We came in along a market street that overlooked a deep arterial drain, chortling with grayish-brown water. Customers stepped daintily on rusted metal stairs to reach the little shops that sold plasma screens and Samsung washing machines. At a major intersection, battered billboards loomed over a stunted cityscape. Satna represented a dystopian vision of urbanity, but it could not be ignored: more and more, every Indian town looked like this. The towns' ugliness was especially painful to contemplate when seen against the background of Hindu culture, with its highly developed aesthetic sense, and its feeling for the earth and the elements. It felt almost like a failure of translation, in which old India was unable to project the germ of its genius into the modern present. It was the utter degradation of this urban landscape—among the most polluted in the world—that made the idyll of village life so enticing.

It was late afternoon when we reached the Hotel Bharhut, a Sovietic behemoth that hulked around an octagonal courtyard of thick overgrown grass. The restaurant was overrun by policemen, who sat at long tables in their dark green uniforms. Shivam had changed into a kurta and jeans, and we sat off to one side, near a glass door, overlooking a shaded lobby that stank of phenol disinfectant.

Shivam was telling me of the violent nature of student politics at BHU, where he was part of the main Hindu nationalist group. Earlier he had described what it had been like to be shot in the leg. The students were demanding an elected union, which the university had been unprepared to grant. The students had occupied one of its buildings and held it until armed men were sent in to expel them. As Shivam was running out, an acting administrator opened fire. "I felt a kick-like sensation," Shivam said, "and my foot was thrown forward. It didn't hurt at first. There was just this stinging. I thought nothing had happened, that I'd just grazed my foot. Then suddenly it began to burn, and when I looked down, I saw that my shoe was sopping with blood. I fainted then and there." When he came to, he was in the hospital.

The incident earned Shivam a certain notoriety. His name appeared in the paper; the leaders of various political parties came to see him in the hospital; and I sensed he regarded it as a turning point in his life, one of those moments when the universe seems to single us out for bigger things.

We had finished our vegetarian lunch. I was rolling a cigarette; tobacco was one of the few vices Shivam and I had in common. The policemen were still eating. I handed Shivam the cigarette and said I would meet him outside on the porch of the hotel after using the bathroom. I went off, the slow coma of an Indian lunch creeping over me. I was thinking of a remark Shivam had made while we ate. He had, out of curiosity, attended a seminar organized by a left-wing student group, though he was a firm adherent of the Hindu right. There, he met young women who greeted him with a hug and a kiss, and this, much more than anything about their politics, had shocked him. He said, "I felt I was among people who did not respect the relationship of a mother or a sister. I felt I was being asked to behave with them as one might behave with one's wife. They were kissing and hugging me. This"—the panic in his voice was still high—"is not a question of politics; this is a question of my culture."

I was turning over what he'd said in my mind, considering the depth of the misunderstanding it revealed—the Western greeting seeming to suggest to him a whole world of lapsed morals, in which all boundaries had broken down—when I came out onto the porch of the hotel and found no sign of Shivam. I began asking the hotel staff where he had gone. They seemed at first not to know whom I was talking about, and only when my inquiries grew more urgent did one say, "Oh, that boy who was with you?"

"Yes."

"The police hauled him over for questioning."

"What?"

I went out and saw that Shivam had been taken off to one corner of the hotel's driveway, where the police were indeed questioning him. A couple of youngish officers seemed to be dressing him down, with that bored cruelty that is the hallmark of officialdom in postcolonial countries.

I went up to them and demanded an explanation in English.

"Oh, he's with you." They grinned. "Then no problem, sir. You please enjoy!"

Shivam walked up to me shaking with indignity and anger. "Do you see what we are put through? If you hadn't been there, he would have given me two or three slaps and taken five hundred rupees off me."

"What was the problem?"

"They said, 'The SP is eating inside, and you dare to stand outside and smoke a cigarette.' I said, 'So what? I was also eating inside with the SP.' They said, 'Is that right? We'll show you, boy.'"

The SP was the superintendent of police. The police officer had been offended on behalf of his superior by Shivam's audacity—what if the SP came out from his lunch and saw a man such as this casually smoking a cigarette?—and thought it fit to show him his place. The incident revealed the workings of yet another power structure, the colonial state, which India had inherited from the British, and which had been designed to treat ordinary citizens like a subject people. Indians had added their own injustices, along the lines of caste and religion; but they had not made the state their own. The caste system may have been grossly unjust, but it was India's, and when the time came to redress its wrongs, men such as the Dalit leader, B. R. Ambedkar, knew how. The modern state was inorganic, an overlay. It contained all the evils of Indian society, but translated into an opaque foreign grammar of civil service, bureaucracy, police, and military. It perpetuated the inequalities of the society while concealing its inner workings. The levers of power, when pulled, did all the wrong things, and rather than serve the people, the apparatus of governance became an instrument of cruelty, a means by which Indians preyed on one another.

I don't know why, but I found myself apologizing to Shivam, and that moment we both recognized that I was inadvertently linked (and yet not subject) to the power at whose hands he suffered daily injuries. There was a BJP government in Madhya Pradesh, and now at the center too, but these injustices did not change with a change in government. Yet it was surely this system that the boatman in Benares had been thinking of when eighteen months before he said, "When Modi comes, we will send this government of the English packing."

But Modi had come, and the attitudes remained.

Shivam's Brahmin sense of self was affronted, but as I went deeper with him into a world governed by the laws of caste, I came to feel less sorry for him. I saw him casually assume the role of perpetrator in a system that is hardwired to degrade other human beings. The world may have known systems of inequality crueler and more unjust than caste, but never, in the history of the world, has one provided a deeper, more metaphysical basis—one sanctified by religion—for why each man must accept his place, and consequently why those who have the audacity to dream of another must be punished.

The unpleasantness from the afternoon carried over into the evening. Everyone seemed to need a little time alone. Mukesh was resting after the long drive from Benares. We were to leave at dawn the next day for Khajuraho. I went to the bar of the hotel, which was in a seedy annex, a dimly lit place of black faux-leather sofas and solitary drinkers. The waiters, who outnumbered the clients two to one, wore uniforms that had been laundered out of shape, but still bore yellow turmeric stains. The sacred precincts of Benares are dry, and the Scotch and soda I drank that night was my first drink in a while. It had a nice salacious quality in the atmosphere of that small-town bar. The sound of traffic filtered in through an evening hush, as if the quiet of the surrounding fields had neutralized the roar of Satna. Now and then, I could make out that most romantic of Indian sounds: the horn of a train carrying mournfully through the night air.

It was a joy to be alone. One is never alone in India, and for those who are accustomed to solitude, those who need it, this is a daily, unorganized form of torture. The barman hovered, wanting to "repeat" my drink with the relish of a bootlegger, and seemed genuinely hurt when I said no.

I returned to my room and found Shivam praying. His eyes were closed, his lips moving silently. When he eventually became aware of my presence, he came to, as if out of a trance. Then he went about his nighttime ablutions, ritually cleaning himself with mineral water, his sacred thread wrapped around his ear.

When he began to speak about his life, I saw that his situation was far more precarious than I had at first realized. He had a young wife and a small child, he now told me. He shuttled aimlessly back and forth between Benares and his village. He was worried about his ability to provide for his family and had considered taking up some basic priestly work in a small temple. His classical education had ill prepared him for modern India. He had no English, no real skills, no knowledge of how the world worked. He was trying to build a political constituency in his area by helping people in the environs—a low-caste man in a neighboring village who needed money to build a house from a government scheme; young Brahmin boys whom Shivam helped into an education similar to the one he himself had received. He was only too aware of how undesirable such an education was: "Today a Brahmin is in no hurry to have his child learn Sanskrit. He would prefer he learn practically anything else, French, Russian, whatever. So, you see, the language of this land, the language that is the mother of all languages, is slowly being run into the ground."

In the middle of telling me this, Shivam's wife called. She, along with their small son, was staying with his in-laws. When Shivam got off the phone, he asked if I was married.

"No," I lied without a thought.

No sooner had I answered than I wondered if someone else, someone such as my husband, say, someone with more distance from India, would have answered differently. I had fought so hard for my life, yet I was so easily willing to deny it. Why? Was it the lurking fear of inauthenticity that plagues the westernized classes in colonized countries? Why was I not more willing to defend what I had become, even as Shivam was so easily willing to defend what he still was?

Shivam said, "Well, when you do get married, you must marry an Indian girl. I tell you, if you make them even a little bit happy, they will reward you a hundred times over, with a lifetime of happiness."

We turned off the light. In the darkness, I returned to New York. I saw the island city, with lines of traffic, gold and ruby red, eddying around it. I saw the yellow rectangle of my apartment on West 86th Street: my husband, our dog, the IKEA shelves, and the takeout dinner. I thought of the towers with their flashing red lights, the dark sea, and the countries in between. Then I came back to Satna, which the map on my phone showed me was a throbbing blue dot on a beige landscape, daubed with fractal lakes and pale splashes of greenery. *To know where you are is also to know who you are*: we have never known better where we are, yet how little it helps us to make sense of the cultural and historical distances that have arisen between people so physically near to us. This young Brahmin dropping off to sleep next to me, talking of good Indian women who reward the little happiness we gave them a hundredfold, was so far away from anything I could relate to. It was as if the space- and time-bending force that had brought the world so near had an undertow of equal force that tore apart what the old unity of a shared geography—and, as an extension, a shared culture—had once made whole.

By morning, a lot had passed unsaid between Shivam and me. The intimacy of the first day and night Shivam and I spent together, like the early days of friendship, affected us both. We developed an understanding that would have been hard to achieve even over several conversations. I feared it dulled my critical faculty. Human beings are never more human than in the mundane details of their lives: the late-night phone call from the wife; the prayers; the nocturnal rituals; the little meaningless conversations that occur on the margins of more serious ones. I thought of travelers I admired—Aldous Huxley, Rebecca West, Octavio Paz, Arthur Koestler, V. S. Naipaul ... Would they have insisted on more distance? The distance might have come naturally to the Europeans; Naipaul, I know, would have actively preserved it. I found it hard to hold India at arm's length. It was encroaching and overfamiliar; but it was also big-hearted and gracious. I found myself susceptible to its embrace. After Amherst, I had planned to come back to India forever, but I was unable to fit back in. My return to the West was an expression of internal exile in India. It didn't feel like immigration; it felt more like a desire to be done with the demands of belonging, and to wait out my time in a neutral place. Perhaps one day a cohesive person would arise from the different societies I had known. But until then, I felt my experience of other places not as some embarrassment of riches, in which I felt at home everywhere, but rather as a betrayal of my own place. I lived with a constant feeling of lack, and my thoughts more often than not returned to what I had left behind.

> On the 24th we drove to Satna in order to pick up Alfred Würfel and then proceed to Khajuraho ... I almost forgot to mention the second evening. I went with Montu and Alfred to the temples in moonlight. Captivated and overwhelmed, we could hardly tear ourselves away from the spot. Montu too shared the enthusiasm of us Europeans, though in a more measured and less enduring way. Finally he slipped away from us and went up a temple. Indeed, from a distance his appearance was in such harmony with the surrounding, a rock of these rocks, a life of these spirits, all this is his, belongs to him, and is not anything alien or mysterious, as for us: this moon, the landscape, these forms, these colours are in his blood, are part of his self; why, then, should the delight extricate him from himself?
>
> —ALICE BONER DIARIES, APRIL 2, 1937

**WE REACHED KHAJURAHO WITH THE** broadening of day. A tourist town of internet cafés and multicuisine restaurants had sprung up around the temple complex. There was a great big airport of steel and blue glass. When Alice was here in 1937, the temples, reclaimed from the jungle a hundred years before, still retained a wildness. Alice described them as "weather-beaten" and "completely black." She had been able to visit them in moonlight. The temples marked the passage of time, but as I was beginning to see, in places where the past is not dead—where no line has been drawn between the classical world and this one—

men do not enjoy contemplating their distance from it. They want instead to eradicate the distance. The Archaeological Survey of India, which had given the temple complex what the writer Neel Mukherjee called a "municipal soul," was frantically erasing the effect of time on the temples. Framed against the wan winter sky, they had been turned into ornaments in a manicured garden with little cemented pathways and flower beds full of dahlias. Some were even being rebuilt.

Shivam had little interest in the historicity of the temples, and yet there was something wonderful in seeing him move among them. He greeted the deities with loud salutations; he touched everything; he sang; he dozed in the sanctum. In one temple, he reached past the iron grille to anoint his forehead with some ash from an incense stick.

The temples were not works of art for him, nor objects of historical importance; they were the articulation of living philosophical truths. "The purpose of the imager," Coomaraswamy writes of the sculptor in traditional India, "was neither self-expression nor the realisation of beauty ... To him the theme was all in all, and if there is beauty in his work, this did not arise from aesthetic intention, but from a state of mind which found unconscious expression." Or, as Alice writes of sacred images: "If they are beautiful, it is because they are true."

The temples enshrined cherished concepts and ideas in stone, and as Shivam moved among them, he looked for these. "We see here"—he looked up at the low relief panel that ran around the base of one of the central temples—"the whole scheme of creation, and destruction. And here"—he pointed to a row of horses and elephants and men with drums—"is life in the middle. This art awakens in us an understanding of death."

My way of looking was closer to Alice's; she had seen in the sculpture an "uninterrupted song of delight over the female body in all its unexpected aspects." She reveled in the playfulness and movement of the sculptures; that "degree of warmth which distinguishes Indian sculpture from Greek." She loved the way the light, as in the apse of a church, reached the innermost recesses of the sanctum. But she also knew that if her intention was to enter into the spirit of an unfamiliar art, then she would have to change her way of looking.

"I always tend to succumb to the temptation to search for the beautiful contour," she admonished herself, "the complete harmony of the composition, the logical distribution of light and shade. Yet this is not enough. It remains external. Every architecture, every image, has to be an expression of the inner life."

Shivam effortlessly sought to work his way back to the philosophical truths that underlay the art. One way to do this was through prayer and concentration, and it unnerved Shivam that the temples were dead. No worship occurred here anymore. Yet the culture that built them, the culture of which Shivam was still a part, was alive. For him, the gods had not been overthrown; the classical world lived on.

"The early humanists," Stephen Greenblatt wrote of fourteenth-century Europe in *The Swerve*, "felt themselves with mingled pride, wonder, and fear, to be involved in an epochal movement. In part the movement involved recognizing that something that had seemed alive was really dead." The acceptance of the death of the classical world was a precondition for renaissance because "once one recognized what was gone, once one had mourned the tragic loss, it was possible to prepare the way for what lay on the other side of death: nothing less than resurrection."

India, on the other hand, was all continuity. The living faith papered over any breaks in the continuum. People sensed in their bones that a great deal had been lost, but they refused to acknowledge the loss. Their instinct told them to revive the continuum. "We must pull the thread of the past forward," Golu told me once, "and tie it to the future."

The past in India is inseparable from the world of belief. Once faith was removed, Indians did not know what to make of their past. As with the dharma of place, what mattered was not antiquity or beauty, but sanctity.

Shivam, once he had honored the gods, began to lose interest in the temples. The site was famous; he had felt obliged to bring me here, but he was not sure what to do next. There was no religious fervor to partake in, and the silence of the past disturbed him. "Keep in mind," Shivam said, wistfully eyeing an active temple outside the complex, "that in those temples where worship no longer occurs, there is not that same *light*."

He spoke no English, but he used the English word, and it reminded me of his earlier remark about the blindness that had come with electrical light.

"Now that"—he looked contemptuously at my green notebook—"is something worth noting down."

**IT WAS EARLY EVENING WHEN** we reached the village of Domhai. A cement road, lined with a fencing of bramble, curled out among fields of young wheat, mustard, and chickpea. The car nosed its way past mud houses with low red-tiled roofs. Shivam's house was pink-washed with high pointed alcoves. A small sacred tulsi plant stood at the center of a forecourt on a whitewashed base fashioned from the earth. Shivam's father, a sturdy Brahmin farmer with a dyed mustache and white stubble, welcomed us with a garland of handpicked flowers. On meeting me, he marveled at the unlikelihood of my being in his village: "Never, in all my life, would I have believed that someone from New York would honor me by being my guest." I begged him not to be so formal. Indian hospitality is excruciatingly gracious, almost as if in anticipation of falling short.

The house was dark, with smooth earth floors and undulating boulder-made walls. The front room, where we put our luggage, contained two beds of rough manufacture covered in bright floral blankets. Near a small window, unable to dispel the darkness of the village house, was a plywood coffee table with chairs draped in a thick begrimed matting. We put our phones to charge at a single electrical outlet, where the current surged and fell. Shivam gave me a lungi to wear and we wandered through the dark house. Down a passage, dinner was being cooked in a kitchen shed of corrugated steel. In a farther room, the walls were covered in bright posters of the gods; the in-built stone shelves were crammed full of sacred books wrapped in red cloth.

The house, though open in places, was airless, and though sparsely furnished, it felt cluttered. The darkness pervading it was like none I had ever known; it was velvety, like the darkness of another time. It was brighter outside, even though the sun had set, and the black limbs of trees were visible against the darkening sky. A violet haze lay over the land. Soon Shivam's mother emerged with a single smoky lamp, a steel plate, and a bell. She honored the tulsi plant outside the house, then went back in. The smell of dung, cattle, and woodsmoke carried through the air. It was a pastoral, and beautiful, but terrifyingly remote. I had never spent a night in a human habitation that had undergone so little change since the advent of agriculture. It was no wonder that the few artifacts of modernity that had made inroads into the village—the phone, the little bit of electricity, the television—were so out of place. They seemed less to herald a new time than to be themselves on their way from the future into the past.

Shivam's village, save for the odd family of the warrior caste, was exclusively Brahmin. I knew this without quite knowing what it implied. What, for instance, did my presence in the Brahmin household denote? My father was Muslim, and since religion in India is patrilineal, my staying overnight in the house should have been an unspeakable defilement, but strangely, it wasn't. I seemed, perhaps on account of my being English-speaking, to be exempt from the rules of caste. Shivam did, however, make one small adjustment as the village approached: he stopped calling me by my conspicuously Persian name and rechristened me with a reliably Hindu alternative: Nitish.

Caste had been with me all the while in Benares. There was no way to write about Brahmins without being aware of the system of which they were a part, but as the village approached, I realized that caste had been an abstraction to me until now. I had spoken to many Brahmins, but we had spoken in isolation. I had not seen them interact with the other castes, and more important, I had not seen the laws of caste pollution at work.

Night fell. Dinner was served. The men were invited to come into the back room with the single weak-rayed bulb and the television set playing news of a terrorist attack in Indonesia. Round steel plates were laid out on the floor. The food appeared, and it was delicious: chutney, mango pickle, salt, lentils, roti, a rustic stew made of chickpea leaves. The pleasure of the food and the evening scene in the village house helped dispel the fog of nerves. I was able to take in my surroundings again, and no sooner had I done so than I realized I had forgotten all about Mukesh, who was certainly not exempt from the rules of caste.

He came trundling in a moment later and sat down with us. As was his wont, he quickly hijacked the conversation, congratulating Shivam's mother on the delicious food and regaling us with tales from Bihar.

The atmosphere in the house seemed fine, even cheerful; but as dinner drew to an end, a terrific tension came over the household. Nervous glances passed between Brahmin father and son; something was murmured in dialect; the room grew so heavy that it even silenced Mukesh. I felt I was in a Buñuel movie, a dark social comedy in which something was amiss, and things were about to go badly wrong. But I knew too little about the world I was in to understand what was going on under the surface. We sat there for many moments, gazing in stupefaction at the mute flashing of the television, when at last Shivam leaned in and whispered in my ear. He explained that his family had made an extraordinary exception in allowing Mukesh, who was of a far lower caste called Yadavs, to eat with them, off their thalis. But now there was something the Brahmins absolutely could not do. "I can wash your plate," Shivam said furtively, "as a favor to a friend. But I cannot"—he gestured to Mukesh—"wash his. If people in the village find out, it will become very difficult for us."

Mukesh's plate, having come in contact with his saliva, was contaminated. It could now only be handled by someone whose social rank was equal to or lower than his. Shivam wanted me to make it clear to the driver that he must wash his own plate, in a separate place from the others.

I froze. A deep shame came up in me, as if from the recesses of childhood, like the shame of wetting one's pants. I found myself paralyzed. I did not have the heart to do either what was asked of me, or the courage to defy the laws of caste and get up and wash Mukesh's plate myself. I just sat there in mute horror at witnessing the concept of caste pollution at work. The idea of pollution was at the heart of the Hindu social system; but pollution, as Taya Zinkin wrote in *Caste Today*, "is not a private but a corporate matter which affects the whole sub-caste and village even."

Shivam was acting not just to protect his family's name, but the entire village from contamination.

Mukesh was still oblivious. His foolish, talkative nature seemed only to add to the pathos. It was a terrible moment. He had been tolerated beyond anyone's expectations. No harsh word had come from the Brahmins, no snide comment, no snub; but now this quiet mechanical acceptance of a much deeper flaw in him was so much more devastating than if someone had just found Mukesh irritating (which he was!) and told him to shut up. Again, it was made to seem, as Mukhopadhyay had, that the repugnant belief could easily be accommodated. After all, it was no big deal to ask someone to clean his own plate. Except that only Mukesh was to be singled out for this task. The others were to stay where they were. It made the idea of spiritual purity feel as real as race or class.

But I was alone in my distress. Mukesh was part of the system that declared him spiritually unclean. When Shivam, seeing my inability to convey the terrible instruction, simply got up and himself told Mukesh, as if telling him where the towels were kept, the driver crumbled at the mere suggestion of the transgression: "You are like gods to me. I would never dream of..."

I couldn't listen. I walked away. A few moments later, I saw him washing his own plate outside, in the weak electric light of the village house.

**THAT EVENING WE WANDERED THE** dark streets of Domhai. The families we visited, many of whom were related to Shivam, now all had televisions. They alternated between the news in Hindi and religious sermons delivered by whitebeards in saffron robes. Politics and faith formed a circle, one feeding the passions of the other. The village had basic electricity twenty-two out of twenty-four hours a day. Everyone had mobile phones. But the village, which had sustained so much, from the connection to the land to the life of tradition and ritual and the social organization of caste, could no longer sustain itself.

We gathered in the village shop as one would in a pub. It was a small cupboard of a place with a flimsy two-leaf door. It sold biscuits and bulbs and practically nothing else. Young men in tracksuits, their blue rubber slippers worn thin, sat about on sacks of grain and wooden benches smooth with wear. There was a palpable sense of distress among them. Modernity had reached the village in the form of technology—which only exacerbated the need among these young men to get out—but it had also come in the form of a changing climate. One handsome farmer, bearded and bawdy, said in thick dialect, "The seasons are no longer on our side." Then, laughing, he added, "The man up there, he either gives with all his heart, or he takes with a stick up your ass."

The young farmer left us a moment later to go water his fields. The old Indian fatalism, which allowed people to accept as karmic justice their lot in life, had died in this younger generation. Those with college degrees—many, in this Brahmin village—were doomed to do "service" at pharmacies and banks in the neighboring towns. Others dreamed of the Indian army as a route of escape. Those like the handsome farmer without a way out of the village were at a breaking point.

The village had been static for centuries. Nothing had changed here since the invention of the plow, but now everything was changing at once. These men, who still lived as men had at the beginning of the Neolithic Age, were the recipients of daily stimuli that were designed to cater to societies at the apex of modernity. We sat in the village shop fetishizing the glamour of life in the West. Our conversation touched on every aspect of that shining world of images and objects, and the life it implied. Every dream that had ever been sold, everything one decried in London and New York as the false effervescence of advertising—chain restaurants, fake bodies, bikinis, shining SUVs—was set free of context; and wafting through the village shop, it all seemed brighter and more beautiful than ever.

But after we had gone over the state of roads and buildings in America, and expressed awe at a society where bribes were not taken, we stumbled into a discussion of comparative values, and here was a gulf no less wide. Karan Singh, who belonged to the warrior caste, could not get over my having left my mother in India and gone to America. Every few minutes he would return to the same point, as if trying to understand the mind of a criminal. "*Aur ma?*"—"And your mother?"—he said, half in fascination, half in horror.

The mother in India—above the father, above the guru, above even the gods—is the supreme object of piety. I almost began to feel bad for mine, until I thought of my actual mother, with her long illustrious career in journalism, her many books, her half a million Twitter followers, her industrialist boyfriend of many years, whom she had never felt the need to marry, and I thought how far away she must be from Karan Singh's sanctified image of the Indian mother.

I had trouble falling asleep that night. The dark village house was vulnerable to even the slightest bit of light. The silence was extreme. A bulb left on in the kitchen, an entrance light, even the rays of the moon, burst through the house, illuminating its low rafters and lumpy walls. The bed was hard, the linen coarse with use, the floral blanket unendurably heavy. Shivam, on the bed next to me, muttered about whether I could help him bring industry to the village, anything that could provide employment for the legion of idle young men; there was the cement plant, but that was not enough. His thoughts in nocturnal free fall, he said suddenly, "I hope you've spoken a little to my father. I don't want him to think that I've come home believing myself to be some kind of big shot." The remark made me realize that Shivam represented an enormous advance in his family's prospects—he had gone to university, after all—and the desperation in his voice was that of a man who needed the hope and resources invested in him to amount to something. He needed to make good.

"My father," he said, as we fell asleep, "wants nothing from this modernity, but the coming generation is moving very swiftly towards it."

In the morning, we took steel vessels to the edge of a chickpea field to defecate. On the cement road that led out of the village, known as a *dharar*, was a steady stream of defecators. We passed an ancient bent-over woman with a plastic vessel—"the oldest person in the village," Shivam said, adding, with that casual Indian disregard for time, "She must be at least a hundred and fifty by now"—and Karan Singh, who greeted us warmly. He was returning with his own steel vessel from the field, and I was struck by the intimacy of these morning rituals.

As we left the spiral confines of the village and approached the open road, we came upon different groups of people. A knot of low-caste laborers, with leathery dark skin and bright-colored clothes, warmed themselves by a straw fire in a steel tin. There were also some Muslims from Rajasthan. Shivam said, "They're from Nagaur, but they have become of this place now, and you see, they live here. There is no problem. They feel safe." What was important, I suspected, as with the low-caste people, was that they remained outside the Brahmin village. It was part of the idea of caste pollution being a "corporate" matter. The village was a living social organism, a unit, a manifestation of caste.

We walked for some time along a thinly tarred road with a red-earth margin. We came to a tall growth of weeds with pretty pink flowers whose interiors were deep purple. Shivam gestured to me to get off the road. We squatted down at a distance of some fifty yards from each other. The sky overhead was scalloped with morning clouds. A pinkish-silvery light gilded their edges. A thin haze lay over the earth, through which I could make out a distant line of trees. The serrated frond of a single palm rose up out of the dark wall of verdure, and religious music drifted across the chickpea field.

Afterward, Shivam said he wanted to take me to his father's "*pharm*house," pronouncing the *p* and taking a dig at Delhi's opulent "farmhouses," which had nothing to do with farming. On the way, a furry black-and-white puppy came up to him and gamboled for a while by his side. When we reached Shivam's father's field, where he had been that morning, moving the hose pipe from one part of it to another, Shivam led me down a dark ridge of earth separating two fields. On one side, the pipe spewed out a foamy pool of water. We knelt down beside it and washed our hands and vessels in the dark wet earth. A white-breasted bird with a long tail, marked orange and black, sat on a line. Shivam hummed a tune. We walked back through fields of stunted wheat, and Shivam lamented the lack of water, which had been a constant theme the night before. We stopped at the farmhouse, a small thatched hut in the middle of the fields with a single bulb and a string bed. Shivam's father slept here for a few hours, in between moving the pipe.

"So, this is village life," Shivam said, in a voice at once wistful and despairing. It was as if he wanted me to accept the poetic aspect of such a life, while at the same time acknowledging that it could not last. His shikha was unknotted; he wore a saffron-colored lungi; and contradictory and difficult as my emotions had been during this time in the village, it was hard to deny the grace and elegance of this Indian pastoral, hard not to feel the tragedy of the old order of things passing away, even as no new order was yet on the horizon.

The village held the institution of caste in place; it gave men security and sustenance, a place to which they could always return; it supported the world of ritual and belief; it cemented the connection to the land and was a bulwark against the dehumanizing anonymity of the city; most of all, the village allowed men to live as their forefathers had lived, free of the gaze of others.

The village was without age. Its buildings could return to the earth, yet the village, as an idea, would remain. The great majority of Indians could still shut their eyes and instantly be returned to that conglomeration of irregularly placed mud houses with whitewashed bases, set in the midst of the fields at a distance from the road and rail track. The village-born taxi driver in Bombay, having lived ten years in the city, might still, in reply to a question about whether he preferred the village or the city, say, "*Gaon gaon hota hai*," "The village is the village after all." Here was one attachment that every village-born Indian could understand.

**THAT MORNING, AS WE MADE** our way back to Benares, the country roads we traveled were crawling with pilgrims. Small open-backed Tempos whizzed past us, containing groups of women whose bright saris hung low over their faces. Occasionally a jolt would reveal a pair of lips painted a dark reddish silver, or a nose laden with jingling bits of gold. It was a day of festival. The night before, on our way into Domhai, we had stopped at a five-village fair. It was set on a steep riverbank, a bare, uneven escarpment leading down to the dark expanse of water. Young men in cheap polyester clothes hung on each other, chewing sugarcane. They threaded their way through stalls that sold everything from kitchen implements of wood and iron to flashing colored sparrows from China, bangles and toys, hair clips, and posters of the one Bollywood actress whose body still conformed to old Indian ideas of beauty. She was wide hipped and buxom, and beneath her image, large letters read POWER FULL SEXY.

The atmosphere of the village fair followed us into the next day.

Shivam and Mukesh, reconciled in their love of holy places, insisted we stop at the ashram of Anasuya at Chitrakoot. Anasuya was the wife of a famous sage, Atri, and a woman of great ascetic power herself. "Once when the world was utterly ravaged by drought for ten years," Atri tells Ram of his illustrious wife in the epic, "it was Anasuya who created roots and fruit and caused the Jahnavi [another name for the Ganges] to flow, for the ascetic power she has acquired is awesome, and mortifications adorn her. She has practiced intense asceticism for ten thousand years, my son, and by her vows all obstacles have been removed."

Ram and Sita are new exiles in the forest, and Ram, perhaps wanting his wife to have female companionship, instructs Sita to go speak to Anasuya, described as very old, her skin wrinkled and loose, her hair white with age, her body trembling like "a plantain tree in the wind."

A moment of tenderness passes between the two women, one old and tested, the other young and about to undergo her terrible ordeal in the forest. Then Anasuya, as if familiarizing Sita with her new surroundings, offers her this description:

> The majestic sun is setting, bringing on the gracious night. You can hear the twitter of the birds that by day range far and

> wide in search of food; now at twilight they are going to their roosts to sleep. And here, carrying their water pots, are the sages returning in a group, wet from their ablutions, their bark-cloth garments soaked with water. The seers have made their fire offerings ... do you see the smoke, pearly as a dove's neck, carried by the wind? Though their leaves are really sparse, the trees all about, even in the distance, seem to have grown dense; the horizons are all lost to view.

That was old India. The modern ashram of Anasuya, though still set deep within the forest, was reached by a crowded thoroughfare. On either side there were little shops that sold everything from religious films to rosaries and Chinese toys. On that festival morning, the crush was prodigious. Groups of young wives in garish silks of lilac and orange, their faces painted and ears dripping with gold, trudged along the dirt street, carrying noisy infants on their hips. Poorer people, village folk, were in hard plastic sandals and loose dusty clothes. Groups of energetic thin men crowded close together. These were the temple-goers, and they were a great multitude, all moving in the direction of the sacred site. On one side flowed the river that Anasuya had summoned with her austerities. Beyond this enchanting emerald river lay the dense central-Indian forest.

As we neared the focus of the pilgrimage, we were met with scenes of total mayhem. The ashram, a white marble monstrosity, leered out at us from a rock face. The surrounding area was covered with white Styrofoam boxes. Cows ate from the boxes and ate the boxes themselves. The pilgrims fed nuts and fruits to a congress of monkeys—black-faced langur and red-bottomed rhesus macaque—while the monkeys snatched food from the hands of children. On the steps of the Mandakini River, a naked child was plashing about. A moment later, he threw himself into the river and was instantly transformed into a seasoned pilgrim. He parted the water with his hands, then folded them, then dunked himself. His parents looked indulgently on, proud at the show of zeal, and I recalled one Brahmin saying to me, "You see, unlike the Christians and Muslims, we don't have to teach our children the religion. They just grow up knowing it."

A moment later, when Shivam directed me to come inside the ashram, I balked. The ashram, with its dark openings and yellow-barred windows, from which people and monkeys were hanging, felt like one of those places that only faith could redeem, and I knew I had none. I did not want to enter its crowded spaces where religious feeling was at a fevered pitch. I made some excuse about not wanting to remove my shoes.

Shivam gave me a look of utter desperation. He had met me halfway in Khajuraho, and now I was refusing to meet him even part of the way. He gave me one last appealing look, then, disappointment turning to resignation, he vanished into the dark grottoed entrance of the ashram.

When he reappeared a moment later, he was a changed man. His contact with the divine had refreshed his patience. He took me down to the steps of the river to show me how it appeared magically from an opening in the stairs: "Look, the entire source for this river is from here." Some older men nearby confirmed this. They said that when Anasuya had summoned the river, it had burst out of the rock in a thousand streams.

I wanted badly to leave, but Shivam insisted we pay our respects at the ancient temple of Anasuya. Certain temples had a miraculous quality for which they were famous, and the magical "proof" of this temple was that only the truly devout were destined to look upon its idol. "So, if I leave without seeing it," Shivam said, "I'll feel I've done something bad, and that is why I am not deserving of darshana."

So up we went. The small temple was on an elevation that overlooked the river, where a maelstrom of submerged trash had collected in a creek. The old stones of the temple were painted in thick coats of pink, and the tiny bug-eyed idol was burdened in fineries. As we made our way down, Shivam said, "I feel you didn't give it a chance. I felt a great power from it."

I was like someone who had been taken to a museum and, instead of looking at the paintings, had spent my entire time reading the instructions on the fire hydrant. I had not even tried to enter into the feeling, the *bhava*, which was no less a way of looking than aesthetic appreciation.

In the car, I mentioned the squalor of the site to Shivam, but even as I did, I knew I was only trying to explain away a deeper sense of unease.

At the next shrine, Kamtanath, we came off a cemented parking lot and into an open-air passage. On one side of this concourse were beggars and lepers; on the other, tiny recessed temples with tiles and crude statuary, the paint garish and bright. In the middle was a great spectacle of faith. One man, who looked as if he could have been a bank manager, was prostrating himself along this stretch of several hundred meters. He had a rock in one hand, which he set down at some distance from himself on the dusty floor. Then he lay down flat on the ground and wormed his large body up to the rock. On reaching it, he picked it up, set it again at some distance from himself, and repeated the prostration. Like this, on and on, bending and slithering, he was circumambulating the entire shrine.

"This," Shivam said, "is bhava." And he was right.

A few paces down, a family had laid their daughter, a polio victim, on a table covered in sacking. She had a pretty face with a little black mark on her forehead. The polio had curled her limbs. She lay flat on her back, her appendages like octopus arms, and her parents collected alms from the display of her pitiful form. On the floor next to her sat a line of women with frazzled faces and harassed white hair, some wearing bifocals with shattered lenses. The passing pilgrims threw coins and rice into their bowls. Faith mingled with poverty, incurable illness, and human degradation. It was as if bhava made people want to bare themselves before their maker. This willingness to be naked before God, which had once been part of the world of worship everywhere, could no longer be found in the West, or even in most parts of the Islamic world.

We carried on. Through an opening, I could see a deep ditch of black water where a concrete slab served as a bank of sorts and a family of hairy boar-like pigs chased each other, mucking about in the dark water.

The eye of faith was blind to all but the shrine. It was scarcely visible. A thick crowd, with arms outstretched, blocked the entrance. Incense wafted out from the bodies, and occasionally, when they readjusted themselves to get nearer the idol, I saw flashes of gold tinsel and red cloth through the gaps.

This time I could not go in, even if I wanted to, and Shivam did not ask. He vanished into the wall of bodies. When he got back in the car, he said, referring to my earlier excuse about catching an infection in my feet, “If you had faith, you would not have caught anything. The tens of thousands who come here are daily proof of this.”

We were due back in Benares that night. On the highway, the sky darkened. The fields of young wheat turned a deep sulky green. A scrawl of lightning raced across the sky, then thunder crackled. Rain at this time of year was bad for the crops. Shivam called home to make sure it was not raining there. It wasn’t. When he hung up, he said, “This again, you see, is the power of faith. So many people would have been praying for it not to rain that in the end it didn’t.”

Shivam’s mood was somber. Something had given way between us, a feeling of trust. I think that he had initially believed my skepticism to be part of the innocence of the uninitiated, and thus forgivable, but now he sensed it was a more sinister and deliberate form of holding out. He said, “Well, I’ve shown you all I have to show you, and now if you were to write something bad about us—about Hindu society—I suppose I would be very angry with you.

"There may be happiness, over there in the West; but there is not peace."

The word he used was *shanti*: the peace of the abyss, the peace that passeth all understanding. Happiness and sorrow, *sukha* and *duhkha,* are part of life and cyclical, like the change of seasons. Those who possess shanti transcended the ravages of these temporal cycles. It would be incomprehensible to a Hindu to make the pursuit of happiness, sukha, the foundation of life. The peace Shivam referred to went much deeper than that. "You must remember," he said, "that every child here grows up knowing that to be born means that you will die..."

The darkness of rain clouds graded into the darkness of night. We drove home in silence, but it was no longer so fraught. Our battles of understanding—or misunderstanding—were at an end. When Shivam grew tired, he put his head on my lap and went to sleep. The intimacy of the gesture made me think again of my distance from India, at times so great, at times so near as to be inseparable from myself.

Waking up, Shivam showed me YouTube videos on his smartphone, which was a constant source of pain and delight to him: a Pakistani extremist declaiming against the "pagan Hindu faith, with its false gods and goddesses"; a white woman singing the Veda. Shivam seemed to like what he saw, but then he quickly checked himself: "It's not right for a woman to recite the Veda. Only an initiated Brahmin has that right."

Outside Allahabad we drove over the confluence of the three rivers. There had been ritual bathing here in the winter month of Magha since the time of the Buddha twenty-five centuries ago. As we drove over the two bridges that spanned the dark expanse of the confluence, I saw Shivam in silhouette fold his hands. Below was a vast encampment, the tented makeshift city of millions bathed in amber street light.

As we approached the outskirts of Benares, Shivam announced that he planned to go back to the village that night itself. The five-hour journey would stretch into eight on a bus. It made no sense, and he gave me no explanation. I put it down to one of the many things I would never understand about him. All I knew was that it was related to his connection to the land, to his ease among crowds, to the deified vision of this country that he carried in his head at all times.

A long time ago, in the context of a novel, I had imagined the temple-going Indian as one who knew his country through its holy places. He knew it from the mountains in the north where the rivers began, and where the rudraksh he wore around his neck came from. He knew the rivers when they broadened and the great temple cities, with their stone steps, that had been set along their banks. He knew the points where those rivers met other rivers and their confluences became part of the nationwide pilgrimages he would make several times in his lifetime. There is no other country, certainly not one so vast, where people are as acquainted with the distant reaches of the land as India, no other country where poor people travel more. They think nothing of jumping on a bus or train, for two or three days, to journey to the temple of Tirupati in the south, or Jagannath in the east. I had written of this imaginary temple-goer long before I met a man such as Shivam, and the reality now did not disprove what the imagination had conjured up.

We reached Benares a little before midnight. The odometer showed that we had traveled just under a thousand kilometers. I paid Mukesh by the kilometer and turned to Shivam. We said goodbye with little expectation that we would see each other again. Then his slight figure disappeared around a corner, retracing his steps in answer to a call my ears were slowly growing deaf to: the dharma of place.

# 11

# THE PROTECTION OF THE SEED

**A TIME OF LEAVE-TAKING** was upon me.

It rained continuously through my last days in Benares. The river swelled. Sky and water turned the same color, blurring the boundary between day and night. I was forced to stay indoors during the day, and in the evenings, when the rain let up, I walked along the now empty riverside, with its parasols under which no astrologers sat, and its little tea and paan stalls wrapped up like Christmas presents in blue tarpaulin. The sky was a pinkish red; the floodlights on the shore left long islands of white reflected light on the river. That great open-air arena was now an empty stage from which all the players and all the spectators had departed. Even the ghat dogs and goats had retreated to places of shelter. All that was left of the pageant were the lone figure of a Japanese photographer in green cargo pants and the imposing sight of a solitary Indian bull, with its ashen hump, newly barred from the inner city by cattle grids, neither sacred enough to be given shelter nor reviled enough to be killed; so, there he stood, the mount of Shiva, black lips and tongue moving in a thoughtful chewing motion.

**ALICE HAD BEQUEATHED HER LIFE'S** work, her legacy, and the care of her house to one of the great doyennes of Benares: the Austrian Indologist Bettina Bäumer. Alice and Bäumer met in the 1960s. Alice had already been living in Benares for some thirty years. "She was a monument in Benares," Bäumer told me. "Very well known, but quite alone."

Bäumer and I sat in her office in the Abhinavagupta Library, where I had heard the Brahmins of Benares hold forth in Sanskrit a decade before. The library, named after the tenth-century aesthetician and logician of medieval Kashmir, was Bäumer's creation; it was what she went on to do after relinquishing charge of Alice's house and foundation. Bäumer sat at a desk strewn with external hard drives and devices, a black-and-white photograph of Swami Lakshman Joo, one of the last great pandits of Kashmir, at her back. She was dressed in a brown sari and sweater.

Here was another face marked with beautiful lines. Her hair, despite her age, was solid gold, and there was a glint of steel in her faintly greenish smile of capped teeth. Bäumer reminded me, in every detail from her dentistry to her clothes to her spectacles, of a quieter, more genteel time in India, when, as Rakesh of Harmony Books had said, there was nothing in Benares save for buffaloes and anthropologists. Even the room, with its cupboard of polished wood and glass, full of books, and its seating on the floor, was reminiscent of this other time, as was the snack of lemon tea and rice flakes I was offered upon sitting down.

I associated this time with a period of innocence in the modern republic of India. When Bäumer came to Benares in 1967 to do postdoctoral research at BHU, Nehru had died only three years before. His daughter, Indira Gandhi, had been prime minister for scarcely a year. She was then still believed to be the "dumb doll" that one of the Congress party elders had called her, easy to manipulate; she was not yet the victor of the 1971 war with Pakistan, nor the tyrant of 1975, who abolished press freedoms overnight and imposed a state of internal emergency in India, jailing the opposition and suspending Indian democracy for two bad years in an otherwise unbroken history of political freedom. The movies then were still full of sweet songs, chiffon saris, and bougainvillea.

At the tail end of this time of innocence, Alice and Bäumer met in Benares. "She was full of ideas and concerns," Bäumer said, "and she had no one to share them with." Bettina lived nearby, and the two women would meet and talk in German about Indian art, about Coomaraswamy, about Alice's fear that India was on the verge of losing her culture. The threat was much less then, but Bäumer was surprised at how prescient Alice had been: "She could see the dangers, and she was very severe and critical of the hypocrisy of Indians."

"How do you mean?"

"You know, the saying you believe one thing, and the living and behaving as quite another. This was part of her disappointment with Uday Shankar too. She felt he was leaving truer forms of dance for kitsch."

As Bäumer spoke, the picture that began to emerge of Alice was of a lonely old woman, surrounded by thieving servants, who rented out the rooms of her house while she was in Europe for the summer. She was also, it seemed, insecure with contemporaries, such as the art historian Stella Kramrisch, and Bäumer wondered if this had to do with Alice's lack of formal academic training and her intuitive, rather than exact, proficiency in Sanskrit. Often the meaning came to Alice, Bäumer said, before the actual words and language.

Alice's diary, which Bäumer read in secret while Alice lay on her deathbed, was a revelation: "She was so reserved that I had very little sense of how powerful her internal life was."

The intensity of that internal life had solaced me during this period of flux in Benares. Alice's and my situations were both alike and diametrical. Her movement had been toward India. As a foreigner, it had been open to her to live in India in a way that would never have been possible for me. I left a modern Indian city, such as Delhi, because I felt it offered a desiccated imitation of life in the West, and because an invisible barrier prevented it from nourishing itself culturally by reaching into the Indian heartland. I had moved toward Sanskrit, Benares, and now the Brahmins because I needed that nourishment myself. But I also knew that I could never overcome the barriers of my upbringing in India. I would never be able to live in Benares as Alice had. I would never be able to pass. People would always be able to place me at a glance—as English speaking, as Muslim, as part of the class of interpreters. The degree of anonymity that Alice had enjoyed in India was only open to me in the West, and maybe all my questing after India had been the precursor to my moving more honestly away from it.

What Alice and I had in common was the late-in-life realization that we could not remain where we had grown up: to be more fully ourselves, to adhere to our dharma, we had to break the bond of place. It was not done in a moment of youthful exuberance, but only after many years of private reckoning, in which the awareness that to grow, one had to leave flickered on the margins of life. The decision to go was quiet, creeping, and final. Europe was to Alice what India was to me: a place she never ceased to love, but one where she could not continue to live.

**ON A DISMAL EVENING IN** January, I found myself climbing the drab staircase that led up to P. K. Mukhopadhyay's flat. Halfway up, I stopped on the landing. Dusk was settling over Gurudham Park.

Inside, Mukhopadhyay was in a lively mood. He wore a gray polo sweater under a white woolen kurta and salmon-pink socks with rubber slippers. He seemed starved of conversation and was keen to talk. Of the new government, he said, "They are Hindus without apology, but they have not yet mastered the challenge of being Hindus without revenge."

Mukhopadhyay was referring to the mass hysteria that had seized India. Every day brought a new incident of chauvinism and misplaced pride, and all the time, as Hindu India reasserted itself, the attacks on Muslims continued. The killings grew more graphic by the day: the lone hunted figure of a dairy farmer lurching and stumbling along the edge of a dusty highway before he is set upon by "cow vigilantes"; a laborer hacked to death and immolated. It was all on social media, so the whole country bore witness. A great clamor surrounded the assertions of pride, even as a great silence settled over the killings.

Mukhopadhyay was intelligent enough to see that this unapologetic revivalism, motivated by historical revenge, would have no more room for him than for me. It was an age that spelled the destruction of the very ideal of the Brahmin. "They have no clear notion of what they are," he said of the people of this new time, "just as they have no clear notion of what they have almost ceased to be. Nor any clear notion of what they've come to be." He added, "I feel sometimes that I have lived too long."

Mukhopadhyay's entire life project had been motivated by the desire to revive tradition with the sap of thought. His aim was to become actively aware of all the beliefs and practices that had come down to him through the unthinking continuities of tradition, and to give them new life through fresh consideration. For a man such as this, the present Hindu revival represented a world turned upside down. Mukhopadhyay dreamed of tradition, imbued with thought, speaking boldly to modernity; what happened instead was tradition itself became the plaything of a violent modern impulse and acted in clean contradiction of itself. The Hindu horror at the taking of life, *any* life, was what underlay India's widespread vegetarianism. It was the same doctrine of ahimsa, or nonviolence, that governed the beliefs of men such as Mahatma Gandhi and Dr. Martin Luther King Jr. Now that same exalted idea had engendered a killing enterprise. It was a perfect inversion of Mukhopadhyay's dream. He wanted autonomy, intellectual life, and renaissance; what he got was revivalism and reaction, his great Hindu past held hostage by the present. Just as the Islam that had appeared in our time—and that killed my father—was not traditional, not even medieval, but utterly new, so, too, was this brand of Hinduism. It was, whether we liked it or not, modern.

But hadn't Mukhopadhyay himself been a little naïve, a little unrelenting, in his rigidity, in his grand vows and stances?

On returning from Benares after the summer election, I relayed the story he had told me of the intercaste marriage to an academic friend in Delhi, who said he knew a man who fit the description of the "boy" in the story. He was now a professor of philosophy at an American university. My friend offered to put us in touch, but I didn't take him up on it.

Some weeks went by. I returned to New York, where I was a private student of Sanskrit at Columbia University. One day my professor told me of an upcoming lecture on Indian logic and hermeneutics. It was to be given by none other than the "boy" in Mukhopadhyay's story.

I thought I had better attend. I took my friend up on his offer of an introduction, and one February morning, weeks after I had returned from India, I found myself in room 754 of the Schermerhorn Extension at Columbia University, listening to a lecture entitled "Moral Epistemic Authority With or Without God: The Meaning of an Imperative Sentence."

Chairing the lecture was the éminence grise of subaltern studies, Gayatri Spivak. She introduced a man in his late fifties with floppy gray hair and a straggly salt-and-pepper beard. Dressed in a kurta and black waistcoat, he was the very picture of a left-wing Indian intellectual, disheveled but vain.

The lecture, not intended for lay audiences, was incomprehensible to me. But I sat through it nonetheless in the hope that, when it was over, I would be able to speak to Mukhopadhyay's former student. We had been in touch by email. He had suggested we have lunch after the lecture, so that I could explain at some length what I was writing about. But no sooner had I approached and mentioned Mukhopadhyay's name than his face became a contorted mask of rage.

"I have no desire to speak about this," he said, and hurried past me.

I thought he must have misunderstood and I tried to explain further. When I mentioned India, he snarled, "I have no interest in India, or the Indian experience, or Sanskrit studies. I am a philosopher. Talk to me about philosophy."

I must have said something about Brahmins because he turned on me and said, "I am not a Brahmin. Perhaps P. K. Mukhopadhyay might see himself as a Brahmin. I certainly do not. For me that word is the same as *Nazi*. It is like your saying to me, 'I hear you're from a Nazi family. Tell me about being a Nazi.'"

With this, the professor vanished into the mouth of the subway at 116th Street, leaving me alone to process the violence of his reaction to India, where a castebound society had sought to extinguish his personal happiness. I thought of Mukhopadhyay and his proposed solution to the moral dilemma in which the couple had found themselves—that simple solution that would "add glory to the life of the boy, glory to the girl, and glory to the system." In that moment, as the great diversity of the American university rushed past me on all sides, the weakness of traditional society had never seemed more apparent. What a grave mistake Mukhopadhyay had made in never leaving that enclosed sphere where his arcane code still held sway! Merely recalling that other place from this intersection in Manhattan, where the fluidity of the world system was at its greatest, and where so many narrower ideas of self had already dissolved, was to feel the full fragility of a closed society whose destruction was all but assured.

Caste now came up again in my conversation with Mukhopadhyay. I was still thinking of the treatment Mukesh had received in Shivam's house, and Mukhopadhyay, speaking of the need for men to give "a theoretical justification" for their beliefs and practices, made me realize that I had never heard one from him: not for the edifice of caste itself, but for the prohibitions surrounding food.

The limited scope of my question startled Mukhopadhyay. I think he would have preferred that I speak more abstractly. He said, "It is the British style that at food time there is all sorts of discussion and socializing. But, in India, eating is a strictly religious activity. You begin by sharing your food with God. Then sharing with your environment. Then with the elements of your body. These are the three stages. All that is there within this practice. The meaning is lost, but the practice remains."

I told him the story of what happened with Mukesh and pressed Mukhopadhyay on this specific point of food.

He said that nothing was wrong with the practice. "I cannot share my food even with my own sister or brother. That's a different thing. A person of a different caste, I will not allow him to touch my utensils or to go into my kitchen." He reminded me of the low-caste student who had once resided with him, and how he fed and taught him. "He had no difficulty living with me."

I was sure he didn't, just as Mukesh had no difficulty with the rules of Shivam's house. "It must be remembered," writes James Baldwin in *Notes of a Native Son*, "that the oppressed and the oppressor are bound together within the same society; they accept the same criteria, they share the same beliefs, they both alike depend on the same reality." I wanted to know from Mukhopadhyay, who claimed to have rethought that reality, with all its criteria and beliefs, who claimed to have taken nothing for granted, what he considered to be the basis for the commensal prohibition: Why could a Brahmin not eat from the same utensils, or even in the company, of a low-caste person?

Mukhopadhyay's mouth tightened. "A person has been born in a particular caste because of some reason, some objective conditions. He is obliged morally to practice what is legitimate within that caste. I can violate the caste only if I convince myself that it is man-made."

He was still not answering the question, but when at last he did, I found myself almost wishing he hadn't.

"If a person is suffering from a communicable disease, you would not let him touch your utensils. You have this one idea of contamination, but you refuse to accept that there might be certain spiritual conditions..." His voice trailed off. He seemed to know he had lost me.

We were speaking during a week when every newspaper in the country was reporting the suicide of a young Dalit student named Rohith Vemula. He was a twenty-six-year-old Ph.D. student at the University of Hyderabad in the south. Vemula was active in student politics and part of a Dalit organization that frequently clashed with the ABVP—the same Hindu nationalist group of which Shivam and Anand were members. In August 2015, Vemula was accused of assaulting an ABVP member. The group wrote a letter, which eventually made its way to the education minister, accusing Vemula of "casteist" and "anti-national" activity. The next month, Vemula, along with four other students, was suspended. In December, the university upheld the suspension, barring Vemula from all public places on the campus, and effectively ending his education.

A few weeks later, Vemula, who had once hoped to become a science writer in the tradition of Carl Sagan, committed suicide, hanging himself from a ceiling fan. The suicide had inspired protests across the country and forced Indians to once more confront the fundamental inequality on which their society had been predicated.

Vemula should have been part of a national healing. Here was a student from among the lowest castes, attending one of India's most prestigious universities. His story could have been about the country's success in overcoming the terrible history of caste. Instead it became a testament to India's inability to do so. In his suicide note, Vemula wrote that he could not move past the "fatal accident" of his birth.

Mukhopadhyay now said, "You have to understand that modern European culture is based on the idea that all men are born equal and later become differentiated. The Indian idea is different. We believe that men are born unequal, but we are all, Brahmin, sage, cobbler, outcaste, heading toward the same destiny."

It was a valiant attempt at a "theoretical justification," but it was absurd. It would mean that millions of lower-caste Indians such as Rohith Vemula would have to forfeit the aspirations of this life in exchange for the promise of some ultimate destiny, many lifetimes away, in which all differences would be obliterated. If men could not be equal at birth, then the only community left for them to be part of was the community of death. No patriotism, no fellow feeling, no notion of the pursuit of happiness—no ambition, no audacity—could survive so systematic a deferral of hope.

Mukhopadhyay showed me to the green metal door for the last time and said, with a hush in his voice, "There may be weaknesses in my argument; but I can tell you one thing: on such occasions, I don't speak a word I do not believe."

**I FOUND ANAND MOHAN JHA** lying back in a boat, just as he had been when I first met him during that election summer. He got up when he saw me, and I almost didn't recognize him in his black-and-white beanie. I asked him if the boat in which he had made himself so comfortable was his.

He grinned, a broad mischievous smile. "What? Even this body is not ours."

Anand was dressed in a white tracksuit top and bright red-and-black socks, and he was loafing about with a young friend from his village called Prakash Thakur. When I asked him his age, Thakur said, "On the certificate, I am fifteen. But in actual fact I am nineteen."

"You won't find him on any voter list," Anand said. "Ask him how many times he voted for Modi."

"Three," Thakur said proudly.

Modi was in town, but Anand hadn't gone to see him. "You know how much I did for him during the election? But this time I haven't so much as gone there. I'm not interested in the posters, the banners, the deluge of people. The mood has gone cold."

The jobs that Modi had promised had not come. There were endless new schemes: smart cities, International Yoga Days, Swachh Bharat Missions, and Make in India programs—in Delhi they were calling it "The Announcement Raj"—but the economy was slowly tanking, and in the months to come, Modi would make gesture after grand populist gesture. He would put 86 percent of the country's currency out of commission overnight in a quest to end black money; he would implement a tortuous new regime of taxes, for which he called a special midnight session of Parliament, such as had never been called since Nehru delivered the "Freedom at Midnight" address that marked the birth of the modern nation.

Modi had promised Kyoto to the people of Benares. He had brought Shinzō Abe to the city, and their pictures had been up at the airport when I first arrived. It was just a little bit of theater. Under Modi, the old Indian disease of symbolic action, such as the washing of feet in Urmila's house, had returned, and an example of what Benares would see of his second Kyoto was the electronic water dispenser, with a cool blue screen and soft silver buttons, which appeared magically one morning amid the dirt and chaos of the riverside. As with all such machines in India—whether they be ATMs or the check-in kiosks at airports—the dispenser did not make men obsolete: it provided employment. It came with a human caretaker, who protected it from the untrained touch. The dispenser's human arm, valet to the great machine, was thereafter to be seen handing out little paper cups of water to pilgrims and tourists as they made their way down to the river. This was the kind of misadventure for which Benares reserved a special laughter, and the jokes had already begun. *Abe* meant "hey" in the local dialect, but more in the sense of "hey, asshole." And, unthinkable as it would have been a few months before, people now said of the prime minister, "Abe, Modi!"

Modi's failure, predictable as it might have seemed to the outsider, was no small matter in India. The election had been an election of hope. The country had felt it was trusting to itself after a long period of "foreign rule," sloughing off the class of interpreters. Modi's coming had implied a reassertion of autonomy, and the end of an age of custodianship. The disappointment he represented now was personal and keenly felt. It was the disappointment of a place that was out of ideas, out of options. The "nerve gas" of contact with the West had paralyzed the life of tradition—that door had closed—but it had not brought the material rewards of life in the West either. "Nationalism," wrote Nehru in his autobiography, "is essentially an anti-feeling, and it feeds and fattens on hatred and anger against other national groups, and especially against the foreign rulers of a subject country." As such, the nationalism that had taken hold in India was not quenched by failure, but fed by it. There would always be other people to blame for why Modi had failed. The culture war on two fronts would rage on.

Anand had just been home to his village, in Bihar, and he described a place where the expectations that Modi had aroused were beginning to curdle. Crime was returning. "And it is very young men who are doing the robberies. They're in debt because they've all bought phones they cannot afford, and now they have to pay back the money from somewhere.

"This new generation is a lost generation."

Thakur agreed, "It's all self-destructiveness, and fashion, and waywardness. The town has come very near, and they're all living with the illusion that they are part of the town. But in fact, they're living off their parents' hard-earned money, and when they try to stand up on their own, they sink back into poverty."

"Their sense has become *disturbed,*" Anand said, using the English word with the flourish for which Biharis were famous.

"Disturbance" was exactly the right word, and Anand instinctively knew what lay behind it: "There is still oneness in our village, still community, but in other villages, it is finished. People have grown distant from each other."

Anand himself was in trouble once again. He had been caught communicating with his girlfriend in the ashram, and the men of the neighborhood had got together and driven him out. He had had to find another place to live. It had been especially galling as he was a BHU student, and a Brahmin to boot.

"This is all mohamaya," Anand said with a smile as we parted. "*Mohamaya*—a darkness, or delusion of mind," the Sanskrit dictionary informs us, "that prevents the discernment of truth and leads men to believe in the reality of worldly objects."

**IN MY LAST DAYS IN** Benares, I was haunted by the memory of a man I had met during that election summer, eighteen months before.

The Samaveda school was in the north of the city. The streets there were of a different quality—quieter, cleaner, the buildings in better shape. It was possible to follow the unbroken line of a cornice along a pale blue façade, or to admire the ironwork of a slim balcony jutting into the street. Pinku and I had come in from the glare of a hot April morning to a shaded courtyard with green-painted columns. The young Brahmin boy who showed us in was dressed in two measures of white unstitched cloth. He led us past great rusting metal cupboards, and through corridors hung with the pictures of former gurus. He explained that his guru, Gyaneshwar Shastri, had a high fever. But he would speak to us nonetheless because he was a teacher, and it was his dharma to teach. Shastri, whom Tripathi had described as living still as Brahmins did hundreds of years ago, taught the Samaveda. And it was all he knew.

I found Shastri reclining near a shrine in the far corner of the courtyard, where the air was smoky. He wore nothing but a loincloth and his sacred thread. His body was wrinkled and sinewy, and his white beard had yellowed in places.

We ran into the old difficulty almost immediately: those in whom tradition was most intact were least able to speak of it.

The world around Shastri was in flux, but without a shared vocabulary, I had no way to ask him about the space- and time-bending force that was encircling him.

What did he have to say to the world beyond the walls of the Vedic school? What did tradition have to say to modernity?

Shastri was not even aware of what was outside the walls of the school. Tradition, like faith, functioned by an internal logic. It was self-contained, and it nourished him completely. The only indication he gave me of even being aware of the passage of time was when he said we were living through Kali Yuga, an age of decline and unrest, followed by dissolution.

Since our conversation was running into dead ends, I thought I would ask him what the value was of teaching the Veda in this age of darkness.

The question roused his interest. This was at last language that meant something to him, and he now knew exactly what I was talking about. He looked at me through the glaze of his feverish eyes, then asked, "Do you know what *beej raksha* is?"

The phrase literally meant "the protection of the seed," but Shastri spoke of it conceptually; and as a concept, I did not know what it meant.

"During the rains, when the land is flooded, the farmer will take the seed"—Shastri made a pouch with his hands—"and he will put it in some high place, where it is safe from the waters. Then, when the flood retreats, there will be farming again."

Shastri held my gaze a moment longer and, looking out at the Ganges, emaciated against a burning plain of beige, said, "This is what we do, and this is all that can be done."

**DEATH, METAPHORICAL AND REAL, HAD** been with me all the while in Benares. I came there from a house of death in New York. My husband's father's death—oblique, numbing, hard to grieve for—contained an echo of my own father's. I was also mourning the end of my life in India, and soon there was Mapu's death from a rare intestinal disease, which happened almost exactly a year after he said it would and seemed in every way to bring my time in Benares to a close.

It was impossible to take death personally in Benares. Here, day and night, the corpses sizzled away on funeral pyres. Upon arrival, one immediately entered into a war of attrition: the universal fact of death wearing away at the particularity of one's own experience of it. But though the community of death had triumphed over what was the supreme source of terror in the modern West—namely, as James Baldwin writes, that "the earth turns and the sun inexorably rises and sets, and one day, for each of us, the sun will go down for the last, last time"—it had found no way to confront the small matter of its own death.

"This thing that goes by the name of life," Tripathi had said, during the summer of the Modi election, "tests our thought." He was referring to the death of his son. He remembered every detail of that morning. Tripathi had been invited to a conference in Trivandrum while his son was ill. He was being treated at a hospital in Delhi, a young man, in the prime of youth. The doctor said he was sure to get well. That put

Tripathi's mind at rest, and he decided to go to the conference, which was quite important. On his way to Trivandrum from Benares, he stopped in Delhi to see his son in the hospital.

It was only 4:00 a.m., but his son was awake. "You seem to have been waiting for me," Tripathi said.

"No, I haven't been waiting. I'm just not feeling very well today." It was October. The seasons were changing. Tripathi thought that might be the reason his son's condition had worsened. Tripathi said he would speak to the doctors when he returned from Trivandrum. With that, he bathed, said his prayers, and set off. He was on a 9:00 a.m. flight, which touched down in Trivandrum a few hours later. Tripathi disembarked to find that everyone from the conference had come to meet him at the airport. They all had sorrowful faces. Tripathi was not sure what the problem was. Then the main theater personality among them came up to him and said, "You must return immediately. We have made a reservation for you on this very same flight. You must go back at once." That was when Tripathi guessed what had happened.

"It is in moments like these..." He left off. He mentioned how he got back on the plane and that his daughter was waiting for him at the airport in Delhi. She took him home, where his son lay dead. He had died within half an hour of Tripathi's leaving. "It is in moments like these..." Tripathi began again. "A line seemed to come up in me from within. '*Dhiras tatra na muhyati...*,'" Tripathi said in Sanskrit, beginning to quote a famous verse from the Gita: "Even as the body passes from boyhood to youth to old age, so, too, does the soul at death pass from one body to another. He of steady mind is not perturbed by such changes."

"This line," Tripathi said, "came up in me again, and again. It reminded me that things went on. Death happens. He who is born has to go. It is decided; but to think it is all over at death ... Well, it is not."

This second untimely death, which bookended Tripathi's life, seemed the spiritual analogue to the more politically significant death of his brother. And death, as I learned when I came to say goodbye to Tripathi, had been an all-too-frequent visitor in his life. It had struck twice in the eighteen months that I had been away, leaving him utterly alone.

We met for the last time in the compound of rain-drenched mango trees and yellow government buildings, which the damp had streaked black. Upstairs, in the brand-new office overlooking a garden where evening fell, the heater was on. Tripathi, wearing a brown woolen cap, a long blue scarf, and a white shawl, was sitting with Bettina Bäumer. The old Brahmin and the Indologist were gossiping when I came in. Their conversation touched on weight loss and advancing age as well as tantric Shaivism in medieval Kashmir. Bäumer, whom Tripathi described as a great *rishika,* or female sage, was saying that tantric Shaivism had, like Buddhism, become fashionable in the West. The remark, I sensed, contained something of the irritation people feel when a subject that has been their life work is taken over by people who know far less about it than they do, but who, in their ignorance, are better able to popularize it than they, in all their knowledge, ever could.

Soon Bäumer left, and Tripathi and I were alone.

We spoke for well over an hour, covering what was now familiar ground: the survival of old India into the present, and the challenge presented by the British—both the rape and the seduction. Tripathi said, "I don't think there was anyone who understood the West like Gandhi. And he understood his own culture too." Tripathi lamented that no one had even tried to follow Gandhi's legacy. "We tried instead to discover India," Tripathi said, taking a swipe at Nehru's book *The Discovery of India,* "as if India was lost. We suffered under the exploitation of the westernized classes. They had their right to pursue their interests, but why were we so stupid to be taken in by them? Why were we not able to save ourselves? This is why I say that I have no faith in the Indian intellectuals, but I have a tremendous faith in the masses."

Those "masses" had now brought about the Modi revolution, and Tripathi could already see a contradiction: these men wanted to save Indian consciousness, but also wanted Western technology. Tripathi believed, as Gandhi had, that the tools of the West were not neutral—that the screen of the smartphone was a portal to alien values, attitudes, ways of life. "Thanks to the superiority of their technology, they have made incursions deep into the Indian village, which is the unit of our culture, and which they will destroy."

When Tripathi and I last spoke, I'd had no experience of the Indian village; I had only just met Shivam. But now I felt a chill hearing Tripathi speak of the village and Gandhi in these idealized ways. I feared that India was in danger of making a catastrophic decision about her future. The country was at a special boiling point: the right quantity of uprooted, semi-urbanized young men; the right kind of populist strongman; the right level of ignorance and heightened expectations, resentment and anger; the right fantasies about the past—who knew what little achievement of nation building and democracy might not yet be sacrificed at the altar of a future too bright to behold?

"Something is bubbling up from within," Tripathi said. "The point we're at right now is critical. The next three years will decide what India will be in the future."

I could not have agreed more: the Indian soul was declaring itself, as the Russian and German souls once had. The trouble then was the same as the trouble now: it was precisely those who were no longer in possession of tradition—those in whom a break had occurred, those whom Rebecca West described in the 1930s as "the mindless, traditionless, possessionless section of the urban proletariat"—who most wanted to bring back what they imagined had been lost. But they themselves had been remade. They were only able to bring back an adulterated version of the past that contained, in far greater quantities than they knew, the alien present from which they were running. Their response to modernity had cut them from their own past. Outside, in one ever louder voice, they were yelling, "Victory to Mother India!"—but the more they stressed their victory, the more one suspected its absence.

Tripathi said, "You see, there is all the difference in the world between being cultured and civilized. Civilization is fundamentally an urban concept, a city concept. This has nothing to do with our use of *sabhya,* or 'cultured.' For us, the people of the forests, or villages—what Europe calls folk culture—are very cultured. Culture is by no means restricted to the city. You see the difference?"

"You mean that, in your view of culture, no man who is in his natural environment can be considered uncultured—only those who have strayed out?"

"Exactly!" He who is among his own, Tripathi explained, is never uncultured. The word *mleccha,* often translated as "barbarian," is not for a Muslim or a Christian, but for someone who has gone out of his cultural norms.

Thomas Mann, in a public feud with his brother Heinrich during World War I, had once said something similar in relation to Germany. "Culture is compatible with all kinds of horrors," Mann wrote. "Oracles, magic, pederasty, human sacrifice, orgiastic cults, inquisition, witch-trials, etc.—by which civilization would be repelled; for civilization is Reason, Enlightenment, moderation, manners, scepticism, disintegration—Mind." In Mann's view at the time, Germany stood for culture, France for civilization. Or, to put it differently, civilization was India, culture Bharat.

Mann, after the horrors of the Nazi years, was forced to recant much of what he believed about the German soul, which, when it found utterance, brought into being a world in which there was no room for Mann—a world in which his books were committed to the fires at the Opernplatz. Hearing Tripathi speak, dabbling level-headedly in political emotions whose intensity he could not grasp, I felt I was listening to a man who would be forced—in the near future—to take back these fond ideas about culture and civilization, a man who was applying the tamer dissatisfactions of an earlier time to one whose crude fury he could never hope to understand. He was by his own definition still "cultured," but he was dealing with a society that was every day more uprooted and adrift.

I was getting up to leave, and as is customary, I asked after Tripathi's family, his wife, his ailing daughter. It was only then, in passing, that I was given a sense of the terrible year Tripathi had been through.

"My daughter, after a five-year struggle with illness, died last year in March. March 20, 2015," he muttered, stanching the flow of emotion through the recollection of precise detail. "My wife followed her some five months ago. She, too, is no more. Those who have gone have gone." He collected himself. "Those who remain, I try to give what I can, with what strength is left me."

Tripathi had taken in a young boy, an electrician who left home at eight in the morning and returned at eight at night. "I was living completely alone, so a relation brought him over to live with me. He is very honest, very hard-working. He makes tea; he answers the telephone. In return, I give him a place to stay, food to eat."

Tripathi stepped into the light to say goodbye, and as he did, his face glistened in the white fluorescent light. It was less a tear than the remains of one, like the gossamer trail left behind by a snail.

"I have many faults," he said. "I had them before, and I still have them now. I must turn my gaze upon myself. Not the egoistic self, but that Self in which you and me both are extinguished. For one thing I know: death is a reality. Death," he said again, as if he had misspoken the time before, "is real."

# ABOUT THE AUTHOR

**Aatish Taseer** was born in 1980. He is the author of the memoir, *Stranger to History: A Son's Journey Through Islamic Lands,* and three acclaimed novels: *The Way Things Were,* a finalist for the 2016 Jan Michalski Prize; *The Temple-Goers,* which was shortlisted for the Costa First Novel Award; and *Noon*. His work has been translated into more than a dozen languages. He is a contributing writer for *The International New York Times* and lives in New Delhi and New York.